DESK REFERENCE ON THE
ECONOMY

BOOKS IN THE DESK REFERENCE SERIES

CQ's Desk Reference on American Courts

CQ's Desk Reference on the States

CQ's Desk Reference on the Federal Budget

CQ's Desk Reference on American Government

CONGRESSIONAL QUARTERLY'S

DESK REFERENCE ON THE ECONOMY

RICHARD J. CARROLL

CQ PRESS

A DIVISION OF CONGRESSIONAL QUARTERLY INC.
WASHINGTON D.C.

For Jay, Grace, and Ted ——————

CQ Press
A Division of Congressional Quarterly Inc.
1414 22nd St. N.W.
Washington, D.C. 20037

(202) 822-1475; (800) 638-1710

www.cqpress.com

Cover designer: Dennis Anderson

Printed in the United States of America

04 03 02 01 00   5 4 3 2 1

Library of Congress Cataloging-in-Publication Data:

Carroll, Richard J., 1957–
    Congressional Quarterly's desk reference on the economy / Richard J. Carroll.
        p.   cm.
    Includes bibliographical references and index.
    ISBN 1-56802-526-2 (cloth : alk. paper)—ISBN 1-56802-525-4 (pbk.)
        1. United States—Economic policy—1993—Handbooks, manuals, etc. 2. United States—Economic conditions—1981—Handbooks, manuals, etc. 3. United States—Economic conditions—1945—Handbooks, manuals, etc. I. Title: Desk reference on the economy. II. Title.
HC106.82.C37 2000
33.973—dc21   00-036016

CONTENTS

Preface   vii

Chapter I: Introduction   1

Chapter II: Major Indicators and Trends in the U.S. Economy from 1946 to 1999   5
Gross Domestic Product   **5**
Employment and Unemployment   **11**
Inflation   **15**
Money and Interest Rates   **18**
Investment and Savings   **25**
Productivity and Compensation   **32**
Poverty   **37**
Stock Market   **41**
International Trade   **46**
Federal Budget Growth   **50**
Federal Budget Composition   **52**
National Debt and Deficit   **57**
Federal Taxes   **61**

Chapter III: Events That Made Today's Economy: Great Depression to Y2K   66
1930s   **66**
1940s   **72**
1950s   **77**
1960s   **81**
1970s   **85**
1980s   **91**
1990s   **96**

Chapter IV: Top Economic Issues: What Matters Most Now and for the Future   103

Fiscal and Monetary Issues   **104**
The Funding and Reform of Social Security   **104**

Tax Reform **122**
Maintaining Low Inflation and Low Unemployment **138**
Saving and Investment Rates **143**
The National Debt **149**
The Pitfalls of Economic Indicators **154**

Private Sector Issues **163**
Technological Advances and Economic Progress **163**
Corporate Restructuring: Stockholder Greed or
Competitive Necessity? **178**
Regulation and Deregulation **185**
The Costs of Civil Litigation **194**
Corporate Welfare **199**

Social and Environmental Issues **202**
Health Care Costs, Reform Proposals, and Medicare **202**
The Economy and Environmental Protection **210**
Poverty and Income and Wealth Distribution **226**
Economic Costs of Illegal Drugs **235**
Natural Resources **239**

International Issues **245**
Globalization **245**
NAFTA and Its Record on Trade and Jobs **253**
Immigration: Costs and Benefits for the United States **260**
The Asian Financial Crisis: Impact on the United States **265**
The Use of Economic Sanctions **272**
The Euro and Its Effects on the U.S. Economy **275**

Chapter V: Evaluating Economic Performance **281**
Setting the Standard to Rate a President's Performance **281**
Tracking the Economy: Truman to Clinton **284**
Political Parties and the Economy **294**
Today's Economy and Priorities for Tomorrow **296**

Reference Materials
Economic Institutions and Resources **301**
Glossary **309**
Statistical Appendix of Economic Indicators, 1945–1999 **317**
Bibliography **327**

Index **332**

PREFACE

In a democracy such as the United States, the more citizens know about the economy, the better it is for the formation of a sound national economic policy. How the United States manages vital issues, such as Social Security, taxes, and health care, depends on what its citizens believe and want. The problem is how can the average citizen figure out economic issues when even the best economic minds disagree. The answer may be that individuals need not fully understand economic issues as much as they need to develop a sense of which economic principles are valid and learn to filter out the "noise" of outlandish economic arguments. One thing is certain: citizens should be able to learn more about the economy given the amount of time they spend thinking about economic issues and the importance of economics in their daily lives.

Most economists do agree on fundamental economic principles, for example, that the price of goods and services should be determined by the interplay of supply and demand in the marketplace and that the forces of competition result in the highest levels of production and consumption in a society. Citizens can deepen their understanding of these fundamental principles and better navigate through economic news and policies. Still, the temptation is to leave economic policy to the professionals. In a democracy, however, it is ultimately the voter who has to decide which politician's plan is better.

Unfortunately, the flow of economic information from professional economists to the public—which would help build this understanding—is not always smooth. Most Americans hear a fair amount about the economy through television, radio, and newspaper reports, which only occasionally provide background to an issue. These media reports are mostly concerned with day-to-day news that is often not put in context. To understand the importance of daily economic news, citizens need context and background to the issues.

Making sense of issues is made more difficult by special interest groups that confuse the public debate with slanted information. These infusions of bias make economic concepts difficult to grasp. The case for well-established concepts of free trade and specialization that are the centerpieces of free-market economics has to be made over and over again. These concepts are often illusive even to policymakers. At the other end, economists themselves do not always make it easy for the nonspecialist. They often write abstract articles that most economists cannot understand and that are not clearly relevant to the real world.

The inability to communicate economic information creates significant costs to society. It is difficult to win political support for policies that have short-term costs but long-term benefits, such as reforming the Social Security system or overhauling the tax system, unless economists and policymakers have credibility and can communicate the benefits.

One way to communicate the costs and benefits of economic issues and policies is to break them into pieces, such as questions and answers, issue by issue, as this desk reference does. In doing so, this volume attempts to present only the essential facts about issues and policy summaries. It provides a professional analysis of the facts in as concise and unbiased a way as possible. Although oversimplification is a risk for such an undertaking, the goal of this reference is to present each issue sufficiently to do justice to various views. Historical perspective is also added to give students, researchers, and interested citizens the critical information needed to understand these economic issues and make democratic choices based on that understanding.

There is a general principle to follow regarding economic news and information. When considering economic news, each citizen should wear the hat of skepticism until the report's significance is clear and it is proven with facts and figures. Beyond that, a three-step method to taking a position might help: (1) get the key facts; (2) use a fair and logical analysis of the facts; and (3) apply your own values to the result.

ORGANIZATION OF THIS DESK REFERENCE

This book is more than a fact finder; it also provides an analysis of the top economic issues and trends of the twenty-first century. The question-and-answer design gradually leads readers through the major economic indicators and U.S. economic history of the past half-century to the major issues of the economy today. It also helps readers develop a critical approach to economic news and presents the economic records of recent American presidents.

Chapter I defines economics and establishes a general consensus on economic thought.

Chapter II explains the major economic indicators that policymakers rely on to make economic decisions and evaluate performance. By presenting long-term trends for each indicator, this chapter creates a historical yardstick with which to judge the significance of reported changes in the indicators. The coverage begins in 1946 because World War II (which ended in 1945) and the Great Depression (which began in 1929) distorted the economic landscape. Before 1929, economic policy was much less developed than after the war when the major monetary and fiscal policy lessons of the Depression had been learned.

Chapter III adds a broader historical perspective by summarizing major economic and noneconomic events starting with the Depression of the 1930s and leading up to the Y2K phenomenon. This chapter demonstrates that the economy cannot be viewed in isolation from the rest of the world and that all of these events have shaped the economy in some way. The economic impact of some of these events, such as the savings and loan crisis, the Vietnam War, and the oil embargoes, although initially large, was not permanent. Other events, such as the construction of the National Highway System, the establishment of Social Security, deregulation, the peace dividend from the end of the cold war, and surges in corporate restructuring have had a more lasting effect on the U.S. economy.

Chapter IV is a detailed look at the major economic issues facing the United States today. This chapter is divided into four policy areas: (1) fiscal policy issues; (2) private sector issues; (3) social and environmental issues; and (4) international issues. Each discussion within these areas provides the key facts necessary for understanding an issue and its significance to the economy. Chapter IV can be used in two ways, either by following the questions and answers sequentially and slowly building a knowledge base for the issue, or as a pure reference.

Chapter V suggests guidelines for evaluating economic performance and presents an economic record of modern presidents (from Harry Truman to Bill Clinton) and political parties. It also gives an overview of the current economy as it moves into the twenty-first century.

The reference materials at the back of the book provide (1) a listing of economic institutions and resources; (2) a comprehensive glossary that explains all important economics terms; (3) a statistical summary of all major economic indicators from 1946 to 1999; and (4) a bibliography for further reading on all policy issues discussed in Chapter 4. A detailed index completes the book.

ACKNOWLEDGMENTS

I am grateful for the many contributions others made to this book. Tiffin Shewmake was primarily responsible for environmental issues. Timothy Kiefer contributed important timeline sections as well as general economic input. George Viksnins and Mark Gallagher provided substantive comments. All of the statistical departments of the U.S. government, especially at the Department of Commerce and Department of Labor, were very helpful in providing data and answering questions. My reviewer, Stephen Nordlinger, gave thorough and thoughtful comments on the completed draft. For production of the book,

I want to thank the staff at CQ Press for their efforts: my sponsoring editor, Patricia Gallagher, for valuable initial feedback and guidance; Jon Preimesberger for a splendid job of editing the manuscript; Jessica Forman for the page layouts; and Grace Hill for her assistance on a variety of matters.

Richard J. Carroll

Introduction

Q **1. What is economics?**

A Economics is "the branch of knowledge that deals with the production and distribution of wealth in theory and practice." The economic challenge for a nation is to allocate limited resources among unlimited demands in the best way possible.

Economics is a particularly interesting field because it is a complex blend of pure and social sciences. It draws from at least five other disciplines: history, mathematics, sociology, psychology, and philosophy.

Q **2. Why is economics so important?**

A Economics is important because of the impact the wrong economic decisions can have on the standard of living, whether for a nation or for a single household. Anyone who lived through the Great Depression knows the consequences of wrong economic decisions by the nation's leaders. Someone who made poor investment decisions twenty years ago and is now faced with retiring with inadequate savings also knows the importance of economics. Today the decisions that policymakers make about Social Security or environmental protection could profoundly affect the nation's well-being in the future.

A strong economic performance creates a high standard of living for a nation. In societies with high standards of living, such as the United States, people have access to abundant food, state-of-the-art medical care, higher education, a multitude of consumer gadgets, and numerous options of what to do with one's life. In nations with low standards of living, as in the third world, families usually must farm just to survive. This is the situation for more than 3 billion people or half of the earth's population. Why are there such great differences between standards of living? Technology is probably one reason for the differences in the living standard, but economic organization under a free market system has led to many of the technological breakthroughs. The development of the financial sector allowed people to invest in research and development that led to technical breakthroughs and in machines that increase productivity and save labor. Today, less than 3 percent of the U.S. population farms but still much of the nation's agricultural production is exported.

Q 3. What do economists do?

A As the economy has grown more complex, economics has become a very broad discipline with countless areas of specialization. The federal government employs economists to analyze the costs and benefits of any change in economic policy, such as how a modification in tax policy might affect all segments of society. Local government employs economists to analyze local and regional economic issues, such as determining whether it would be economically viable to construct a new road or bridge. The private sector (business and industry) needs economists to analyze potential contracts, investments, and more efficient means of production. Whatever the area of specialization, economists all have one central duty: to assess the costs and benefits of an economic activity. This is how economists determine whether an activity is worthwhile or not.

Economists identify the economic actions that lead to the stated goal of policymakers or business executives, while maximizing efficiency. Policymakers often require economists to evaluate the costs and benefits of value considerations in their analysis, such as determining whether the poor are sufficiently protected by a progressive tax system or whether social safety nets are adequate. In the private sector, value considerations might include the environmental and employment impacts of a business investment, such as a new construction project in a local area.

Q 4. Is economics an art or a science?

A Economics is a fairly strict discipline with established research methods and standards. With all the numerical data and calculations that economists employ, economics would clearly seem to be a science, if merely a social science. In order to carry out their principal duty of assessing the costs and benefits of economic decisions, economists try to use the best information and tools of economic analysis. They generally do not try to be overly "artistic" by wearing the hat of the sociologist, engineer, psychologist, or politician in the process, even though those disciplines are implicit in the field of economics.

Dealing with future uncertainty would seem to be an area of economics that would be less reliant on scientific methods. But economists seldom deal artistically with this challenge. Rather, economists who try to predict future economic happenings tend to qualify their conclusions and make heavy assumptions. Sometimes econ-

Q **12. What was the average rate of economic growth during each of the previous five decades?**

A The average rate of economic growth by decade was

1950s	4.0%
1960s	4.3%
1970s	3.2%
1980s	3.0%
1990s	3.0%

Q **13. What is considered a "good" economic growth rate for today?**

A Given recent and historical growth rates, a "good" growth rate would be between 2.5 and 3.5 percent. A "slow" growth rate would fall below 2.0 percent, while rapid growth would be more than 4.0 percent. During the 1980s and 1990s, the highest growth rate was 7.3 percent in 1984, while the lowest was -1.9 percent in 1982. The growth rate in 1998 was 4.0 percent.

Q **14. What is the difference between GDP and the gross national product?**

A In addition to what GDP covers, GNP includes payments by foreigners to domestic residents for labor and property that is supplied *abroad*. GDP is confined to production from domestic resources. (Both GDP and GNP include payments for such services supplied *domestically* by nonresidents.) The difference between GDP and the gross national product (GNP) for the United States is small.

Q **15. Why did the federal government switch the official gauge of the U.S. economy from GNP to GDP in 1991?**

A The United States switched from GNP to GDP to be more consistent with the measures that other major industrial countries were using.

Q **16. Why are other indicators needed to capture economic performance?**

A The main reason to look beyond mere average GDP growth rates is that a broader set of indicators provides insights into whether GDP growth *would* have been higher or lower *under a given set of economic conditions*. For example, if GDP growth were below average but saving and investment rates were high, then the higher saving and investment rates might lay the basis for future GDP growth.

Q 17. Does GDP measure the value of every good and service produced in the United States each year?

A GDP is only an estimate of total annual production. It is calculated from data taken from a wide variety of federal agencies, such as the Census Bureau and the Bureau of Labor Statistics, and many private industry trade associations. The margin of error of the GDP estimate is not known.

Q 18. Does GDP growth define the business cycle?

A A number of measures go into tracking the business cycle. Other leading economic indicators, such as housing starts and business equipment orders, precede the peaks and troughs of the business cycle by six to twelve months. A trough is usually a recession, which is defined by two successive quarters of contraction of the economy. The peak of the business cycle is the point just before GDP growth begins to decelerate. GDP is, however, the determining business cycle measure, because GDP growth defines peaks and troughs.

Q 19. Has the business cycle changed during the past half century?

A Business cycles have changed in frequency, magnitude, and duration during the previous 50 years. They have had troughs with only slightly negative growth, such as occurred in 1960 with -0.1 percent growth in two quarters during that year, to as deep as -1.9 percent GDP growth in 1981–1982. Peaks have been as low as 2.5 percent (1981) and as high as 8.9 percent (1950). Cycles, which can be measured from peak to peak, or trough to trough, have been as short as 5 quarters (1980–1982), or longer than 35 quarters (1958–1969 and 1991–1999).

(See 11 How many recessions occurred in the United States from 1946 to 1999?)

Q 20. Do the president's and Congress's policies affect the business cycle?

A The actions of the president and Congress have an effect on the economy, but usually a minor one. Annual budget deals with moderate tax increases or cuts usually have a modest impact on the business cycle. A large tax cut (of the size of the

Kennedy tax cut of 1964 or the Reagan tax cut of 1981) is probably enough to increase the peaks and prolong the expansion phase of the business cycle. Tax policy, not just increases and cuts, can also affect economic activity by changing the incentive structure in economic behavior, but it is not known how much such interventions alter the business cycle. Suggesting that Congress was often left behind by economic events, Martin Feldstein, chief economic advisor under President Ronald Reagan, used to say that one could tell when a recession was over by the passage by Congress of a jobs bill. As historical events have shown, the economy is often dominated by forces beyond a president's and Congress's control.

(See 172 What and how much was the "Kennedy Tax Cut"? 628 Who has more influence on the economy, the president or Congress?)

EMPLOYMENT AND UNEMPLOYMENT

Q 21. What is unemployment and how is it measured?

A Anyone who is part of the workforce and who is ready, willing, and able to work but does not have a job is considered unemployed. The workforce consists of people who are employed and self-employed but does not include the military, the retired, or those under age 16. Unemployment is most commonly measured by the unemployment rate, which is the percentage of the workforce looking for work but not finding it. This indicator is compiled by the Bureau of Labor Statistics.

Q 22. What causes unemployment?

A Changes in unemployment are very closely related to GDP, so almost anything that causes an economic contraction also causes unemployment: a downswing in the business cycle, a drop in the level of investment (with delayed effects), a recession in other countries that buy U.S. exports, and high interest rates (which reduces investment). Rigid or artificially high wages, as might occur if minimum wages or union contracted wages are too high, can also increase unemployment. Generally, when wages are higher than the value of worker-produced goods or services, unemployment increases.

Q 23. What was the overall trend in growth of employment from 1946 to 1999?

A From 1946 to 1999, employment grew at an average rate of 1.8 percent. During the same period, the civilian labor force participation rate—that is, the percentage of the population in the labor force—increased from 57.3 percent to 67.1 percent. The participation rate accelerated in the 1960s with the large influx of women into the labor force. With the participation rate rising, it has become more difficult for the economy to keep the *unemployment rate* low, since a higher percentage of people want to work. The official growth rate of employment takes this phenomenon into account by simply measuring the net increase in the total number of employed people, and, thus, provides a useful complement to the unemployment rate.

Figure 4 illustrates the annual growth rate per year during this period. The main employment trends were the high degree of fluctuation of employment growth from 1946 to 1960 (as also seen with GDP growth), the moderate and sustained growth of employment between 1962 and 1973, erratic growth and decline from 1974 to 1982, and the moderate, steady growth from 1983 to 1999.

Figure 4   Employment Growth, 1946–1999

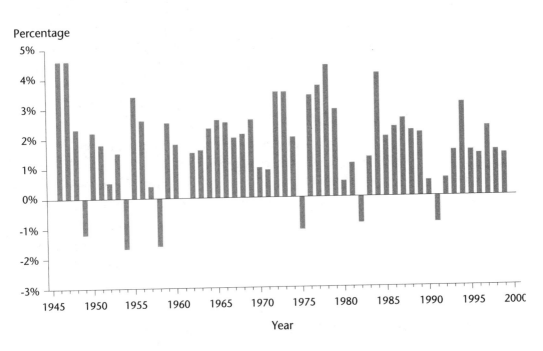

Source: U.S. Labor Department, Bureau of Labor Statistics.

Figure 6   Inflation Rate, 1946–1999

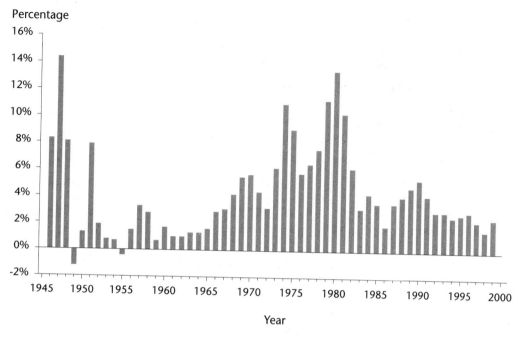

Percentage

Source: U.S. Labor Department, Bureau of Labor Statistics.

(See 178 What was President Johnson's tax surcharge? 179 What were the major economic changes that President Nixon imposed?)

Q 32. What was the average inflation rate during each of the previous five decades?

A The average inflation rate by decade was

1950s	2.0%
1960s	2.3%
1970s	6.8%
1980s	5.4%
1990s	3.0%

33. What is considered a good level of inflation for today?

A The inflation environment of the 1980s and 1990s certainly improved from that of the double-digit inflation of the 1970s. Under President Ronald Reagan, the average inflation rate was lowered by 5.5 percentage points, under George Bush, another 1.1 percentage points and under Bill Clinton, yet another 1.4 percentage points. After Federal Reserve Chairman Paul Volcker and the Reagan administration campaigned to defeat inflation in the 1980s, a new attitude of intolerance of inflation became prevalent. A 3.0 percent rate, which is lower than what was considered good in the 1970s and 1980s, is now considered good, even though it is higher than the 2.2 percent of 1999.

Even at these historically low inflation levels, economists have shown by a preponderance of evidence that the CPI still overstates actual inflation by up to 1 percent. When the 1999 inflation rate of 2.2 percent is adjusted for this overstatement, a near zero inflation rate is achieved, an excellent performance.

(See 325 What is the central controversy over the Consumer Price Index?)

34. Could the United States ever experience hyperinflation?

A Hyperinflation is generally understood to be extremely high inflation to the point that people begin to resort to bartering to obtain goods and services. In the current U.S. context, anything above 15 percent would be extreme. Hyperinflation is extremely unlikely because it can only be generated by excessive growth in the money supply. The agencies of the federal government devoted to managing the economy, such as the Treasury Department and Federal Reserve, work diligently to prevent this from happening. However, to take an extreme hypothetical example, if the entire $5 trillion gross federal debt were monetized, that is, paid off by newly printed money, hyperinflation would result. Monetizing the entire debt would cause currency in circulation to increase by tenfold and M1 by fivefold.

(See 36 What is the money supply?)

MONEY AND INTEREST RATES

35. What is the Federal Reserve?

A The Federal Reserve (Fed) is the central bank of the United States that (1) conducts U.S. monetary policy; (2) regulates banking institutions and protects the credit rights

Still, the Fed can influence the money supply in the short run, and investors are keenly interested in the Fed's plans for the money supply. Investors want to be the first to respond to or anticipate the Fed's interventions so they can exploit the financial opportunity. The Fed's announcements and interventions are also signals of future Fed intentions.

Q 47. What is the gold standard?

A The gold standard is the system by which a country gives gold in exchange for any of its currency when demanded. The gold standard has special significance for international trade, because adherence to the gold standard means fixed exchange rates for all participating countries. For example, if gold is redeemed for $300 per ounce in the United States and 600 marks in Germany, then the exchange is 2 German marks per $1, and that rate remains fixed. Under a gold standard, all international debts are settled in gold. A balance of payments surplus means an inflow of gold to the central bank's reserve.

Q 48. What is the effect of interest rates on saving, investment, and growth?

A Interest rates have a strong effect on investment because they represent an "opportunity cost for investment." The opportunity cost is the return investors could have received by placing their money in the next best investment. High interest rates have a strong dampening effect on investment. Interest rates have a much less pronounced effect on saving. People save as a residual to their consumption, which is mainly based on their expected income during their lifetimes, rather than on interest rates. Interest rates provide an incentive to save, but actual saving works primarily through people's estimate of what they can afford to consume. High interest rates damage growth through their effects on investment and excessively high interest rates can contribute to recessions as in 1981–1982 and 1990–1991.

(See 306 Do interest rates really matter to saving and investment?)

Q 49. Why are interest rates a measure of economic performance?

A Interest rates are the economy's way of discounting the future, that is, they represent investors' expectations of how well the economy will perform. In order to induce people to invest, the return on investment has to exceed the interest rate. Interest rates thus cover a risk factor and a natural discount rate to compensate savers for postponing consumption. The higher the interest rate, the higher the perceived risk in, and the lower the expectations for, the economy.

Q 50. What was the overall trend in interest rates from 1946 to 1999?

A The average real prime interest rate was 2.6 percent for 1946–1999. There are four distinct interest rate subperiods. (See Figure 8.) The first period covers 1946 to 1952 and was characterized by grossly negative real interest rates, which were as low as -11.3 percent in 1947. This phenomenon was a result of low rates, combined with 14.4 percent inflation, hence the sharply negative real interest rate. The prime rate should not be confused with *deposit* rates, which were strictly controlled under interest rate ceilings. These interest ceilings meant that real deposit rates were essentially determined by the inflation rate, as there was only very limited possibility for the regulated nominal rate to adjust. Only the low and moderate inflation of the 1950s and 1960s guaranteed "reasonable" real returns on deposits. As nominal deposit rates were gradually deregulated during the 1970s and early 1980s, nominal deposit rates were initially quite volatile and high.

Figure 8   Real Prime Interest Rate, 1946–1999

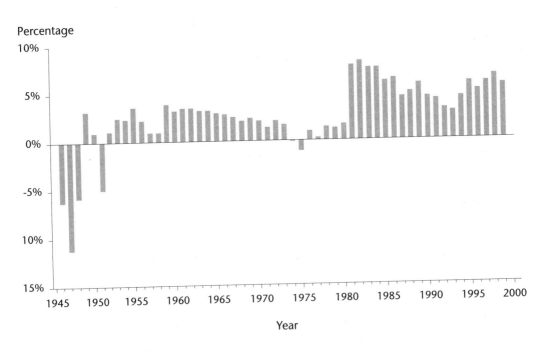

Source: Federal Reserve.

During the second period (1952–1980), interest rates increased modestly and inflation was low to moderate. The range of real prime interest rates was rather narrow, between -1.1 and 3.8 percent. This period included a 16-year stretch, 1959–1975, in which rates declined fairly steadily from 3.8 percent to -1.1 percent. The second period closed out with the real prime rate in the 1.2 to 1.6 percent range for the three years 1978 to 1980. The third period began with a quantum leap in 1981 (actually beginning in late 1980) in which the real interest rate jumped to 7.8 percent and peaked at 8.1 percent in 1982. Thereafter, rates steadily declined to 2.9 percent in 1993. The fourth period recorded a gradual rise to 6.6 percent by 1998 and dropped to 5.7 percent in 1999.

Q **51. What was the average prime interest rate during each of the previous five decades?**

A The average prime interest rate by decade was

1950s	1.3%
1960s	2.9%
1970s	1.1%
1980s	6.0%
1990s	4.8%

Q **52. What is considered a good real interest rate, that is, consistent with growth, for today?**

A Real interest rates in the late 1990s were far above the historical average of 2.6 percent or even the average of the previous 40 years of 3.6 percent, which is a bit perplexing given the otherwise benign economic environment. A real interest rate should probably not exceed 4 percent (over and above inflation), otherwise investment might be too costly and growth could be reduced in future years. The real interest rate in 1998 was 6.6 percent, quite high by historical standards.

INVESTMENT AND SAVINGS

Q **53. What are the measures of investment?**

A Investment is defined as expenditure by business on physical assets with a life of more than one year. The major components of gross investment are gross private domestic investment, gross government investment, and net foreign investment. These investment measures are part of the National Income and Product Accounts (NIPA) that are compiled by the Department of Commerce. The major components of gross private domestic investment (GPDI), their dollar amounts, and percent of total investment in 1997 are illustrated in the following table:

Category	$ billions	Percent of GPDI
Gross Private Domestic Investment	$1,256.0	100%
Fixed Investment	1,188.6	95
Nonresidential	*860.7*	*69*
Residential	*327.9*	*26*
Business Inventories	67.4	5

Gross private domestic fixed investment is determined by subtracting the change in business inventories from GPDI.

Q 54. What is gross versus net investment?

A Gross investment is simply the total amount of investment in the economy during a year. Net investment is the amount of investment over and above the amount of capital consumption, or investment used up (depreciation). Net saving is needed to finance net investment.

Q 55. What are the main measures of saving?

A Personal saving is the most popular indicator of how thrifty individuals are. Gross private saving includes undistributed corporate profits, which are retained earnings, that is, profits after companies pay taxes and dividends. Gross saving adds government saving to private saving. As the federal deficit disappeared in the late 1990s, the government was transformed from a big dissaver to a saver.

Capital consumption, or depreciation, which is the value of the capital asset divided by its years of useful life, appears as a component of savings in "gross" savings measures. For example, in government savings because the NIPA measure of federal deficit takes out depreciation, it is a net savings measure. Depreciation or capital consumption at both the federal and state and local levels is added back in to create gross savings measures.

Measurements of Saving

Personal saving	Gross private saving	Gross government saving	Gross saving
Personal income minus taxes and consumption	Personal saving	Federal capital consumption	Gross private saving
	Undistributed corporate profits	Federal surplus or deficit	Government saving
	Inventory valuation	State and local capital consumption adjustment	
	Capital consumption	State and local surplus or deficit adjustment	
	Noncorporate fixed capital consumption adjustment		
	Wage accruals minus disbursement		

Q **56. What do savings and investment measures exclude?**

A Generally, savings is income not spent and investment is expenditure that produces a future income stream. But this is not always the case. Investment measures do not cover education, even though it is clear that the more educated a society is, the greater is its stream of future income. Savings excludes real estate appreciation (which affords the benefit of financial leverage) and stock appreciation. Both are seen as increases in wealth that is not spent.

(See 335 What is the controversy about the standard saving rate measure?)

Q 57. Why is it said that businesses invest, but households save?

A It is simply a convention under the standard NIPA system that what an individual buys is considered consumption (because it must be for personal use) and what a business buys that lasts more than one year is considered investment (because it must be for production). For example, when a business buys a computer, NIPA records it as investment. When an individual buys a computer, NIPA records it as consumption. Yet, NIPA treats a homeowner as a business in which he rents the home to himself. The rental value of owner-occupied housing is actually part of GDP. Depreciation on the home is also factored into the national accounts.

Q 58. Does this mean that measuring savings and investment is worthless?

A It is certainly not worthless to measure savings and investment, but it is very important to know their limitations and what they can and cannot be used for.

(See 337 Are these exclusions of the NIPA a big problem?)

Q 59. Does the share of investment in GDP indicate how well the economy is going to do?

A Market analysts view investment as a "lagging indicator" of economic activity, that is, if there is a high level of investment relative to GDP, then the economy is already doing well. But there are other investment indicators that are considered "leading indicators," that is, they indicate how the economy is going to perform. Leading investment indicators include housing starts, imports of capital goods, construction spending, and announcements of investment intentions. Increasing business inventories can also be a leading indicator if the increase in inventories is due to an expectation of increasing demand, but not due to a decline in business sales (in which case it would be a lagging indicator). Generally, because the lead time of investment to increased output can vary by years, investment as a percent of GDP is of little value to forecasters as a "leading indicator."

Q 60. Why is capital consumption part of savings?

A Capital consumption is counted as savings because it measures the funds set aside for future depreciation.

61. What was the overall trend in saving rates from 1946 to 1999?

A From 1946 to 1999, gross private saving rates varied between 11.0 and 21.0 percent. (See Figure 9.) The lowest rate, 11.0 percent, occurred in 1947, and the lowest in the past 40 years, 14.9 percent, occurred in 1999. Three identifiable subperiods in Figure 9 are: (1) 1948–1969, which was typified by moderate and steady saving rates ranging between 14.2 and 18.1 percent; (2) 1970–1988, characterized by higher saving rates, with 16 of the 19 years having rates of 18 percent or higher, and a peak of 21.0 percent in 1984; and (3) 1989–1999, in which saving declined to below 15 percent by 1999. The average for the entire third period was 17.1 percent.

For personal saving rates, the saving by individuals and households, there are no trends that last more than four years in a positive or negative direction until 1997. (See Figure 10.) The lower and upper bounds of saving rates are 2.4 percent and 10.9 percent. For the period 1950–1986, the saving rate levels are similar in both the earlier years and the later years, that is, individuals' inclination to save did not change significantly during 1950–1986. However, from 1987 to 1998 personal saving rates

Figure 9   Gross Private Savings as Percentage of GDP, 1946–1999

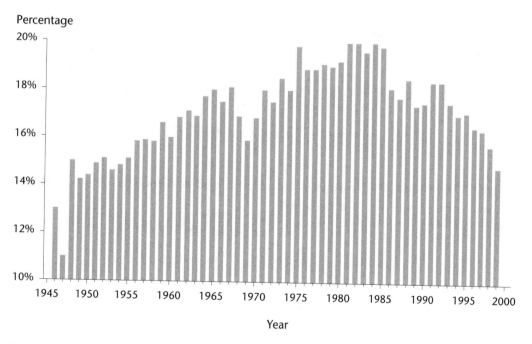

Source: U.S. Commerce Department, Bureau of Economic Analysis.

Figure 10   Personal Savings Rate, 1946–1999

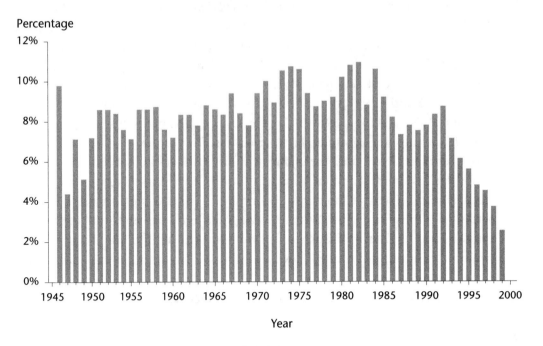

Percentage

Source: U.S. Commerce Department, Bureau of Economic Analysis.

were lower than in previous years with a sharp decline in the latter part of the 1990s. The average saving rate for 1946–1999 was 8.1 percent.

(See 55 What are the main measures of saving?)

Q 62. What were the average gross private and personal saving rates during each of the previous five decades?

A The average gross private and personal saving rates by decade were

	Gross private saving	Personal saving
1950s	15.0%	7.7%
1960s	17.0	8.3
1970s	17.9	9.4
1980s	19.5	9.4
1990s	17.5	6.8

Q 77. What is considered a good compensation growth rate for today?

A Compensation growth, in principle, should match productivity growth, but competition has dictated that real compensation lag behind productivity. Compensation has fallen behind productivity by 0.6 percent per year for the entire postwar period. If a good productivity growth rate is between 1.5 and 2.0 percent, then a fair minimum compensation growth would be between 0.9 and 1.5 percent annually (although this could extend as high as the full, reasonable productivity increase, or 2.0 percent).

Q 78. At the end of the 1990s, were people working harder for less money than they were at the beginning of the decade?

A Despite the good economy of the 1990s, aggregate compensation declined for three straight years from 1993 to 1995. Lower skilled job compensation declined even more sharply during this same period. So yes, the lower skilled segments of the workforce were working harder for less money than they were at the beginning of the decade.

POVERTY

Q 79. How does the government define poverty?

A The federal government defines poverty as falling below the level of income needed to purchase the goods and services, mostly food, clothing, shelter, and medical care, required for "basic human" needs. The main indicator for poverty is "the percentage of the population below the poverty line." The poverty line indicator was conceived in 1964, and the series was estimated back to 1959 (the earliest year available). The poverty line of income is called the "poverty threshold."

Q 80. What is a poverty threshold and how was it developed?

A The official calculation of the point at which a person's or family's income falls below the poverty line is called the poverty threshold. The poverty threshold is based on two items: (1) the most economical of four nutritionally adequate food plans designed by the Department of Agriculture; and (2) a 1955 survey by the Department of Agriculture that found that families of three or more spent about one-third of their income on food. Therefore, the poverty level was set at three times the cost of the least expensive food plan. Adjustments were made for families of one or two persons in order to make up for the higher fixed costs of rent, utilities, and other household costs. From 1969 onward, the poverty threshold for nonfarm families was adjusted by the CPI and the threshold for farm families was raised from 70 to 85 percent of the nonfarm thresholds. These changes resulted in an increase of 360,000 families (1.6 million individuals) counted as poor in 1967. Further changes were made in 1980: (1) separate thresholds for farm families were eliminated, (2) thresholds for female household heads and "all other families" were averaged, and (3) the poverty matrix was extended to families of nine or more.

Q 81. How are the poverty thresholds calculated?

A Since the smallest economic units are families (of one or more people), thresholds are calculated specific to family size. The poverty threshold is compared with the family's total *money* income, that is, earnings, interest income, Social Security, public assistance payments, unemployment and workers' compensation, and all pensions. The estimate of family income excludes nonmonetary transfers such as food stamps, subsidized school lunches, subsidized housing, Medicaid, and Medicare. Families whose income falls below the threshold are considered poor. Thus, there is a poverty threshold for each family size and, of course, that threshold increases as family size increases. If, for example, a family of nine fell below the poverty threshold of $32,556 (1997 level), then all nine members of that family were said to be below the poverty line. The yearly percentage below the poverty line measures poverty through March of the following year. Annual statistics are released in the following September.

Q 82. What was the overall trend in the population below the poverty line from 1959 to 1998?

A The percent of the population below the poverty line was first estimated for 1959 at a rate of 22.4 percent. This indicator did not fluctuate much, but moved in fairly smooth waves during long time spans. (See Figure 14.) This pattern is due in part to the fact that this indicator is measured in *levels* rather than *growth rates*, which fluctuate much more. The percent below the poverty line declined during the next 14 years, from 1959 to 1973. It was interrupted by a minor increase during 1970–1971 and recorded the lowest level of the period in 1973 at a level of 11.1 percent. The declining trend in the poverty share ended in 1975 when it rose to 12.3 percent, but it then fell again for the next three years, from 1976 to 1978, to 11.4 percent by 1978. For the next five years, from 1979 to 1983 the percent of the population under the

(See 373 Why do corporations restructure? 379 Is corporate restructuring a short-sighted way to hike stock prices?)

Q 99. Why does the stock market sometimes interpret good news as bad?

A Frequently, upon news of higher than expected GDP growth, or a drop in the unemployment rate, the stock market will react negatively. If the stock market is a barometer of the expected future of the economy, then how could such good economic news—such as a drop in unemployment—be seen as bad? The simple answer is that market traders are reacting to the fear of inflation, and, perhaps more importantly, the anticipation of action by the Fed to counter inflation, such as raising interest rates. Traders, wanting to achieve higher returns, may sell in anticipation of Fed actions that might temporarily reduce stock prices. But this initial negative reaction is often short-lived. Despite the continuous reduction in unemployment during 1992–1999, the stock market continued to rise as inflation fears were quickly erased. Thus, the initial negative market reaction owes to fear of inflation, but over the longer term, the generally bright economic prospects are reflected positively in the stock market.

(See 296 Is there a trade-off between inflation and unemployment?)

Q 100. Why is it good to have a high stock market?

A Higher stock prices mean that firms can raise more investment funds by selling company-owned shares of their stock. With greater supplies of investment funds, companies have more options to grow, to develop new products, to compete in more markets, and to achieve economies of scale. To some extent, the higher stock prices have been self-sustaining because they have given a strong advantage to U.S. companies in accessing investment funds that has driven up expected future earnings, and, therefore stock prices. In other words, higher stock prices can beget higher stock prices.

Q 101. Did all stock market measures rise sharply in the 1990s?

A Most measures that cover predominantly large companies, such as the S&P 500, followed the DJIA upward in the 1990s. Lower-valued companies did not appreciate as fast during the second boom in the 1990s. So, the great stock market boom of the 1990s, although fairly broad, was not marketwide.

Q **102. Was the market overvalued in the late 1990s?**

A Overvaluation is sometimes indicated by the price-earnings (PE) ratio—the ratio of the company's stock price to its earnings. PE ratios were the highest in history, with the PE of the S&P 500 stocks reaching 30 in 1999. Without a proportional change in the real value of the companies, it was reasonable to conclude that the stock market was overvalued at this time. But value is in the eyes of the market, and the prices of stocks, like the prices of most everything else, are determined by supply and demand, and, more specifically, the expected value of companies' future earnings.

Q **103. What did Federal Reserve Chairman Alan Greenspan mean by "irrational exuberance" in describing the financial markets in 1996?**

A Greenspan was addressing the role of monetary policy in an environment of "asset bubbles" in the financial markets. Asset bubbles are assets that appreciate rapidly, but are vulnerable to collapse. His term, "irrational exuberance," suggested that some financial assets were overpriced. From 1997 to 1999, however, the stock market increased another 4,000 points.

INTERNATIONAL TRADE

Q **104. What are the components of international trade?**

A International trade can be as narrow as the simple import and export of goods and as broad as all international transactions including all cross-border financial dealings. Generally, *trade* is understood to refer to the import and export of goods and services. Services are traded, for example, by having American tourists go to Europe (which would be recorded as a U.S. import of services from Europe), or Chinese students earning a graduate degree at a U.S. university (which would be recorded as a U.S. export of services to China). Services also consist of banking and insurance and are traded electronically.

The Balance of Payments (BOP) is a more comprehensive measure of international transactions than is trade. BOP is divided into a current account and a capital account. The current account consists of visible and invisible trade, that is, exports and imports of goods (visibles) and services (invisibles), and profits earned overseas and interest payments. The capital account is made up of the actual investment by Americans in foreign countries, as opposed to just the profits from investment, as well as foreigners' investment in America, and international grants and loans.

105. Why is trade important?

A Increased trade raises the consumption, and thus standard of living, of the trading countries. For the United States, as for any country, this consumption is sustainable if the United States can pay for it, which is best done by exporting at a comparable level as importing. U.S. exports also support U.S. companies and increase employment and purchasing power. Trade also acts as a kind of economic stabilizer. If one country sinks into recession and its currency value falls, its exports become more competitive. The resulting increased foreign demand for products of the country in recession can help jump-start the economy, making the recession briefer and lighter.

Q **106. What is the trade balance?**

A The narrow definition of the balance of trade is the excess of visible (tangible) exports over visible imports. A broader definition includes products of factors of production, including services, workers' remittances, royalties, and income from international investments. Through most of the 1980s and 1990s, the U.S. balance of trade was negative. The United States had a deficit of $150 billion in 1998, and more than $250 billion in 1999. Economists disagree on whether such large trade deficits are healthy or unhealthy. The positive side of the negative trade balance is that the large excess of imports over exports has helped keep inflation in the United States low as more goods have flooded in to absorb American purchasing power. Consumers reap benefits through a wider choice of less expensive goods and services. The negative side is that, at a minimum, foreigners build up claims on U.S. resources through their accumulation of dollars. In another phase of the business cycle, foreigners cashing in their dollars could drive up inflation, but also create a large additional demand for U.S. produced goods.

Q **107. What was the trade balance from 1946 to 1999?**

A The trade balance (exports minus imports) was positive for all except two years in the first 22 years after World War II. By 1968, that all changed. For the next 31 years, the trade balance was negative in all but three years. (See Figure 16.) The trade deficit increased sharply in the mid to late 1980s, fell substantially from 1989 to 1991, but increased steadily thereafter with very large increases in 1993, 1998, and 1999.

Figure 16   Real Balance of Trade on Goods and Services, 1946–1999

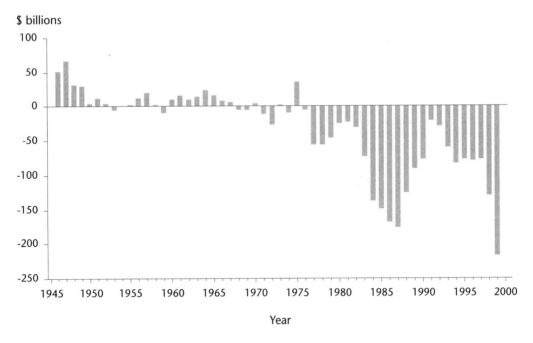

$ billions

Year

Source: U.S. Commerce Department, Bureau of Economic Analysis.

Q 108. What percentage of GDP were the average export and trade volumes during each of the previous five decades?

A The average export and trade volumes as a share of GDP by decade were

	Trade volume % of GDP	Export volume % of GDP
1950s	8.4%	4.3%
1960s	9.4	4.9
1970s	14.8	7.2
1980s	18.6	8.4
1990s	22.3	10.6

Q 109. What is considered a good balance between exports and imports today?

A A trade balance surplus of any size, or even a zero balance, would be fine historically. That was not realistic for the United States at the end of the 1990s. The strength of the dollar, because of relatively good economic conditions and prospects in the

	1999	1946–1999
Human resources	62.2%	41.4%
Defense	16.1	36.6
Net interest payments	13.5	9.9
Other	5.8	9.0
Physical resources	4.8	7.3
Undistributed offsetting receipts	2.4	4.1

Note: Undistributed offsetting receipts are subtracted from the total percentage of all categories to arrive at 100 percent.

Q 119. What makes up these categories?

A Most of the major categories of federal government expenditure can be further divided into subcategories, listed below in descending order of expenditures for 1999:

• Human resources: $1.058.9 billion
  (1) Social Security (on- and off-budget): $390.0 billion
  (2) Income security: $237.7 billion
  (3) Medicare: $190.4 billion
  (4) Other health: $141.1 billion
  (5) Education, training, employment and social services: $56.4 billion
  (6) Veterans' benefits and services: $43.2 billion

• Defense: $274.9 billion

• Net interest (on- and off-budget): $229.7 billion

• Other functions: $98.1 billion
  (1) Administration of justice: $25.9 billion
  (2) Agriculture: $23.0 billion
  (3) General science, space, and technology: $18.1 billion
  (4) General government: $15.8 billion
  (5) International affairs (which includes foreign aid): $15.2 billion

• Physical resources:$81.3 billion
  (1) Transportation: $42.5 billion
  (2) Natural resources and the environment: $24.0 billion

(3) Community and regional development: $11.9 billion

(4) Commerce and housing credit (on- and off-budget): $2.6 billion

(5) Energy: $0.9 billion

The category entitled "Undistributed offsetting receipts" consists of receipts collected by the government that are not attributed to any functional category. The current sources of these receipts include employee retirement contributions, royalties from oil leases, and proceeds from the sale of federal assets.

Q 120. Why are these shares important?

A To some extent, these shares represent the priorities of Congress and the president. Historically, they also reflect exigencies, such as war and transfer payments related to recession.

Q 121. How much of the budget is composed of transfer payments and how much is composed of government purchases?

A About 70 percent of the total federal budget is money that is taken in taxes and sent back out to others in the form of transfer payments. The remainder, or about 30 percent, is government purchases and is counted as part of GDP. Transfer payments are not part of GDP.

Q 122. What was the overall trend in the composition of the federal budget from 1946 to 1999?

A The most striking change in the federal budget over time is the shift of resources out of defense and into human resources. (See Figure 19.) Only during the Korean War, the Vietnam War, and the military buildup during the Reagan administration was this resource shift interrupted. Human resources increased during 1953 to 1976, from 15.6 percent of the federal budget to 54.8 percent, leveled off, then dropped to 48.6 percent in 1986, and increased thereafter reaching 62.2 percent in 1999. Defense, between 1953 and 1965, fell from 69.4 percent of the budget to 42.8 percent. Defense expenditures began to increase because of the Vietnam War, but only for three years, reaching 46.0 percent in 1968. Afterward, however, even as the war continued, defense expenditures fell to 34.3 percent by 1972, the last year of American involvement. Defense expenditures continued to fall to 22.7 percent by 1980. Beginning in 1981, defense expenditures' share of the federal budget increased, reaching 28.1 percent by 1987, reflecting the Reagan buildup. Soon afterward, the cold war was over, and defense expenditures plummeted to 16.1 percent by 1999, the lowest level since before World War II. The peace dividend in terms of defense expenditure reductions has therefore probably reached its limit. However, the avoidance of higher defense expenditures every year constitutes an annual peace dividend.

Another major trend is the increase in interest payments as a share of the total budget. In 1948, as the United States was paying off the expenses for World War II, interest payments on the debt were 14.6 percent of the budget. The U.S. economy was able to pay off the debt of World War II and the Korean War astoundingly quickly and interest payments were down to 6.3 percent by 1959, albeit under the controlled interest rate regime of the Federal Reserve and the Treasury. Interest payments were in the 7 to 8 percent range for most of the 1960s and 1970s. Interest pay-

Figure 19 Composition of the Federal Budget, 1946–1999

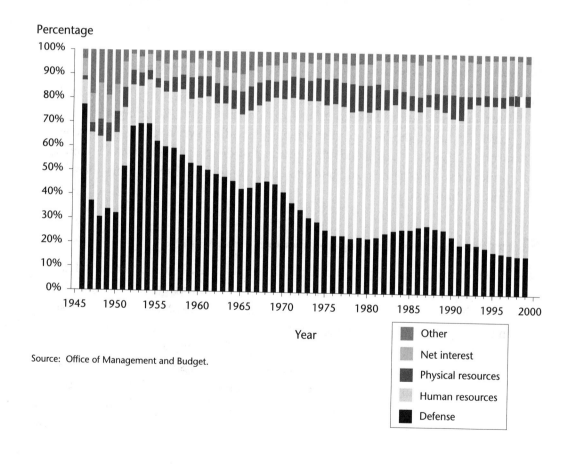

Source: Office of Management and Budget.

ments on the debt began to rise in 1975, going from a 7.0 percent share of the budget to 15.4 percent by 1996, as the federal debt soared. In the late 1990s, interest payments started to decrease. It is important to remember that interest payments are not only a function of the size of the debt, but also of the prevailing interest rates and the term structure of the debt.

(See 317 What is the term structure of the national debt and why is it important?)

Q 123. What is the difference between "on" and "off" budget items?

A An off-budget item is spending or revenue that is excluded from the budget totals by law. Off-budget outlays are mostly funded by revenues collected for specific off-budget programs. For example, the revenues and outlays of the Social Security trust fund and the transactions of the Postal Service are off-budget. Nevertheless, on- and off-budget items are routinely lumped together when budget outlays, deficits, and surpluses are reported in the press.

Q 124. What is discretionary versus nondiscretionary spending?

A Discretionary spending is federal money spent for programs whose funding levels are determined and controlled in annual appropriation acts. Congress, thus, has the power to change the level of discretionary spending every year. Nondiscretionary spending, also known as mandatory spending or direct spending, is money spent on entitlements, food stamps, and budget authority provided by laws other than annual appropriation acts.

Q 125. How much of the budget is spent on foreign aid?

A In the federal budget, foreign aid is called "International Development and Humanitarian Assistance." In 1999, $9.0 billion was spent on foreign aid, making up five-tenths of one percent of total federal outlays. The United States does give military and other aid to foreign nations, but that aid is given almost entirely to achieve the strategic, self-interested goals of the United States and, therefore, must be put in the category of aid from which the United States receives some reciprocal benefit. It should be added that even U.S. foreign aid for third world development is given for political reasons to countries most cooperative to U.S. interests, although the general goal is economic development.

NATIONAL DEBT AND DEFICIT

Q **126. What is the national debt?**

A The national debt is the total value of the federal government's interest-bearing securities. The national debt does not include coin and currency in circulation. The debt is different from the deficit, which is, roughly, the *annual increase* to the debt. The deficit consists of operating expenditures that exceed operating revenues, additional borrowing to service the existing debt, and, for the unified on- and off-budget deficit, net drawdowns of any government trust funds.

Q **127. How much was the national debt in 1999?**

A First of all, there are actually two versions of national debt: the publicly held federal debt and the gross federal debt. The publicly held debt was $3.7 trillion in 1999. The gross federal debt was $5.6 trillion. The publicly held debt includes all government debt instruments held by the public ($3.1 trillion) plus debt held in the federal reserve system ($0.5 trillion). Gross federal debt is higher because it includes publicly held debt plus debt held in federal accounts. The largest component of debt in federal accounts is the Social Security Trust Fund, which accounts for more than $850 billion. In this section, the *gross federal debt* is used, except where otherwise indicated, because it captures federal borrowing from the trust funds.

(See 224 How high was the balance in the trust fund in 1999? 316 What types of securities does the government sell to make up the national debt?)

Q **128. Which measure of the national debt is more important, absolute dollars, or percent of GDP?**

A Reporters and economists in the media love to use the absolute dollar figure to wow the public. They say that the U.S. debt is more than 5 trillion dollars, with a mighty emphasis on trillion, as if to dramatize this monster burden on the American people. However, a better measure is the debt as a percentage of GDP, because that gives a more accurate picture of whether the economy is big enough to "carry" the debt load. Economists would call this "normalizing" the debt, that is, putting it within a frame of reference to show its true size, and allowing more meaningful comparisons with other countries. A $5 trillion debt to any other country would be a multiple of its GDP and the interest payments on the debt would be insupportable. While the U.S. debt is large in relation to GDP by recent standards, a few years of balanced budgets and, perhaps, surpluses will allow the economy to grow relative to the debt and reduce its relative burden.

Q **129. What was the overall trend in the growth of the federal debt from 1946 to 1999?**

A The gross federal debt levels are adjusted for inflation using government budget deflators. Real national debt trends show four distinct periods. The first period runs from 1947 to 1961, which is characterized by declines in the real level of national debt. The second period runs from 1962 to 1981 in which the debt remained virtually constant. The third period, from 1982 through 1995, experienced uninterrupted and rapid increases in the national debt. The final period showed a leveling off, and slight decline.

Q **130. What was the overall trend in the federal debt as a percentage of GDP from 1946 to 1999?**

A The federal debt expressed as a percent of GDP gives a clearer idea than does the growth of the debt burden on the economy. The real growth of the debt leaves out the fact that the economy has also been growing. Debt measured as a percent of GDP compares the level of debt in each year to the level of output in the economy for that year (gross federal debt divided by GDP). Debt as a percent of GDP follows a similar pattern to that of the real debt level (see Figure 20), but with a more pronounced decline in the first period, 1946–1974, and a less pronounced increase in the second period, 1981–1996. At the very end, 1997–1998, debt as a percent of GDP began to decline slightly. The reason for the difference in slope is that GDP, the denominator of the indicator, was rising throughout the period, thus increasing the steepness of declines in debt as a percent of GDP, while reducing the increases. During the entire 1946–1999 period, the gross federal debt averaged 56.4 percent of GDP.

Q **131. The national debt composed what percentage of GDP during each of the previous five decades?**

A The percentage of GDP composed by the national debt by decade was

1950s	70.3%
1960s	47.8%
1970s	35.6%
1980s	42.9%
1990s	63.9%

Figure 20   Gross Federal Debt as Percentage of GDP, 1946–1999

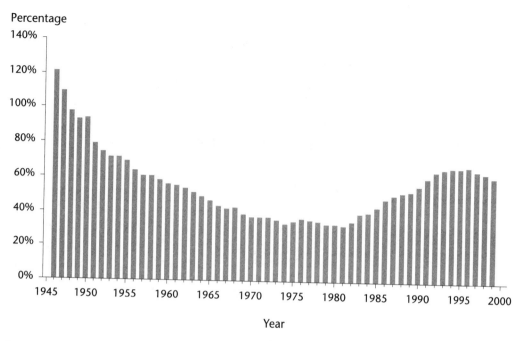

Source: Office of Management and Budget.

Q **132. Is there a relationship between the real interest rate and the size of the debt and/or deficit?**

A The real prime rate does not appear as closely linked to the size of the deficit and debt as some claim. During the Bush administration when the United States recorded the highest deficits, the prime rate actually dropped from 5.8 percent in 1989 to 2.9 percent in 1993. As deficits began to decline and turn into surplus, the real prime rate increased to 6.6 percent by 1998, before ending the decade at 5.7 percent in 1999. Therefore, a relationship developed between deficits and interest rates in the 1990s that was opposite to what was expected. Nevertheless, some politicians claim a close link between eliminating the deficit and lowering the interest rate in order to stimulate investment and growth. This link did not exist in the 1990s. The stronger relationship is between the real interest rate and the levels of economic activity. High growth can push interest rates up.

A Figure 21 depicts surpluses on the unified federal budget as positive percentages of the budget (deficits are negatives). There are four distinct periods: (1) the volatile years 1946–1951 during the Truman administration when the budget oscillated between large then small surpluses and deficits; (2) the period 1952–1974 of small to moderate deficits in all but four years; (3) the period 1975–1995 of high deficits with nearly all deficits falling in the range of 11.6 to 25.7 percent of the budget (with the largest deficits occurring under the Reagan and Bush administrations); and (4) rapidly falling deficits from a $290 billion deficit in 1993 to a $124 billion surplus in 1999.

(See 123 What is the difference between "on" and "off" budget items?)

Figure 21   Federal Deficits as Percentage of the Federal Budget, 1946–1999

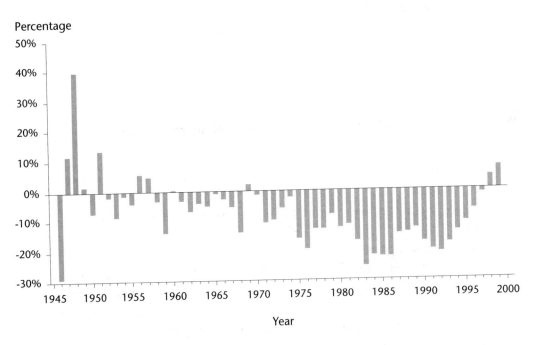

Source: Office of Management and Budget.

Q **134. What was the average deficit share of the federal budget during each of the previous five decades?**

A The average deficit share of the federal budget by decade was

1950s	-1.8%
1960s	-4.1%
1970s	-10.1%
1980s	-17.6%
1990s	-9.9%

Q **135. Is there a relation between deficits and the business cycle?**

A There is a strong relationship between the size of deficits and the trends in GDP or business cycles. When the economy goes into recession, deficits are increased in two ways: by reduced tax revenues because employment and income are lower, and because there is a greater need for transfer payments such as unemployment compensation and other forms of income security transfers. Policymakers are also reluctant to curtail government expenditures for fear of deepening the recession. Accumulated federal debt also follows the business cycle, but because the debt is so much larger than the deficit, percentage-wise it does not fluctuate as much during the business cycle.

FEDERAL TAXES

Q **136. What are the major types of federal taxes?**

A The major federal taxes are the personal income tax; the payroll tax, including Social Security and Medicare; and the corporate income tax.

Q **137. Why is taxation important to the economy?**

A Taxes are a reallocation of a portion of marketed production from the private sector (the tax base) to pay for activities of the public sector. The level of taxes collected is important for two main reasons: the level must be high enough to ensure adequate funding for the government, but not too high to hurt incentives for maximizing production in the private sector.

138. What was the overall trend in federal taxes (measured by taxes' share of GDP) from 1946 to 1999?

A The share of GDP taken in federal taxes did rise during the postwar period, but not as rapidly as many claim. (See Figure 22.) The relative stability is evidenced by the fact that most years' tax shares fell within fairly narrow ranges: All years (54) were within the 14.4–20.0 percent range, 89 percent (48 years) of tax shares fell between 16.0 and 19.5 percent of GDP, and 76 percent (41 of the 54 years) fell within the 17–19 percent range. The 19 percent level was reached eight times: during the Korean War (19.0 percent, 1952), at the height of the Vietnam War (19.0–19.7 percent, 1969–1970), during 1980–1982 (19.1–19.6 percent), and in 1997–1999 (19.3–20.0 percent). Low tax share years by decade were 1949–1951 (14.4–16.1 percent), 1965–1966 (17.0–17.3 percent), 1976 (17.2 percent), 1983–1984 (17.3–17.4 percent), and 1992–1993 (17.5–17.6 percent). The average tax share for the 1946–1999 period was 17.8 percent, while the annual average real growth rate of tax receipts was 2.7 percent.

Figure 22   Federal Tax Receipts as Share of GDP, 1946–1999

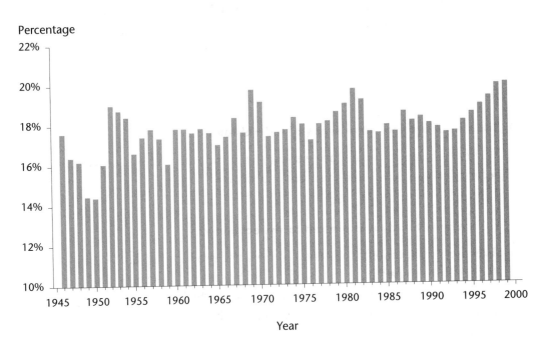

Source: Office of Management and Budget.

In 1929, one key measure of the money supply, called M1, stood at $26.4 billion and by 1933 it had fallen to $19.8 billion, a drop of 25 percent in nominal terms. The tight money policy resulted in rapid *deflation* (over 8 percent annually). The nominal interest rate was only 1 to 2 percent, but the real interest rate soared to more than 10 percent, which depressed investment and, therefore, the economy.

On the fiscal side, even in the midst of the Depression, President Herbert Hoover's administration was still very concerned about budget deficits. The fear of insolvency through deficits led the administration to adopt a tax policy that would have led to a doubling of tax revenue at full employment at a time when the economy was trying to struggle out of the Depression. A tax *increase* was actually instituted in 1932 in an attempt to eliminate budget deficits. With the high unemployment that prevailed, this tax increase was not successful in eliminating budget deficits. Tax increases occurred not only at the federal level, but also at the state and local levels. At the time, state and local taxes accounted for substantially more revenue than did federal taxes. Although the tax increases occurred well after the

Federal Government Receipts and Expenditures Compared with GDP, 1929–1945

Year	Receipts ($ billions)	Expenditures ($ billions)	Expenditures as % of GDP	Surplus or deficit ($ billions)	Real GDP ($ billions)	Real GDP growth
1929	$3.9	$3.1	3.0%	$0.7	$791	
1933	2.0	4.6	8.0	−2.6	577	
1934	3.0	6.5	10.7	−3.6	641	11.1%
1935	3.6	6.4	9.2	−2.8	698	8.9
1936	3.9	8.2	10.5	−4.3	790	13.1
1937	5.4	7.6	8.6	−2.2	831	5.3
1938	6.8	6.8	7.7	−0.1	801	−3.6
1939	6.3	9.1	10.3	−2.8	866	8.2
1940	6.5	9.5	9.8	−2.9	941	8.6
1941	8.7	13.7	12.0	−4.9	1,102	17.1
1942	14.6	35.1	24.4	−20.5	1,309	18.8
1943	24.0	78.6	43.6	−54.6	1,523	16.4
1944	43.7	91.3	43.7	−47.6	1,645	8.0
1945	45.2	92.7	41.9	−47.6	1,627	−1.1

Source: Office of Management and Budget, *Historical Tables, Budget of the U.S. Government, Fiscal Year 2000* (Washington, D.C.: Government Printing Office, 1999).

Depression had started and GDP had already fallen by 30 percent, these increases served to deepen and prolong the Depression and indicated a further lack of understanding, in addition to the monetary policy mistakes, of how economic variables respond to economic policies.

There were also important external events contributing to the Depression that were beyond Hoover's control. In September 1931, Britain abandoned the gold standard. Other countries, which held U.S. dollars, feared the United States was going to follow Britain. With the low and declining interest rates in the United States, these foreign countries decided to cash in their dollars for gold. The ensuing run on U.S. gold exacerbated the Depression because the Federal Reserve, concerned about the gold drain, actually increased the rediscount rate to member banks. The timing of this move was particularly destructive as it occurred during a wave of bank failures. This policy continued under Franklin D. Roosevelt as the discount rate was also increased in 1933 and 1937, the latter contributing to the major recessionary setback of 1938.

Tariffs were raised and quotas were instituted. In 1930, the Smoot-Hawley Tariff was passed, which raised the tariff rate to 50 percent on all imports. The result of this tariff and the high barriers to imports imposed by other countries was to seal off what employment relief might have been realized from the expansion of international trade.

Under Hoover, monetary, fiscal, and trade policies were what is called pro-cyclical, that is they exaggerate the trend that policy should try to ease.

(See 47 What is the gold standard? 293 How does the Fed keep inflation low?)

Q 146. What was President Franklin Roosevelt's economic strategy?

A Although monetary policy was greatly eased under Roosevelt, tax policy did not change much from that of President Hoover. The taxing and spending structure that continued throughout Franklin Roosevelt's administration in the 1930s was designed more to eliminate the deficits than to nurture the economic recovery. The tax increase of the early 1930s, which, as mentioned, would have doubled revenues at the full-employment level of national income, was not rescinded by Roosevelt. Moreover, in 1936, in order to finance the new Social Security programs, additional taxes had to be imposed. Thus, taxes grew faster than expenditures, holding down economic recovery long before full employment was attained. The course of unemployment on the establishment of an international economic order based on Western principles of free trade and competition.

(See 168 What were the developments in the cold war?)

Q 158. What was the Bretton Woods Agreement?

A The Bretton Woods Agreement was signed on December 27, 1945, in Washington, D.C., following the United Nations Monetary and Financial Conference at Bretton Woods, New Hampshire, in July 1944. The agreement established the International Bank for Reconstruction and Development, commonly known as the World Bank, and the International Monetary Fund (IMF). The purpose of the World Bank, which began operation on June 25, 1946, was to make loans for development projects, primarily infrastructure, in war-torn countries and in developing countries for the benefit of poor people, while the IMF was to maintain exchange rate stability and facilitate exchange rate adjustment.

The Bretton Woods Agreement also attempted to establish a stable international environment through: (1) fixed exchange rates; (2) currency convertibility; (3) a gold standard that maintained a gold price of US$35 per ounce; and (4) a provision for orderly exchange rate adjustment in the event of "fundamental disequilibrium" between major currencies. The IMF would oversee the system and provide medium-term loans to countries with temporary balance of payments difficulties, which would, therefore, help preserve the system of fixed exchange rates and provide more stability. Currency convertibility meant that one major currency could buy or be bought with another at the fixed exchange rate. (Currency convertibility did not come about until the end of the 1950s. Currency convertibility was a precondition for freedom of capital mobility and ultimately led to the integration of global financial markets, as shown later by, among other things, the rise of the Eurodollar market. Balance of payments crises were also worked out at the IMF through ad hoc arrangements.)

(See 529 What are some of the more notable examples of globalization?)

Q 159. What was the General Agreement on Tariffs and Trade (GATT)?

A GATT was important in setting up the rules of trade, especially for industrial countries. GATT consolidated a series of bilateral trade agreements and created a liberal trade regime based on: (1) nondiscrimination in trade in that a privilege extended to one signatory was extended to all, that is, "the most-favored-nation clause"; (2)

industry protection through tariffs rather than quotas or other nontariff barriers; and (3) a mechanism to work out trade disputes. Much of the rapid growth of international trade following the war has been attributed to the principles on which GATT was based. The rapid trade expansion, in turn, is cited by many economists as the engine of both European recovery and sustained growth in the United States. From 1950 to 1970, U.S. exports more than quadrupled in nominal terms.

Q **160. What was the Marshall Plan?**

A The Marshall Plan for European Reconstruction (officially called the European Recovery Program) was carried out from 1948 to 1952 and was the largest foreign aid program ever launched by the United States. The plan, motivated by the concern that economic collapse would invite the spread of communism, cost $13.2 billion (equivalent to $100 billion in today's dollars) over the four-year period. Another $1 billion went to east and southeast Asia. The primary recipients of aid were Great Britain ($3.2 billion), France ($2.7 billion), West Germany ($1.4 billion), and Holland ($1.1 billion), which were followed by, in order of amount received: Greece, Austria, Belgium, Denmark, Norway, Turkey, Ireland, and Sweden. There were four additional recipients that received modest amounts. The plan helped to rebuild these countries by financing raw materials, semifinished goods, agricultural inputs, machinery, vehicles, fuel, etc. The Marshall Plan largely replaced the World Bank in its role as an "International Bank for Reconstruction." Rather, the World Bank became a development institution for third world countries.

Q **161. Was the Marshall Plan similar to foreign aid today?**

A No, the Marshall Plan was much more successful. The main reason for its success was that, at the end of World War II, Europe was in the unusual position where its physical capital lay in ruin, but its human capital and know-how were substantial and intact. Because of the good stock of human capital, the infusion of capital from the Marshall Plan could be effectively absorbed. The economic success of the recipient countries, especially West Germany, is consistent with this view. The vast majority of developing countries, on the other hand, lack the human capital, that is, an educated, skilled, healthy workforce, needed to make effective use of foreign aid today.

Q **162. What was the arrangement between the Treasury and the Federal Reserve on interest rates during World War II?**

A In April 1942, in order to help the Treasury keep the cost of borrowing low for the war effort, the Federal Reserve fixed the rate at which it bought Treasury debt at 3/8 of 1 percent, which held until 1947. The rate was adjusted upward thereafter, but the Federal Reserve continued to fix interest rates during 1948–1951, respecting the deal it had made with the Treasury. With the higher inflation of the 1950s, monetary policy became more active, with open market operations becoming the primary tool. Some interest rate ceilings remained in effect into the 1970s.

(See 293 How does the Fed keep inflation low?)

1950s

Q **163. Why did President Truman impose price controls in 1951?**

A At the end of World War II, price controls in effect during the war were removed. During 1946–1948, the U.S. inflation rate was substantial, averaging more than 10 percent. The recession of 1949 seemed to knock out inflation. However, inflation was rekindled with the military build up for the Korean War, and President Harry Truman saw the need to impose new controls. In January 1951 he imposed wage and price controls for the purpose of moderating "violent waves of general price increases which marked the second half of 1950." President Dwight Eisenhower abolished the controls in 1954, the year after the Korean War ended.

Q **164. How did the Korean War come about and how did it end?**

A At the end of World War II Korea, which had been occupied by the Japanese, was divided in half with the Soviet army occupying the area north of the 38th parallel and U.S.-led forces the south. This military division became political when the Soviets set up a Communist government in the North, while the United States recognized the Republic of South Korea. The Korean War began in June 1950 when a force of Soviet-supported North Koreans crossed the 38th parallel invading South Korea. President Truman successfully obtained a United Nations (UN) Security Council Resolution (the Soviets were boycotting the UN at the time) to resist the aggression.

Most of the fighting occurred during the first year of the war. In the early going, UN forces, nearly driven into the Sea of Japan, counterattacked under the command of General Douglas MacArthur to push the North Koreans back to the Chinese border. At this stage Communist Chinese forces entered the war in support of North Korea and drove the UN troops back to the 38th parallel. A stalemate ensued and, after many lengthy rounds of truce talks, an armistice was signed on July 27, 1953, drawing the border of the two nations at the 38th parallel. U.S. troop strength in Korea peaked at 350,000, with 33,600 U.S. soldiers killed in action over the course of the war. The United States spent approximately $18 billion ($110 billion in today's dollars) on the war effort.

Q 165. What impact did the Korean War have on the economy?

A The Korean War had at least two effects on the economy. First, the increase in defense spending triggered an economic boom, especially in 1950 and 1951. Second, the increase in government spending drove up inflation, particularly in 1951. Concerned about inflation, Congress gave Truman broad power over the economy, including power to impose wage and price controls. The end of the war was followed by a brief recession in 1954. An interesting sidelight to the Korean War is that the United States ordered thousands of military trucks for the war effort from a relatively unknown Japanese company named Toyota, a transaction that provided an important early boost to the Japanese vehicle manufacturer.

(See 163 Why did President Truman impose price controls in 1951?)

Q 166. What was the significance of the Interstate Highway Act of 1956?

A It is thought that when General Dwight Eisenhower marched through Germany, he became so impressed with the Autobahn, Germany's main highway system, that he made building a similar U.S. highway system a priority when he became president. After much debate about funding and scope, the Interstate Highway Act of 1956 was passed, making possible the largest construction project in history. A national interstate highway system was created to cover 41,000 miles of road. The federal government's share of paying for interstate highways increased from 60 percent to 90 percent. (The rest was funded by state and local governments.) The federal share was raised through a gas tax. Initial funding for the project was $27 billion, but that figure was soon raised to $41 billion. The act was to provide funding until 1972 and set up a Highway Trust Fund.

an "incursion" into Cambodia, which proved disastrous to that country. In January 1973, a peace agreement was signed and the remaining U.S. troops and prisoners of war returned to the United States.

Q 177. How much did the Vietnam War cost the United States?

A The cost of the Vietnam War for the United States was almost 58,000 American lives lost and more than $100 billion in military spending. Through both the Johnson and the Nixon administrations, the war coincided with sustained economic growth and low unemployment on the one hand, and larger budget deficits and increasing inflation on the other. The deficits and inflation persisted for several years after the end of the war.

Q 178. What was President Johnson's "tax surcharge"?

A The Johnson surcharge was a tax increase on personal and corporate income. Passed in June 1968, it authorized a 10 percent tax on individuals retroactive to April 1968, and on corporate income retroactive to January 1968. The surcharge was reduced to 5 percent in 1970 and eliminated on June 30, 1970. The purpose of the surcharge was twofold: to battle inflation and to generate revenue for the Vietnam War. At the time, inflation was accelerating, increasing from 1.9 percent in 1965 to more than 3 percent in 1966 and 1967, and 4.7 percent in 1968. The growth of the inflation rate was fueled by the economy nearing full employment, the escalation of the Vietnam War, and substantial increases in federal funding of Johnson's social programs. The surcharge was geared to reducing "demand pull" inflation by cutting the disposable income of consumers and businesses. However, the surcharge proved ineffective as inflation continued to rise to 5.4 percent in 1969 and 5.9 percent in 1970. Despite U.S. spending on the Vietnam War, the surcharge did contribute to achieving a federal budget surplus in 1969, the last one the United States would record for the next 30 years.

1970s

Q 179. What were the major economic changes that President Nixon imposed?

A President Nixon instituted wage and price controls and changes in the rules of international economic exchange. In addition to freezing wages and prices, the measures permanently rescinded dollar-gold convertibility and fixed exchange rates, thus removing two pillars of the Bretton Woods system. Also as part of the program, Nixon levied a surcharge on imports as a means to force other major countries to revalue (increase the value of) their currencies with respect to the dollar, created an investment tax credit, deferred certain government expenditure increases and eliminated the excise tax on automobiles. The program lasted from August 15, 1971, until April 10, 1974. The actual price and wage freezes lasted only about 90 days. The measures were in response to persistent and relatively high inflation along with the concern, which had been developing since the 1960s, of a run on the U.S. dollar in the foreign exchange markets.

Q 180. What was the public reaction to Nixon's wage and price controls?

A The Nixon wage and price controls were enthusiastically received by the public; the Dow Jones Industrial Average rose 32.9 points the day after the program's unveiling, the largest one-day increase in history up to that point. Public support (as represented by the stock market) was apparently undisturbed by such bold interventions in the free economy. The public's acceptance of the controls did not change during the nearly three years that the controls were in effect. The program, however, lost the battle with inflation. A new cabinet committee, the Cost of Living Council, was also created to manage the program.

Q 181. Why did the Bretton Woods system fail and what replaced it?

A The world economic system embodied in the Bretton Woods Agreement ceased to reflect the reality of the time. Bretton Woods had established a fixed exchange rate system in a world where economic forces required exchange rates to change constantly. This phenomenon was known as "fundamental disequilibrium" because "real" exchange rates differed from the fixed exchange rate. Different inflation rates between countries, as well as other factors, made it impossible to maintain a constant value of some currencies with respect to others. Fixed exchange rates could not be maintained even with substantial interventions from major central banks. Furthermore, on average, countries felt more pressure to devalue their currencies than to revalue them with respect to gold and therefore the dollar. Without the other currencies revaluing, the United States could only support the exchange rate of the dollar by selling gold. U.S. gold reserves were depleted from $17.8 billion in 1960 to $11 billion in 1971, a decline of 38 percent. The result was a deterioration of the U.S. balance of payments and a dollar crisis, creating a liquidity problem that thwarted the ability of the system to adjust.

Nixon was forced to sever the dollar-gold link and, later, to replace the system of fixed exchange with floating exchange rates in 1973. Although the Bretton Woods Agreement essentially ended as an operational system of international exchange when the United States left the gold standard and abandoned fixed exchange rates, its legacy lives on in the two institutions it created: the IMF and the World Bank.

Q 182. What led to the oil embargo of 1973?

A The seeds of the energy crisis of 1973–1974 were sown in the 1950s and 1960s, when most of the industrialized countries became dependent on oil imports for sizable portions of their energy consumption. Every year since 1958, the United States has consumed more energy than it has produced. The immediate crisis in 1973 was precipitated by the Organization of Petroleum Exporting Countries' (OPEC) oil embargo of countries supporting Israel in the Arab-Israeli war of that year. The embargo was in effect against the United States from October 1973 to March 1974 and led to a tripling of the U.S. price of oil. A number of measures were taken by the United States to manage the scarcity, including asking the public to voluntarily lower thermostats, placing restrictions on gasoline purchases, and authorizing a standby plan for rationing.

(See 185 What was President Carter's energy strategy?)

Q 183. Why was there a significant recession during 1974–1975?

A A number of negative factors struck at once to cause the 1974–1975 recession: the oil embargo of 1973 that tripled the price of oil; the end of the Vietnam War in early 1973, which took away a large fiscal stimulus to the economy; the lifting of policies to suppress inflation by direct price controls during 1971–1974; and perhaps also the mood of malaise of the Nixon Watergate scandal during 1973–1974. The stock market also took a nosedive in 1973 and 1974, losing half its value in real terms during the two years. The effects of these events were felt a year later. With the economy contracting (negative growth) in three of the four quarters of 1974, continuing into the first quarter of 1975, GDP declined by 1.0 percent during the 1974–1975 recession. The worst effect of the recession was the increase in unemployment to 8.5 percent (up 2.9 percentage points) in 1975, and the increase in inflation to 11.0 percent (up 4.8 percentage points) in 1974 and remaining high at 9.1 percent in 1975. After the recession, the next 10 quarters had substantial positive GDP growth and there was not another recession until 1980.

(See 94 What has been the overall trend in the DJIA from 1946 to 1999?)

Q 184. What was stagflation?

A "Stagflation" was a term coined in the 1970s to describe an economic situation of high inflation and slow or negative growth. Until the 1974–1975 recession, there had never really been such a pronounced combination of the two. Stagflation ended in 1976 with the return of strong growth of 5.4 percent, a reduction in inflation to 5.8 percent and a reduced, but still high, unemployment rate of 7.7 percent. Stagflation returned in 1980 with a 0.3 percent GDP decline, and 13.5 percent inflation. There have been no real cases of stagflation since 1980, although in the 1991 recession (-0.9 percent growth), inflation was a little higher than it had been at 4.1 percent.

Q 185. What was President Carter's energy strategy?

A Throughout the 1970s, imports of petroleum as a percent of consumption rose steadily, reaching a peak of 46 percent in 1977. The oil embargo of 1973 did not seem to have dampened the U.S. appetite for foreign oil. This increasing dependency on foreign oil caused President Jimmy Carter to refer to solving this vulnerability as the "moral equivalent of war." In response, he launched a series of measures to lower oil consumption, reduce dependence on imported oil, and increase the production of energy. The measures included controlling imports of crude oil and phasing out price controls on domestic oil and natural gas. The resulting windfall profits to energy companies were subject to a special tax. The Carter plan also promoted alternative energy sources such as solar, geothermal, nuclear, and synthetic fuels. The energy program was administered by the newly created Energy Department.

The results of Carter's energy strategy were mixed. In general, since the 1973 oil embargo, the United States has substituted coal and nuclear power for petroleum and natural gas, and has generally achieved more growth with less energy consumption (also a by-product of expanding the service sector's share of the economy). The oil and natural gas share of energy consumption dropped from 77 percent in 1973 to 63 percent in 1997. Shortly after the Carter administration launched its plan, domestic production of energy increased, while the growth of consumption slowed. After the second oil shock in 1979, the extremely high price of oil, coupled with the deregulation of domestic markets, apparently depressed demand and encouraged domestic supply. By 1981, the price of crude oil increased to 5 times its 1972 level (adjusted for inflation). By 1985, oil imports had declined to just 27 percent of consumption. But the general decline in oil prices since the mid-1980s reversed the decline in imports. In fact, imports of oil have increased sharply, reaching a record 48 percent of total consumption in 1997. The goal of energy independence, seemingly so critical in the 1970s, receives scant attention today.

Thus, in the long run, the plan did not meet the goal of reducing the dependence of the U.S. economy on foreign oil. It should be noted that there was a policy shift during the Reagan and Bush administrations, which cut federal programs for energy and sharply curtailed government intervention in energy markets. Domestic production was encouraged by permitting oil fields in environmentally sensitive areas and by encouraging pipelines.

(See 182 What led to the oil embargo of 1973?)

Q 186. When was the second oil shock and how was it resolved?

A The second oil shock of the 1970s occurred in the aftermath of the overthrow of the Shah of Iran. During the turmoil leading up to the Shah's flight from his country in January 1979, Iranian oil workers went on strike. Iranian oil exports, which accounted for 12 percent of the noncommunist world's oil supply, were severely disrupted. Taking advantage of this situation, OPEC raised the price of crude oil by almost 15 percent during 1979. Increases in production from such countries as Saudi Arabia probably prevented a greater crisis. Within the United States, a series of gasoline shortages swept the nation, beginning in May in California and extending to the East Coast by summer. Unlike the 1973–1974 oil crisis, several features of the 1979 crisis suggested that the crisis might have been more of a misallocation than of a real shortage: (1) supplies of crude oil in the United States were actually higher in 1979 than in 1978; (2) some regions of the country never experienced any shortages; and (3) regional shortages often disappeared quickly.

Q 187. Could an oil crisis happen again?

A By the end of the 1990s, no immediate geopolitical events suggested that the United States faced the risk of another oil crisis. However, the U.S. dependency on imported oil in the late 1990s hovered at nearly half of its total consumption compared with 45 percent in 1973.

188. What is bracket creep?

A From the late 1960s, throughout the 1970s, and leading up to the Reagan administration, individuals' income rose rapidly in money terms, largely due to inflation. Although individuals' *real* income and purchasing power had not risen nearly as rapidly, because tax brackets were not adjusted for inflation, they nevertheless found themselves in ever higher tax brackets, paying higher percentages of their income to the government. In effect, this phenomenon, known as "bracket creep," gave the government automatic tax increases, which were geared to the rate of inflation. The Congress was also not forced to pay the political price for enacting these tax increases. An example of a middle-class family in the 1970s illustrates. A family that had a household income of $20,000 in 1970 was in a 25 percent tax bracket. By 1980 that family was vaulted into a 40 percent tax bracket simply because of inflationary increases in income. Thus, their taxes increased by about 50 percent just because of inflation. Lower income families that earned $10,000 in 1970 were pushed from a 15 percent bracket into the 25 percent bracket by 1980.

(See 190 What was the Reagan tax cut?)

Q **189. What important decision did the Federal Reserve make in October 1979?**

A On October 6, 1979, the Federal Reserve made a substantial policy switch from trying to achieve certain interest rate levels, to a monetarist position that targeted the growth of monetary aggregates, or various types of money supply. The Fed's former policy of targeting interest rates had failed and left the economy in double-digit inflation. The new policy was not very successful in the goal of managing the narrowly defined money supply (M1) as the relationship between the narrow money supply and GDP broke down (although the broader money supply, M2, remained fairly stable). However, the intentions of the Fed, the interest rate policy, and the painful recession in 1982 appeared to wring most of the inflation out of the economy that had plagued the 1970s.

(See 43 What are the major issues in measuring the money supply in recent decades?)

Q 190. What was the Reagan tax cut?

A One of the pillars of Ronald Reagan's 1980 campaign was general tax reduction, following the supply-side premise that such a tax reduction would increase resources and incentives for production, much needed after the seesaw economic performance of the 1970s. President Reagan's plan, known as the Economic Recovery Act of 1981, included substantial income tax reduction, cuts in social programs, and accelerated defense spending. The act achieved an across-the-board reduction in individual income tax rates phased in over three years, a concept that had received attention in its incarnation as the Kemp-Roth tax cut. The income tax rate reductions amounted to 5 percent in 1982, 10 percent in 1983, and 10 percent in 1984, for an overall rate reduction of 25 percent over the three years, although, due to technicalities in the process, the total cut worked out to only 23 percent over the three years. The top tax rate was reduced from 70 to 50 percent. Prior to the tax cut, an individual with a taxable income of $20,000 in 1981 was in the 34 percent tax bracket. By 1985 the person was in the 26 percent bracket. An individual with a taxable income of $40,000 fell from a 49 percent bracket to a 38 percent bracket. An individual with a taxable income of $60,000 fell from a 63 percent bracket to a 48 percent bracket. The resulting change in tax liability was substantial.

Effects of Reagan Tax Cut at Various Income Levels, 1981–1985

Income	Filing status	Federal tax liability				
		1981	1982	1983	1984	1985
$20,000	Single	$ 4,105	$ 3,752	$ 3,369	$ 3,205	$ 3,124
	Married	3,225	2,893	2,606	2,461	2,414
$40,000	Single	12,657	11,408	10,313	9,749	9,527
	Married	10,226	9,195	8,304	7,858	7,640
$60,000	Single	23,943	21,318	19,473	18,371	17,946
	Married	19,678	17,705	16,014	15,168	14,856
$100,000	Single	50,053	41,318	39,473	37,935	37,444
	Married	41,998	37,629	34,190	32,400	31,886

Note: Tax cut was phased in during 1982–1984.

Perhaps an equally important aspect of the tax package was the indexing of income tax rates to inflation to solve the problem of bracket creep. Starting in 1985, the Economic Recovery Act required the IRS to increase the income tax bracket levels by the increase in the Consumer Price Index, thus ending years of progressively higher tax rates on inflation-induced increases in income. The slight reductions in taxes paid by income bracket for 1985 reflect the indexation. Consequently, the hidden revenue source of the government of inflation-induced tax increases was ended.

The 1981 act also contained benefits to businesses, including cuts in tax rates at the lower levels of corporate income and a new system of depreciation, known as the Accelerated Cost Recovery System (ACRS). This system provided for much faster write-offs of capital expenditures and consequently lower taxes to companies making such investments.

(See 188 What is bracket creep?)

Q 191. How deep was the 1981–1982 recession?

A This recession was the deepest since the Great Depression, but nowhere near as severe. GDP declined 1.9 percent and unemployment reached an annual average 9.7 percent for 1983–1984, compared with the Great Depression when GDP declined 36 percent during 1929–1933, with unemployment reaching 24.9 percent in 1933. The recession also marked the beginning of years of high budget deficits. There was also a positive outcome to the 1982 recession, which was the defeat of inflation.

Q 192. Why did such large deficits emerge in the 1980s and how high were they?

A The standard explanation is that the Reagan tax cut reduced revenues, while his accelerated defense spending trend canceled out much of the social spending cuts. In fact, government expenditures did increase every year of his administration, while revenues decreased in 1982 and 1983. However, revenues increased in 1984, the third year of the tax cut. A large part of the reason that deficits increased initially was the recession in 1981–1982 (fourth quarter 1981 and first quarter 1982). Still, even when the economy shot out of recession recording 4.2 percent real growth in 1983 and 7.3 percent in 1984, deficits were still 5.9 percent (the post–World War II peak) and 4.7 percent of GDP, respectively. As growth continued throughout the 1980s, the deficit gradually declined as a share of GDP, down to 2.8 percent. This share was still high for peacetime by historical standards.

193. What was the structural deficit?

The structural deficit was a hypothetical deficit that economists believed would exist even if the economy were at or near full employment. In the 1980s the structural, inflation-adjusted budget began to display chronic large deficits for the first time. The significance for policy was that something should be done about the systematic imbalance between revenues and expenditures. Otherwise, debt would grow to too large a share of GDP, macroeconomic policy would be handcuffed, and debt servicing would leave too little discretion in the federal budget.

194. What did the term "voodoo economics" mean?

This term, used by George Bush as he battled Ronald Reagan for the Republican presidential nomination in 1980, meant to ridicule Reagan's contention that large tax rate reductions would benefit the economy and actually increase tax revenues.

195. What was the Laffer Curve?

The Laffer Curve, developed by economist Arthur Laffer, represented a supply-side view of the relationship of government revenues to taxation. Laffer argued in favor of the Reagan tax cut as a means to actually increase government revenue. The theory states that above a certain level of taxation, increasing the tax rate actually reduces tax revenue because tax rates are so high that people have less incentive to work and, therefore, earn less taxable income. Laffer contended that, prior to the Reagan tax cut, tax rates had exceeded rates at which government revenue was maximized.

196. How did the savings and loan crisis of the 1980s materialize?

The seeds of the crisis were sown in the 1960s. By law, savings and loans (S&Ls), or thrifts, were limited to financing home mortgages with 30-year maturities and taking in deposits with zero maturities. That imbalance in maturities became a problem in the late 1960s when inflation started to increase and thrifts were holding 30-year mortgages at very low interest rates and could not afford, and were not allowed, to keep depositors with higher interest rates. This unhealthy situation went on for more than a decade until the thrift industry was actually worth less than nothing (*negative* $100 billion was one estimate in 1982). In 1980 and 1982 there were two phases of deregulation that allowed S&Ls to diversify both their assets and liabilities. S&Ls

could offer credit cards and consumer loans, and they could invest in commercial real estate. S&Ls also no longer faced interest rate ceilings.

S&Ls now had some freedom. The problem was that many had already sunk too far and now had new opportunities to survive by engaging in moral hazard, that is, pursue high-risk investments and pray they would pay off, without being any worse off if they failed. The other problem was that despite the increased freedom for the thrifts, the authorities did not increase the supervisory and regulatory effort. In the early to mid-1980s, some S&L executives—perhaps the most famous being Charles Keating—went berserk investing in new assets. Assets of the industry grew 56 percent during 1983–1985. During this period, the S&L crisis got very expensive. With real estate prices falling in parts of the United States where S&L investing was especially rabid, the bottom soon fell out for the thrifts. By the late 1980s, it was evident that a major cleanup operation was ahead. (See box on page 191.)

Q 197. How much did it cost?

A Although by the end of the 1990s, expenditures were still ongoing, the cost to pay off creditors, and high-ranking debtors, and the loss of the use of financial assets, by some estimates, amounted to nearly half a trillion dollars. This estimate is the present value of past, present, and future expected outlays. Wall Street seemed to accept the loss fairly well, viewing it in accounting terms largely as a transfer to depositors with insurance. The real economic costs were the unused buildings and other facilities such as malls and marinas, and the tied-up financial resources during the resolution of the S&L crisis.

Q 198. What major funding changes were made to the Social Security program in the 1980s?

A In 1983 a blue-ribbon commission, headed by Alan Greenspan (future Federal Reserve Chairman) and including the Speaker of the House of Representatives, Tip O'Neill, and Senators Bob Dole and Howard Baker, dealt with an urgent funding problem in the Social Security Program. The trust fund had run out of money and outlays exceeded revenues. The commission recommended increasing the payroll tax to fund Social Security, taxing Social Security benefits, and increasing the eligibility age for benefits from 65 to 67. The latter would be phased in gradually during the first decades after the year 2000. The result was huge surpluses, which exceeded $100 billion annually by the end of the 1990s. The trust fund that is built from these surpluses is intended to provide a cushion between 2018 and 2034 during which deficits in the program would be financed by drawing down the trust fund. Management of the trust fund has raised serious questions as to whether this "cushion" is real or not.

(See 234 Why does the program collect large surpluses if it is a pay-as-you-go program?)

Q 199. What were the elements of the Tax Reform Act of 1986?

A The 1986 Tax Reform Act was one of the most important pieces of financial legislation since 1913, when the Sixteenth Amendment to the Constitution, authorizing modern-day income taxes, was ratified. It took two years to enact, and was signed into law by President Reagan in October 1986. The 1986 tax reform substantially reduced the number of tax brackets for individuals and eliminated many cherished tax breaks. Prior to 1987, there were 15 tax-brackets for single taxpayers and 14 for married taxpayers. Maximum tax rates were 50 percent in both categories. This system was replaced by a five-bracket system in 1987 (considered a transitional year) and a two-bracket system thereafter. Under the two-bracket system, married and single individuals were taxed at 15 percent up to a certain level of income and 28 percent thereafter. At higher levels of income, the benefits associated with the 15 percent rate were phased out. Among the significantly curtailed or eliminated tax deductions were for interest on consumer loans, medical expenses, sales tax, political and charitable contributions, and unreimbursed business expenses.

The 1986 act also curtailed tax shelters. For many years, tax shelters had gained notoriety as unfair tax dodges available only to the very rich. The 1986 act changed the tax code to significantly reduce the attractiveness of tax shelters by: repealing the investment tax credit; scaling back the depreciation schedules of the 1981 Economic Recovery Act; and eliminating deductions for losses from tax shelters. Through these changes, the tax reform is credited with significantly improving the efficiency of investment because fewer investment decisions would be based on tax benefit considerations. Businesses did receive some benefits in the 1986 act including a reduction in the general corporate tax rates from 46 to 34 percent. It was estimated that the tax reform shifted $120 billion of tax burden from individuals to corporations.

Q 200. What was the magnitude of the stock market crash of 1987?

A The stock market crash of 1987 occurred on October 19, "Black Monday," when the Dow Jones Industrial Average (DJIA) dropped 508 points, 22.6 percent of total market value, the largest one-day percentage loss ever. An overlooked aspect of this crash is that the market had already fallen over 250 points in the previous week. Over the weekend prior to "Black Monday" investors apparently became increasingly nervous about the rapid decline and by Monday the stock market was primed for a crash.

Q 201. What caused the 1987 crash?

A The many possible explanations for the crash range from international causes such as Treasury Secretary Baker's announcement that the United States would not prop up the dollar and indications that foreign holders of U.S. debt were becoming uneasy with financing U.S. deficits, to technical causes such as think-alike MBAs locked into automatic sell points, or "programm trading." The market did recover partially in the following days and by mid-July 1990 had regained its precrash level.

1990s

Q 202. What were the Gramm-Rudman targets and how did they affect the 1990 budget deal?

A Gramm-Rudman targets were federal budget deficit targets, which, if exceeded, would have forced automatic spending cuts. These targets forced President Bush and Congress into dealing more seriously with the budget deficits in 1990 than they had in the previous year, Bush's first year in office. With the economy slowing down and the estimates of the budget deficit rising, the automatic spending cuts would have been huge to meet the Gramm-Rudman targets. Thus, there was a great deal of pressure on Bush to reach a major compromise with Congress that would attack the deficit on *both* the expenditure and revenue sides.

Q 203. How did President Bush violate his "no new taxes" campaign pledge?

A In accepting the Republican nomination for president in 1988, Bush emphasized his economic goal as president: "Read my lips. No new taxes." In the ensuing political battle with Congress over the federal budget deficit, Bush faced an embarrassing repudiation of his "read my lips" promise on the one hand, while Democrats wanted to avoid the label of "big tax and spenders" on the other hand. During 1990, two major budget agreements were drafted. The first budget agreement between the president and Congress was based on excise tax increases on gasoline and home heating oil and spending cuts, largely on Medicare, but avoided both the much-discussed capital gains tax cut and upper income tax increases. When this first agreement was resoundingly defeated in the House by a vote of 179–254, with many Republicans voting against it, a second budget agreement had to be drafted.

The House put together its plan that included higher taxes on the wealthy and eliminated the regressive gas tax. The Senate Democrats found the House version desirable, but created their own budget plan, which was modified to get the needed Republican support. The choice was shifted considerably to the left compared to the earlier budget agreement as, in the end, greater Democrat support was sought. The agreement that finally passed included: an increase in the tax rate in the high-income brackets (strongly fought against by Bush) and other indirect tax increases on the better-off (that is, elimination of some deductions), no capital gains tax cut, a smaller increase in gas taxes, and smaller cuts in Medicare compared to the previous version. On October 28, 1990, the final agreement, which purported to decrease budget deficits by $490 billion over a 5-year period, was passed in the House and Senate and was later signed by the president under the name of the Omnibus Budget Reconciliation Act of 1990, also known as the Budget Enforcement Act (BEA). The story behind this budget deal is also interesting in that only three years later President Bill Clinton faced a similar situation in forging his first budget in 1993.

Q 204. When was the Persian Gulf War and how much did it cost?

A In the early morning hours of August 2, 1990, a large Iraqi force invaded Kuwait and took Kuwait City by midday. On January 17, 1991, after months of posturing and sanctions, U.S.-led coalition forces launched the Gulf War, known from the U.S. side as "Operation Desert Storm." It was an intense, but brief, conflict that lasted less than two months. The U.S.-led coalition, including Great Britain, France, Saudi Arabia, and Kuwait, began the effort to liberate Kuwait by waging a withering aerial attack. On February 22, Iraqi troops destroyed over 100 Kuwaiti oil wells in less than 24 hours unleashing the worst environmental disaster the region had ever seen. This act was followed by a ground force invasion by 270,000 coalition troops on February 23, which successfully drove Iraqi forces out of Kuwait. The technological superiority of the U.S. forces kept coalition casualties extremely low, in spite of dire predictions by Gulf War opponents in the United States.

Iraq was forced to accept unconditional terms of surrender on March 3, which allowed the continued elimination of Saddam Hussein's arsenal of weapons of mass destruction. With some interruptions, inspection teams supervised the further destruction of chemical and biological weapons. The cost to prosecute the war was about $50 billion. Damages to Kuwait from the Iraqi invasion and the destroyed oil wells, and the damage to Iraq, far exceeded this amount. While the United States was the major anti-Iraq combatant, it received financial support from some Arab states, Japan, and Germany to reimburse the United States for its military expenses, including about $20 billion from Saudi Arabia.

Q **205. What sparked the national health care debate early in President Clinton's first term?**

A Two main factors were involved in the national health care debate: the long-term rapid growth in health care costs that had been outpacing general economic growth for decades; and President Bill Clinton's top priority of consolidating the health care system and improving portability of health insurance, and achieving universal coverage and a means to control costs.

Q **206. Why did President Clinton's health care plan of 1993 fail?**

A Many factors contributed to the failure of the Clinton health care plan (the Health Security Act of 1993). One may have been the alienation of the media by restricting its access to information during the earlier, formative phase of the plan. It is true that many hearings were held and many viewpoints aired, but many who later opposed the plan were not convinced that their viewpoints were carefully considered. The plan included features that were not new in the health care debate, and far more radical alternatives, such as the single-payer plan, had been floated about. In any case, the Clinton plan did provide for a much stronger government role such as in capping insurance premiums and requiring insurance companies to provide standard single price plans under the "community rating" system. Early enthusiasm waned as the high degree of government involvement became apparent to Republican legislators and an effective public information campaign featuring "Harry and Louise" whittled away at public support. The proposal died before being brought to a vote before the 1994 elections. The Health Insurance Portability and Accountability Act of 1996, however, did enact some of the changes attempted earlier, including maintaining health insurance despite job changes. The "Patients' Bill of Rights" was also passed that permitted patients to sue health maintenance organizations.

(See 440 What were the major elements of President Clinton's Health Security Act of 1993?)

Q 207. What is the North American Free Trade Agreement and who signed it?

A The North American Free Trade Agreement (NAFTA) is a trade agreement between the United States, Canada, and Mexico. NAFTA went into effect on January 1, 1994, having been signed two years earlier by President Bush, and eliminates all tariffs and drops most other trade barriers between the three countries over a 15-year period. The bill made numerous changes in U.S. law to conform to the trade pact. In addition to tariff reduction, NAFTA has provisions governing investments in other NAFTA countries, establishing environmental and safety regulations, and opening up the markets for services.

(See 539 What does NAFTA do?)

Q 208. What is the Family Leave Act?

A President Clinton signed the Family and Medical Leave Act (FMLA) in February 1993 as one of his first acts as president. The stated purpose of the act is to "support families in their efforts to strike a workable balance between the competing demands of the workplace and the home." It took effect on August 5, 1993, and is administered by the Wage and Hour Division of the Labor Department. Eligible employees are entitled to 12 weeks of leave in a 12-month period to care for newborn, or adopted children, relatives with serious medical conditions, or their own health problems. The act applies to companies with 50 or more employees. Eligible employees are those who have been with the employer for 12 months and worked at least 1,250 hours during that time. The employer does not have to pay wages during the leave, but must offer health benefits as if the employee continued to work. Employees may have to use accrued sick or vacation leave to cover some or all of the family leave.

Q 209. What is the impact of the Family Leave Act?

A Compared with other developed countries, coverage under the FMLA is limited. It is estimated that about half of U.S. workers qualify for FMLA leave, but only 19 percent of new mothers, mainly because they do not meet the work requirements. In addition, the patterns of leave-taking in establishments that are exempt from FMLA are roughly the same as those covered by FMLA, implying that FMLA has had little impact on increasing work absences for maternity, or caring for family members. The main reason for the limited impact is the limited scope (it is unpaid and relatively short) and that most workers would have been able to take leave without FMLA. Possible expansion of the FMLA includes extension to smaller firms (25–49 employees) and partial pay with the leave.

Q 210. What was the Balanced Budget Amendment of 1995?

A The balanced budget amendment was a significant nonevent: although it reflected the economic thinking of a large segment of America, it did not pass Congress. It was a proposed amendment to the Constitution to require that the federal budget be in balance within seven years of passage and remain in balance thereafter. To pass the amendment required two-thirds of both the House and the Senate and three-quarters of the 50 state legislatures. The amendment passed the House, but failed in the Senate. The vast majority of Republicans supported it and most Democrats opposed it. The few Republicans that opposed it were enough to kill the initiative.

Q 211. What were the pros and cons of the balanced budget amendment?

A There were strong governance arguments for the balanced budget amendment, while there were strong economic arguments against it. The arguments in favor of the amendment were mainly that the executive and legislative branches could not be trusted to move toward and maintain a balanced budget. At the time of its consideration, the amendment was seen as an answer to the large annual deficits that were quickly raising the national debt to a worrisome level.

Opponents of the amendment argued that it would take important macroeconomic tools away from policymakers. For instance, under the amendment, if economic growth slowed (which would increase the deficit as government revenues dropped), Congress would not be able to stimulate the economy with tax cuts or spending increases because either would further raise the budget deficit. In fact, policymakers would be forced to do the opposite, that is, raise taxes and/or cut spending while the economy was declining. These are called procyclical policies, which means they accentuate the current trend in the business cycle. So-called "automatic stabilizers" would be negated. (Automatic stabilizers are fiscal measures, such as welfare and unemployment compensation, that increase during a recession and therefore compensate for some of the loss in market demand that occurs during a slowdown.) The balanced budget amendment would call for contractionary policies during a slowdown that would serve to deepen the recession. Among the greatest accomplishments in economic policy since the Great Depression has been the ability to smooth out the business cycle, to lessen downswings, and to control upswings, in favor of sometimes lower but more sustainable growth. These results were most evident during the Reagan and Clinton administrations, both of which had prolonged periods of moderate growth. In the end, the economic arguments carried the day and defeated the amendment.

In hindsight, the balanced budget amendment was not needed, at least for the business cycle of the 1990s. The deficit fell ahead of schedule, achieved surplus on the unified budget in fiscal year 1998 and recorded a small surplus on the operating budget in fiscal year 1999. The balanced budget amendment would have been superfluous at best, and tied policy makers' hands dealing with subsequent swings of the business cycle.

Q **212. What was welfare reform and what did it do?**

A The welfare reform bill, "Personal Responsibility and Work Opportunity Act of 1996," turned control of welfare over to the states; limited lifetime benefits to five years; required adults to work after two years; and denied many benefits to noncitizens. Food stamps were also cut. The rationale behind this legislation was to break the cycle of dependency, which sometimes extended to successive generations. The potential harsh effects of the bill were softened by the low unemployment rate in the years following its enactment.

Q **213. Did the investigations and impeachment of President Clinton have any economic impact?**

A President Clinton's scandals over his affair with White House intern Monica Lewinsky and his dubious testimony in the Paula Jones sexual harassment suit against him, and the subsequent investigations of his conduct by the special counsel and his impeachment by the House of Representatives, unlike the Watergate affair, did not seem to disturb the economy. While the scandals broiled during almost all of 1998, the Dow Jones Industrials stock index climbed from 7,908.25 to 9,181.43, and GDP grew at 4.3 percent. Judging by economic growth before (growth in 1997 was 4.5 percent), during and after the scandal (1999 GDP growth was 4.0 percent), the scandal did not appear to have any adverse effect. Of course, it is always possible that GDP and stock price growth could have been substantially higher, but the year dominated by scandal, 1998, was more or less in line with economic performance in 1997 and 1999.

Q **214. What was the Y2K phenomenon?**

A The year 2000 computer problem, or Y2K, resulted from software and chips that represented years with only two digits. The year 1999 was represented as 99 and the year

2000 as 00. The trouble was that 00 was interpreted as 1900, rather than 2000. It was this misinterpretation that would result in failed applications or wrong answers. An application measuring intervening years from 1990 to 2000, instead of measuring a plus ten years, would measure a negative 90 years. The Y2K problem was not limited to mainframes but also involved personal computers, local area networks, and microprocessors in medical equipment and process controls.

Q **215. What did the Y2K phenomenon do to the economy?**

A As Y2K approached, the predicted consequences ranged from minor glitches to global recession. The threatened possible collapse of electrical power, water services, telecommunications, and essentially anything that depended on computers—including the breakdown of safeguards of the nuclear arsenal—spurred some people to stockpile food and supplies in anticipation of a crisis. Experts in major industries assured the public that no major failures would occur. Intelligence agencies were also able to reassure Americans that an inadvertent nuclear strike would not happen.

Besides the costs of malfunctions, compliance posed a real economic cost to organizations. Even if an organization complied, noncompliance by a supplier or customer could pose serious costs. Perhaps as an incentive to comply, there was much discussion of legal liability for failures resulting from the Y2K problem.

In the end, problems associated with Y2K were minor. Shutdowns of major services, shortages of consumer goods, and even disruptions in work did not materialize. On New Year's Eve 1999, people in the United States received early reassurance that Y2K was of little concern as they watched satellite broadcasts of the year 2000 dawning first in Australia, then throughout Asia, Africa, and Europe without incident. Although the Y2K alarm seemed excessive in retrospect, it did serve as an impetus for many organizations to review and update their computer systems.

IV

Top Economic Issues: What Matters Most Now and for the Future

Economics is useful only when applied to the real world. Similarly, economic policy must be linked to the effects on people's lives. Applying economics to the top unfolding issues of today ties the study of economics to the daily life and long-term prosperity of the nation. This chapter looks at the most important economic issues facing U.S. society at the beginning of the twenty-first century.

Any list of top economic issues is going to vary depending on what the analyst views as "important." The issues presented were chosen because they ranked high in some or all of the following areas: Does the issue greatly affect American lives? Does the issue involve a lot of money? Does the issue have long-term implications for the U.S. economy? Is the issue one that will likely demand some action in the near future by the president or Congress? Will something terrible happen if the issue is not managed well in the future? And, finally, has the issue appeared so frequently in the media that it is currently on the minds of many people?

The top economic issues in this chapter are divided into four categories: fiscal and monetary, private sector, environmental and social, and international. These issues are not necessarily presented in order of importance, and every attempt has been made either to present both sides of the issue, provide a reasonable consensus, or simply provide a briefing on the issue.

FISCAL AND MONETARY ISSUES

THE FUNDING AND REFORM OF SOCIAL SECURITY

On the issue of Social Security funding and reform, the stakes are high and the rhetoric is plentiful. From labor unions and Gray Panthers, to anti–New Dealers and reform zealots, the debate has become dominated by various interest groups and partisan personalities who use media sound bites to influence public opinion.

Q 216. What is Social Security?

A Social Security is a federal entitlement program designed to protect Americans from the financial risks of income shortfall during old age, or after the death of an income-earning spouse and/or parent. In terms of financing, the program was originally conceived as a "pay-as-you-go system," that is, every year the revenues from Social Security taxes would be roughly equal to payments to beneficiaries, with a trust fund serving only as a contingency fund.

(See 234 Why does the program collect large surpluses if it is a "pay-as-you-go" program?)

Q 217. When did the Social Security program start?

A Social Security was created when President Franklin D. Roosevelt signed the Social Security Act in 1935. Payroll taxes were first paid in 1937 and old-age benefits began in 1940. Initially, the program covered 60 percent of the workforce. In 1939, the act was amended to include benefits for the dependents and survivors of retired workers.

Q 218. When was Disability Insurance approved and how does it fit into the Social Security program?

A Disability Insurance was added to the traditional old-age and survivors-based Social Security in 1957. The government broadened the mandate of the program to protect a new class of beneficiaries from income shortfall related to their disability. In 1998 disability insurance covered 6.3 million beneficiaries with an annual outlay of $49 billion, 13 percent of the total Social Security outlays, averaging $7,808 per beneficiary.

Q 219. What is the Social Security trust fund?

A The Social Security trust fund is a financial account in the U.S. Treasury that is funded from surplus Social Security taxes from employers, employees, and the self-employed and interest income on trust fund assets. Surpluses in the trust fund are, by law, taken by the Treasury in exchange for "Special Issues" of the Treasury, a financial instrument traded by the Treasury to the Social Security Administration, an independent federal agency. Social Security has two separate trust funds, Old-Age and Survivors Insurance (OASI), which pays retirement and survivors' benefits, and Disability Insurance (DI), which pays disability benefits. The combined programs are called the Old-Age Survivors and Disability Insurance (OASDI) program.

Q 220. How have Social Security expenditures grown during the past half century?

A There are two ways to track the growth in Social Security outlays: real Social Security outlays and outlays as a percentage of the federal budget. Real expenditures rose continuously throughout the period, especially rapidly during the Eisenhower administration in the 1950s and the Nixon/Ford administrations in the 1970s. Figure 23 illustrates the trend in Social Security outlays as a share of the budget.

Q 221. What is the average annual growth in and share of the total federal budget of Social Security outlays during each of the previous five decades?

A The average annual growth and share of the total federal budget by decade were

	Average annual growth	Share of total budget
1950s	24.9%	6.0%
1960s	8.0	13.9
1970s	6.6	19.2
1980s	2.7	20.6
1990s	2.3	21.8

Q 222. What has been the trend in the Social Security trust fund during the past half century?

A While the Social Security program has always been officially a pay-as-you-go program, the level of the Social Security trust fund varied widely during the 1946–1999

Figure 23 Social Security Outlays as Share of the Federal Budget, 1946–1999

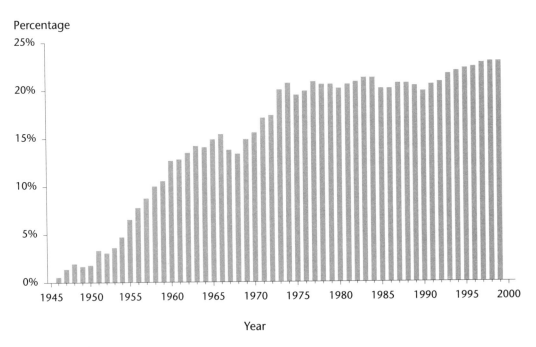

Source: Social Security Administration.

period. *(See Figure 24.)* The real (deflated by the CPI) trust fund levels had five distinct subperiods:

1. 1946–1957: the trust fund grew moderately in real terms (average growth was 6.1 percent), although from a low trust fund base.
2. 1958–1966: the trust fund declined (average growth was -1.9 percent).
3. 1967–1972: the fund increased at about the same rate as in the first period (average growth of 6.6 percent).
4. 1973–1984: the fund declined rapidly (average growth for the period was -10.2 percent) leaving a very small balance.
5. 1985–1999: the fund increased very rapidly, although the first several years' high percentage growth rates were from a small base (average growth of 19.1 percent).

The average growth rate of the fund for the entire period was 4.0 percent. Clearly, the pay-as-you-go approach is no longer operative. The 1999 estimate of maximum trust fund balance (in the year 2021) is $4.5 trillion.

Figure 24   Social Security Trust Fund (Adjusted for Inflation), 1946–1999

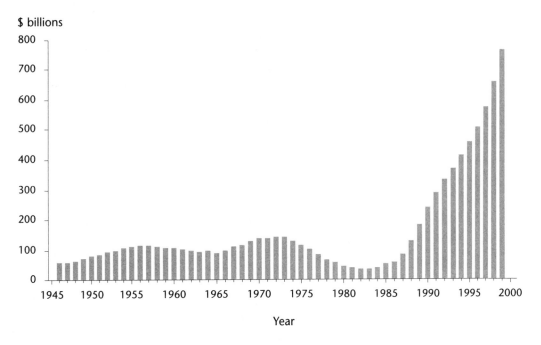

Source: Social Security Administration.

Q **223. What is the average annual growth in the Social Security trust fund during the previous five decades?**

A The average annual growth by decade was

1950s	4.2%
1960s	2.1%
1970s	-8.0%
1980s	11.5%
1990s	13.9%

Q **224. How high was the balance in the trust fund in 1999?**

A At the end of 1999, the Social Security (OASDI) trust fund stood at $880 billion, which was equal to two years' outlays, or 9.0 percent of GDP. The balance was increasing at a rate of more than $100 billion per year at the end of the 1990s.

Q **225. Why is the funding of Social Security a top priority issue?**

A First, because of the sheer size of the Social Security program in terms of dollars and the number of people who rely on it, Social Security has a tremendous effect on the U.S. economy. In 1998 the program received $515 billion in receipts from taxpayers (29 percent of all federal revenues) and paid out $390 billion in benefits (23 percent of all federal outlays). There were 148 million contributors (96 percent of employed workers) while there were 44 million beneficiaries (16 percent of the population or 95 percent of people over age 65). Underscoring the importance of Social Security is that most taxpayers (nearly 80 percent) pay more in Social Security and Medicare taxes than they do in income taxes. In addition, on average, almost half of the income of people over age 65 comes from Social Security.

Second, how the program is managed or reformed will have profound implications for taxpayers and beneficiaries in the coming decades. The issue here is whether Social Security's ability to meet future liabilities will be adversely affected by how the trust fund has been invested. There are other, even longer-term issues about whether Social Security can meet its goals of providing adequate insurance and antipoverty benefits to subsequent generations of Americans. *The Economist* expresses the issue more bluntly in the box below. The long-term demographic issues are also briefly summarized in the box, but the focus here is the management of the Social Security trust fund.

THE ECONOMIST'S VIEW OF THE SOCIAL SECURITY PROGRAM

"It is neither a pension plan nor a genuine trust fund. It is, rather a redistribution system: the federal government taxes the young and gives to the old, plain and simple. Of course, the payoff to the young is that they will one day retire themselves, and will then begin feeding off tomorrow's taxpayers. . . . As long as incomes and the workforce are growing, each generation can give its predecessors a secure retirement, and expect to enjoy still greater comforts when its turn comes along. But if wages and population growth stagnate—or if beneficiaries become greedy—the virtuous cycle turns vicious."

Source: "Anti-Social Security," *The Economist*, January 21, 1995, 58.

Q 226. What are the sources of Social Security revenue?

A Of the $578 billion in total receipts for the Social Security program in 1999, 88 percent ($515 billion) came from payroll taxes, 10 percent ($51 billion) from interest, and 2 percent ($12 billion) from taxation of Social Security benefits.

Q 227. How do Social Security outlays compare to other federal social program outlays?

A With $390 billion in outlays in 1999, Social Security was the largest federal social program. The next largest was Medicare, which had about $191 billion in annual expenditures. Medicaid followed with more than $108 billion (not counting the individual states' portion). Other social programs include Supplemental Security Income (SSI) with $28.2 billion; Temporary Assistance to Needy Families (TANF)—formerly Aid to Families with Dependent Children (AFDC)—with $19.2 billion; food and nutrition assistance with $33.6 billion; and unemployment insurance with $23.6 billion. Social Security differs from the other programs in that it is not needs based. However, its benefits formula favors retirees whose income was lower than average.

Q 228. How is the trust fund used?

A The *Annual Statistical Supplement to the Social Security Bulletin* describes the uses of the trust fund as follows:

> All taxes are credited to the OASI and DI trust funds, which by law may be used only to meet the cost of: (i) monthly benefits when the worker retires, dies, or becomes disabled; (ii) lump-sum death payments to survivors; (iii) vocational rehabilitation services for disability beneficiaries; and (iv) administrative expenses.

Q 229. How long does it take beneficiaries to recoup Social Security contributions?

A Beneficiaries recoup their Social Security contributions based on two factors: (1) their retirement dates, and (2) how much they earned during their lifetimes. Generally, the later the retirement date and the higher the income, the longer the recovery period. For example, a person with average income who retired in 1970 required only 20 months to recoup all Social Security tax contributions and interest; a person with an average income who retired in 2000 required 122 months, or more than six times as long as the 1970 retiree.

Payback Periods for Social Security, 1970–2040

Year	Earnings category	Accumulated taxes (with interest)	Initial benefit	Months to recover
1970	High	$3,977	$190	22
	Average	3,205	168	20
	Low	1,442	107	14
1980	High	14,557	562	25
	Average	10,770	451	23
	Low	4,847	271	18
1990	High	58,115	913	75
	Average	40,787	720	66
	Low	18,354	437	47
2000	High	147,905	1,272	142
	Average	100,277	982	122
	Low	45,124	594	87
2020	High	460,140	3,013	196
	Average	287,588	2,284	154
	Low	129,415	1,382	109
2040	High	1,011,469	6,823	189
	Average	632,168	5,186	148
	Low	284,476	3,133	105

Note: This table uses the example of an employee who works from age 22 until the year before his or her Social Security retirement age. It does not include the employer's contribution. High earnings equals 160 percent of the average earnings; low earnings equals 45 percent of the average earnings.

Source: Social Security Administration.

Q 230. What is Supplemental Security Income?

A A separate program for individuals who have low incomes, Supplemental Security Income (SSI) provides support to persons 65 or older, blind or disabled adults, and blind or disabled children. Congress established SSI in 1972. It replaced the former federal/state program of Old-Age Assistance (OAA), Aid to the Blind, and Aid to the Permanently and Totally Disabled. Although the Social Security Administration administers the SSI program, SSI does not have a trust fund and is not involved in the Social Security/Medicare funding issue. The 1998 benefit rate for an individual living in his or her own household and with no other countable income was $494 monthly. In 1997, the Social Security Administration paid out $29.1 billion (from the federal budget) in SSI benefits to 6.5 million people.

Q 231. When did the Social Security Administration become independent?

A In August 1994, Congress passed legislation making the Social Security Administration a separate agency (no longer under the Department of Health and Human Services). Under this legislation, the Treasury must issue debt instruments directly to the agency for the Social Security surpluses.

Q 232. How much does it cost to administer Social Security?

A It costs the Social Security Administration, which has 64,900 employees, $3.7 billion to administer the program, or about 1.0 percent of benefits paid out.

Q 233. What are the key dates for the Social Security trust fund?

A The following are recent and projected milestones for the trust fund:

1983	Payroll tax increase.
1984	Surpluses begin.
2012 (projected)	Surpluses end.
2021 (projected)	Trust fund reaches maximum value at $4.5 trillion.
2022 (projected)	Outlays exceed taxes plus interest income.
2034 (projected)	Trust fund at $0.

Q 234. Why does the program collect large surpluses if it is a "pay-as-you-go" program?

A Social Security was originally conceived as a pay-as-you-go program, meaning that any year's benefit payments would be funded by the same year's revenue from Social Security taxes. It was not intended to accrue a large trust fund. So why did policy-makers set up taxes to build such an enormous trust fund beginning in 1984? Policy-makers in the early 1980s saw two major problems with Social Security as a pay-as-you-go system: (1) the program was about to go into debt under the tax and benefit

Figure 25   Social Security Trust Fund, 2000–2034

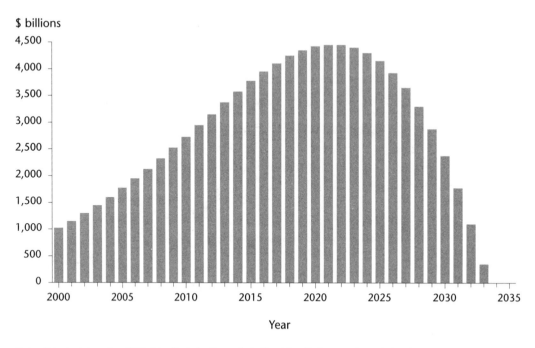

Note: This chart, based on 1999 data, illustrates the projected trust fund balance at the end of each year.

Source: Social Security Administration.

formula at the time; and (2) the program would become a severe strain on working people in the next century because there would be too many long-lived beneficiaries relative to Social Security taxpayers.

A commission headed by Alan Greenspan (who later became the chairman of the Federal Reserve) recommended raising Social Security tax rates, taxing benefits, and increasing the benefits eligibility age in order to build up a trust fund. The implemented tax increases amounted to 0.8 percent each for employees and employers (for a total of 1.6 percent) and 4.35 percent for the self-employed. At the same time the payroll tax for Medicare was also raised (0.15 percent each on employees and employers and 1.3 percent on the self-employed). Essentially, the trust fund would help spread the costs of payments to future retirees over more years, so that children of the 1980s, 1990s, and 2000s would not have to pay suffocating Social Security taxes to fund their parents' and grandparents' retirements.

(See 448 What are the major government health programs?)

235. Where are the surpluses invested?

A By law, cash surpluses are taken by the Treasury in exchange for Treasury "Special Issues" that are nontradeable debt instruments exclusively issued to the Social Security program. The rate of return on Special Issues is equal to average market yield on all interest-bearing obligations of the United States that are not due or callable until after the expiration of 4 years from the date of rate determination. Although some politicians have tried to change the system, the practice of exchanging the large surpluses of the trust fund for Treasury "Special Issues" has been entirely bipartisan, taking place in the Reagan, Bush, and Clinton administrations and regardless of which party was in control of the Congress.

Q **236. Do other pension funds invest this way?**

A No. A typical low-risk corporate pension fund would invest only about 10 percent in government securities. Such a pension fund, in addition, would put 60 percent in stocks, 20 percent in corporate and other bonds, and the rest in other investments.

Q **237. How will the investment strategy of today affect the contributors and beneficiaries of Social Security tomorrow?**

A First, because the return on the "Special Issues" is low, lower than the most conservative pension funds, the compounding effect will also be low, which means a reduced future principal. For example, investing $1,000 per year at 5.0 percent yields $120,800 after 40 years. If the same amount is invested with a 9 percent annual return, the yield after 40 years is $337,882.

HOW MANAGING THE TRUST FUND AFFECTS TAXPAYERS
AND THEIR CHILDREN

The most important change to the Social Security trust fund was the 1.6 percent increase (4.35 percent if self-employed) in Social Security taxes initiated in 1984. An employee with a gross income of $50,000 per year (along with his or her employer) now pays an additional $800 annually. Over 40 years, with no change in salary and compounding at 5 percent—far below stock market returns—this additional 1.6 percent would be worth $96,640. Because the contributions have been used to cover general expenses of the government, younger generations, today's children, may still have to pay substantially higher taxes to fund their parents' retirement.

Second, from a federal financing standpoint serious revenue issues will arise in the second and third decades of the twenty-first century. Because the trust fund holds only "Special Issues," it will have to rely on the Treasury's ability to pay back approximately $4.5 trillion in "Special Issues" during the 13-year period from 2021 to 2034. To raise the necessary cash for the redemptions, the Treasury can either raise taxes, issue additional debt instruments (or in other words, raise the national debt), print money, or a combination thereof. Therefore, the trust fund will not provide a cushion and taxpayers will bear the full burden of retiring baby boomers and their increasing longevity early in the next century.

(See 243 How do budget projections affect plans for the Social Security trust fund?)

Q 238. Is managing the Social Security receipts this way fair?

A One effect of the policy of incorporating Social Security receipts into general revenues has been to shift the composition of taxes over time. The relatively regressive Social Security payroll tax has been financing general government expenditures in recent years, while general revenues will have to finance Social Security benefits payments in later years. So the fact that regressive taxes are funding government expenses that should be funded by progressive taxes raises the fairness issue. The situation is made worse by the fact that while the Social Security program appears sound *actuarially* on paper through 2034, there will likely be very serious funding problems in Social Security for the Treasury Department early next century as the OASDI trust fund begins to cash in its special Treasury issues unless long-range projections of federal budget surpluses hold true.

Q 239. Why is there so much concern and confusion about the state of Social Security?

A First, there is the "on-budget" vs. "off-budget" confusion. The U.S. budget is divided into on-budget and off-budget portions. On-budget is most of the budget and includes general operating expenses for health and human services, defense, and so on. Off-budget includes separate programs like Social Security and other programs that have federal trust funds. The confusion occurs with the standard practice of quoting the budget balance for the "unified" (combined on- and off-budget deficits) budget (which lumps in the Social Security surpluses), rather than just the "on-budget" deficit. The on-budget deficit for 1998 was $42 billion (considerably less than the Social Security surplus), whereas on the much more commonly reported unified

THE GULF IN THE SOCIAL SECURITY DEBATE

VIEW NO. 1

"The unfunded liability of the nation's largest entitlement program is twice the national debt, and if Social Security solvency is preserved simply by raising taxes and cutting benefits, the cost will exceed the combined cost of all the wars fought in our nation's history. The looming Social Security crisis is more than a financial crisis, it is a human tragedy that will force us to choose between economic opportunity for our children and retirement security for our parents."

Source: National Center for Policy Analysis Policy Report No. 220, December 1998.

VIEW NO. 2

"The widespread analytical neglect of productivity in favor of financial flows has obliterated the capacity of the nonbeneficiary population to provide the necessary material support for Social Security retirees. The essence of support capability is production, and there is every reason to estimate that production will be adequate to substantially increase the per capita consumption of both beneficiaries and non-beneficiaries in the peak retirement period. . . . All current projections of long-term income growth exceed current projections for long-term population growth. In a period where income per capita increases for the whole population, it is illogical to say some part of the total population *must* suffer a decrease."

Source: Harold G. Vatter and John F. Walker, "Support for Baby-Boom Retirees," *Journal of Economic Issues,* March 1998, 85.

budget deficit there was actually a surplus, leaving the impression that general government operations were carried out within budget. Misunderstandings over the significance of the unified budget deficit may have had a material effect, such as decreasing political pressure for deficit reduction and/or increasing pressure for tax cuts and/or spending increases. The box above shows just how wide the gulf between the two positions can be.

Another source of confusion may stem from some special interest groups' fear of privatizing Social Security. Institutions such as the American Association for Retired Persons (AARP) and organized labor prefer to keep the status quo. They want to minimize concerns about Social Security's future solvency by citing conservative assumptions of economic growth. They de-emphasize the practice of using the trust fund for general government expenses.

Those who might like to see Social Security replaced with a voluntary or private alternative often advocate tax cuts. This position may be, in part, to increase the likelihood that saving will take place in the private sector rather than in the form of government surpluses. Government surpluses would make Social Security in its current form more credible, while increased saving by individuals would make a private alternative to Social Security more feasible. There is also the recognition that a big pot of money does not sit around for long before people with ambitious spending ideas begin to tap it. In either case, the agenda is somewhat hidden, which complicates the public policy debate.

Even information disseminated by the Social Security Administration itself can create confusion because of its incompleteness. In particular, the Personal Earnings and Benefit Statements (PEBES), which are mailed out to 120 million people over the age of 25, give participants an incomplete cost and benefit summary. PEBES omits employers' cost of the program. This cost is equal to that of the individual and no doubt reduces the wage that the employer is able and willing to pay the worker. PEBES includes estimated future benefits, but omits an accounting of all the future taxes that the participant pays. Thus, there is no way to judge whether Social Security is a good deal for the participant.

Q 240. Why is there a surge in interest in Social Security policy?

A Social Security always gets attention because it is the largest of all government programs and entrenched political forces battle over it continuously. The Social Security program has been increasingly in the news because the federal budget, thanks to a large extent to Social Security surpluses, recorded a surplus in 1998 for the first time since 1969. The issue suddenly became what to do with the surplus. Cut taxes? Increase spending? Pay down the debt? And last, but not least, save Social Security for the future?

Q 241. Are these questions relevant?

A Initially, these questions were premature because the budget surplus relied on the Social Security surplus, which was required to be held in the trust fund. Since there has emerged a real surplus on the on-, or operating, budget in 1999, whether to pay down the debt, or cut taxes, or establish a true, diversified Social Security trust fund with tradeable assets, are now pertinent questions.

Q 242. Why do some believe that Social Security is not in crisis?

A Some economists argue that the Social Security program and the economy would not be any better off had the program actually saved the surpluses (without creating a debt elsewhere in the government). Why should it matter that one part of the U.S. government borrows from another? These economists argue that although the federal government has taxed Americans enough to build a $880 billion trust fund (end of 1999), it is unnecessary and even undesirable to have a trust fund. Rather, it is cheaper to pay a return on "Special Issues" to the Social Security program than to have to borrow an additional $880 billion on the capital market. It might also be preferable that the Social Security Administration not have to manage a trust fund that is projected to approach $4.5 trillion, because of political pressures on investment decisions. So, from a fiscal point of view, the current management of the trust fund is not a significant economic issue. Some economists also believe that some analysts of Social Security program have ignored productivity increases, which has led to pessimistic financial predictions for the program. (See box on page 115.)

Q 243. How do budget projections affect plans for the Social Security trust fund?

A Unified budget projections by the Office of Management and Budget (OMB) through 2030 forecast federal budget surpluses declining to virtual budget balance. During 2030–2050 OMB forecasts modest and manageable deficits. (The Congressional Budget Office (CBO) projections are not quite so optimistic.) These projections imply that there will *not* have to be any higher taxes, borrowing, or expenditure cuts as the Social Security trust fund is drawn down. This goes for Medicare and other trust funds as well. However, projections that go far into the future are unstable and unreliable. For example, as recently as 1996 the OMB forecast a (unified) budget deficit of $197 billion for Fiscal Year 1999, when a (unified) surplus of about $124 billion actually ccurred. The euphoria or pessimism of the immediate present seems to dominate projections of distant and not-so-distant years.

Projected Budget Deficits (-) and Surpluses as a Percent of GDP

Source of estimate	2010	2020	2030	2040	2050	2060
OMB (1999)	3.6%	1.8%	-0.1%	-0.7%	-1.3%	-2.5%
CBO (1999)	3.0	1.0	-1.0	-3.0	-6.0	-14.0
CBO (1996)	-4.0	-8.0	-12.0	-	-19.0	-

Q 244. How has the management of the trust fund reduced deficits, but increased the national debt?

A A strange quirk of the management of the Social Security program is that when surpluses are used the deficit appears to go down, and the debt up. This happens because the trust fund surpluses, which are "off-budget," are added into the total unified budget. If the on-budget has a $150 billion deficit, and the off-budget Social Security program a $70 billion surplus, then the total deficit is reported at $80 billion. The off-budget side has been in surplus since 1984. When the two are added together, the deficit appears reduced.

On the debt side, taking in the surplus Social Security payments from taxpayers and then trading them for Treasury "Special Issues" creates additional debt for the U.S. Treasury. This act increases the *gross federal debt.* In the end, what has happened is that the "reported" deficit is lower, but the total federal debt has increased. Moreover, this management of the trust fund has produced two liabilities for the federal government, the Special Issues (a liability for the Treasury) *and* the benefits claims of future beneficiaries, against one asset, the Special Issues held by the Social Security Administration. Thus, under current practices, faster accumulation of the trust fund just means faster accumulation of gross federal debt for the Treasury.

(See 126 What is the national debt?)

Q 245. Why is there pressure to reform Social Security?

A In addition to the trust fund management issues, the increasing age of the U.S. population is putting pressure on the Social Security program. The number of workers per beneficiary is projected to decline from 3.4 to 2.1 by 2030, then decline more gradually to 1.8 by 2075. This demographic trend has led many policymakers to propose changes to Social Security that they feel will help it meet the challenges of the twenty-first century. Most proposals involve partial or total privatization.

Q 246. What is the Social Security advisory council?

A The provisions of the Social Security Act, prior to the 1995 law that established the Social Security Administration as an independent agency, required the appointment of an advisory council every four years. The last advisory council, appointed in June 1994, examined funding options for Social Security. The council was composed of a chair and 12 members who represented employers, employees, and the public. Under the 1995 law, a permanent seven-member advisory board advises the president, Congress, and the Social Security Administration on the Social Security and Supplemental Security Income programs.

Q 247. What are the major alternatives for reforming Social Security?

A Three proposals by the advisory council all include some form of privatization: (1) a "maintain benefits" plan that would invest part of the trust fund in the stock market in order to raise returns; (2) an "individual account" plan that would require workers to contribute 1.6 percent of their pay to new individual savings accounts to make up for Social Security cuts that may be required to ensure long-run solvency of the program; and (3) a "personal security account" plan that would redesign the system by gradually replacing Social Security benefits with a "flat-rate" government benefit for each worker and individual private savings accounts funded with 5 percent of pay (part of which would take the place of Social Security taxes).

In addition, the national retirement program in Chile is gaining attention in the United States. Chile replaced its state-run, pay-as-you-go system with one requiring most workers to invest a portion of their earnings in individual savings accounts through government-approved private pension funds. Similar, but scaled-down, approaches that would run in conjunction with the current system have been introduced in recent Congresses.

Q 248. What are the arguments why Social Security should be fundamentally reformed?

A Critics of Social Security cite its contradictory mix of insurance and social welfare goals. Social Security benefits are not based on a person's contributions as in a private savings program. Many well-to-do recipients also receive benefits. Privatization, say proponents, is a way for Americans to gain greater ownership over their retirement savings, achieve higher returns, and generally promote national saving and economic growth. Privatization would curb the practices of the government using the trust fund surpluses to camouflage borrowing and avoid raising taxes to pay for other programs.

Q 249. What are the arguments why Social Security should *not* be fundamentally reformed?

A Opponents of changing Social Security maintain that privatization would undermine the social insurance feature of Social Security and expose low-income retirees, survivors, and the disabled to poor investment decisions. Current workers would not only have to support current retirees, but save for their own retirement as well. Privatization would not increase national saving because governmental borrowing and spending would have to increase.

Q 250. Why have some policymakers proposed changing the method of cost of living adjustment for Social Security?

A Benefits under Social Security and other entitlement programs are adjusted annually by the cost of living adjustment (COLA) that is based on the consumer price index (CPI). The CPI is the most common measure of inflation. Because the CPI is said to overstate inflation, it leads to too high an increase in benefits from entitlement programs. The CPI does not take into account the degree of flexibility in consumers' purchases. Rather, it simply assumes that regardless of how much the price of a good increases, the consumer will continue to buy the same quantity of the good (until the expenditure weights are updated). For instance, if the price of tomatoes increases 20 percent, the consumer will likely buy other vegetables whose prices have not increased as sharply. The CPI does not reflect this adjustment, nor quality improvements, and, so, overstates inflation. Thus, the annual COLAs for entitlements programs are higher than they should be. Revising the COLA downward would result in large savings for Social Security and improve its actuarial soundness. Advocates for the elderly maintain that the CPI does not overestimate inflation and that retirees would suffer a real decline in their benefits payments if the COLA were reduced.

(See 29 What is inflation? 325 What is the central controversy over the consumer price index?)

Q 251. How would the introduction of means-testing affect Social Security?

A Means-testing of Social Security benefits would introduce personal income and assets as a determinant of benefits and have the goal of curbing the rapid growth in entitlements, which account for half the federal budget. The Concord Coalition, a proponent of means-testing, observed that the wealthiest 40 percent of Social Security recipients receive less than 35 percent of their income from Social Security, but receive almost half of all Social Security benefits. Means-testing proposals have included reducing benefits for persons whose annual income exceeds $50,000 ($100,000 for a couple). However, means-testing might have only a small effect because 50 percent of Social Security benefits are already taxable for recipients in the

$25,000–34,000 income range, and 85 percent of benefits are taxable above an income of $34,000. Opponents of means-testing argue that it breaks the link between earnings and benefits. Means-testing, they argue, would unfavorably alter the public perception and support for Social Security, making Social Security look like welfare and adversely affect people who had sacrificed by saving for their retirement.

Q 252. What was President Clinton's proposal to save Social Security?

A In 1999 President Clinton proposed allocating the long-range projected federal budget surplus during the following 15 years to a combination of debt reduction ($1.8 trillion) and investment of Social Security in the stock market ($560 billion).

Q 253. Why did Federal Reserve Chairman Greenspan oppose President Clinton's proposal?

A Maintaining that "investing the Social Security trust funds in equities does little or nothing to improve the overall ability of the U.S. economy to meet the retirement needs of the next century," Alan Greenspan opposed investing Social Security trust funds on three grounds. First, the returns would not meet expectations and would be lower than private retirement funds. Second, investing a large additional amount in the stock market would raise equity prices and reduce net returns. Also, private portfolios would have to buy Treasury securities sold by the Social Security trust fund in order to raise cash to buy stocks. These portfolios would demand higher returns on Treasury notes to absorb the extra volume, thus raising the cost of servicing the federal debt. Finally, Greenspan stated it is not "possible to secure and sustain institutional arrangements that would insulate, over the long run, the trust funds from political pressures." He added, "Those pressures, whether direct or indirect, could result in suboptimal performance by our capital markets."

Q 254. By the end of 1999, were there any pending legislative changes to Social Security or Medicare?

A Various modifications and alternatives to Social Security were proposed in the late 1990s, but none passed. In 2000 Congress voted not to eliminate the tax on Social Security benefits for people earning above certain income thresholds. Previously the last major modification in Social Security benefits occurred in 1983, when the age at which a recipient could receive full benefits was increased from 65 to 67 (to be phased in beginning in 2003, adding one month to the eligibility age each year until 2027).

Q **255. Does the present use of Social Security trust fund surpluses affect the economy as a whole?**

A Some analysts argue that, in a fiscal sense, use of the trust fund does not affect the economy. If Social Security surpluses were not transferred to the Treasury to purchase "Special Issues," the Treasury would simply have to (1) run larger deficits financed by more Treasury debt on the open capital market, or (2) increase income taxes. On the other hand, with the Social Security surpluses masking recent deficits, the pressure to cut spending or increase taxes may have been reduced. The policies of using Social Security surpluses versus borrowing in other forms or increasing taxes are not necessarily equivalent economic choices. Moreover, the trust fund "cushion" that is supposed to exist during 2022 to 2034, the years in which the trust fund would be drawn down, will, in effect, not provide a buffer at all to taxpayers, because revenues from other sources will be needed to cash in the Treasury "Special Issues."

Q **256. Are there any tax allocation issues with using the Social Security trust fund to fund general government?**

A The Social Security tax is a regressive tax because above a certain income ($72,600 in 1999), the taxpayer pays no additional Social Security tax. Normally, more progressive federal *income* taxes fund general government expenses. (For the 2.9 percent hospital insurance tax rate, there is no income limit.) On the benefit side, however, the structure of Social Security favors beneficiaries who had lower incomes.

The policy question then appears to be whether to change the law to allow the trust fund to accumulate real funds (without increasing the debt elsewhere in the government—that is, no longer trading Social Security funds for Treasury "Special Issues"), or to reduce the payroll tax so that a substantial trust fund is not generated.

TAX REFORM

Every April 15, many taxpayers and small businesses yearn for a simpler tax code. For a large segment of taxpayers, the current code is relatively simple, but the overall cost of complying with the tax code, in terms of both hours and dollars spent, is a driving force behind proposals to change the code.

However, none of the recent, more simple tax reform proposals—the flat tax, the value-added tax, the personal consumption tax, and the national sales tax—have gained sufficient support for passage in Congress. These tax systems would mean big changes in the incentive structure governing consumption, saving, and investment. Have these reforms not advanced because Americans fear a new tax system with its unknown consequences? Is the current tax system perpetuated because politicians are rewarded for maintaining the status quo? Or do Americans really prefer the current tax system, for all its faults, to the proposed alternatives?

This section looks at these questions in the context of recent proposals to change the way federal income and payroll taxes are assessed. It also examines the issue of who receives tax breaks in U.S. society, whether it is those who have children, those who own a home, those who rent, those who contribute to charities, or those who invest in different types of financial instruments.

Q 257. What is tax reform?

A Tax reform is a fundamental change in the way the government assesses taxes on individuals and organizations. Tinkering with tax rates to meet a fiscal policy goal, or adding or subtracting a few deductions is not real tax reform. For example, an increase in the tax rate at each income bracket is not a fundamental reform, nor is increasing a deduction for child care expenses. On the other hand, changes in the philosophy of taxation, such as indexing tax brackets for inflation, or a wholesale elimination of personal and corporate deductions, do constitute tax reform. Federal taxes are considered here, but tax reform could be applied to state and local taxation as well.

(See 190 What was the Reagan tax cut? 199 What were the elements of the Tax Reform Act of 1986?)

Q 258. Why is tax reform a crucial issue?

A Tax reform is crucial because of the vast amount of money involved; its potential for changing the way people consume, save, and invest; and the controversy in deciding what is equitable and even what is efficient. Taxation, along with the power to print money, are the two most important economic powers of government. How a government taxes influences what consumers buy, how much they save, and what companies invest in. Almost every financial decision has tax implications. In recent years, the taxes paid at the federal, state, and local levels have been more than 30 percent of the gross domestic product—about $3 trillion per year. Two-thirds of this amount was collected at the federal level. Collecting the right amount of money needed to run the type of government that its citizens want is one goal of taxation. What is the right amount of taxation, and what is equitable is where controversy arises. The ultimate question is whether the current tax system, with all its interventions, is the best system for the long-term survival, prosperity, and fairness of the U.S. economy.

Q 259. What are some of the major types of tax reform?

A Tax reform proposals include very different alternatives to the current tax system. Major alternatives are the flat tax, the value-added tax (VAT), the national retail sales tax (NRST), and the personal consumption tax (PCT) or unlimited saving allowance (USA) tax. While these proposals are all different, they have two things in common: they represent major simplification of the tax code and they reduce the role of government in influencing consumption, saving, and investment decisions, while increasing autonomy of individuals and companies.

The proposals would lead to less progressive taxation than in the current system. The proposals, with the exception of the flat tax, would also shift taxation from income to consumption. Under these reforms, the rich would pay the same amount of tax for each additional dollar of consumption (the same marginal rate) as the middle or lower classes. The rich would pay more taxes by consuming more, but the rate would be the same. There are adjustments that can be made to restore some progressivity in some of the proposals.

Q 260. Do the proposals increase or decrease taxes?

A The proposals aim to be "revenue neutral," which means they are supposed to generate the same amount of revenue as the current tax system. However, because the tax methods are unproven, in practice, they may well bring either an unanticipated revenue shortfall or surplus. Over time, if any new tax method is more efficient than the current tax system, then the economy will gain by reducing compliance costs, and reducing the distortions caused by incorporating the tax considerations into various economic decisions.

Q 261. How did the current tax system begin?

A The 16th Amendment, which authorized the federal government to tax personal and business incomes, was adopted in 1913. The income tax was set up with progressive tax brackets. This meant that those businesses or individuals who earned more paid taxes at a higher rate. Before the modern income tax system began with legislation passed in 1913, the government generated revenue from "sin" taxes (taxes on alcohol and tobacco) and taxes on trade. These taxes constituted a much lower percentage of GDP than became the norm in the latter half of the twentieth century.

Q 262. What were the major milestones in the evolution of the U.S. tax code?

A Since its institution in 1913, the tax code has undergone several major changes. In 1942 employers began to withhold income taxes from workers' paychecks. Thus, workers paid taxes as they earned, and businesses collected taxes for the IRS. Some economic historians have pointed out that the institution of withholding had the effect of desensitizing people to paying taxes, because they no longer had to actively give a portion of their assets to the federal government, but rather passively received less in take home pay.

In 1954 the tax code was revised to allow personal and other deductions. Over time, the personal exemption has declined as a proportion of income, while other types of deductions have increased. The net effect from 1955 to 1970 was that taxable income as a share of total income increased slowly but steadily. After 1970, taxable income was a fairly constant share of total income.

With the advent of indexing the tax rate structure in 1985 by the CPI, the federal government no longer gained additional revenues through inflation.

In 1986 the tax code was simplified by reducing the number of tax brackets from 14 to 2. Many individual and investment deductions were also eliminated. The elimination of deductions meant that the federal government pulled back from intervening in many consumption and investment decisions by the public and companies.

(See 188 What is bracket creep? 199 What were the elements of the Tax Reform Act of 1986?)

Q 263. What are the major criticisms of today's tax code?

A Many taxpayers, especially individuals who itemize deductions and small businesses, are dissatisfied with the current tax code because it (1) is overly complex; (2) costs too much to comply with; (3) usurps the American brainpower that has to be employed to figure out tax implications and optimize economic decisions; (4) interferes excessively in private economic decisions; and (5) strongly favors consumption over saving.

264. What is the evidence of the tax system being overly complex?

A The complexity of the U.S. tax code is evident in a number of ways. Although most people may only deal with a half dozen or so forms, there are 480 separate forms and 280 separate instructions. In 1993, almost three-quarters of Form 1040 tax returns (which accounted for 58 percent of all returns) were prepared by paid preparers. Virtually half of all returns filed were signed by a paid tax form preparer. Even people educated in a quantitative discipline often find it necessary to hire professional tax preparers. The tax code has increased in complexity since the 1993 survey. The easier forms, 1040A and 1040EZ, had much lower percentages of paid preparers and would probably not be simplified by any of the major tax proposals.

Tax Returns Signed by a Paid Preparer

Form	Number of returns filed (millions)	Number with paid preparer's signature (millions)	Percentage with paid preparer's signature
1040EZ	20.4	1.5	7%
1040A	27.9	5.8	21
1040	66.4	49.2	74
Total	114.6	56.6	49

Source: Government Accounting Office, *Tax Administration-Potential Impact of Alternative Taxes on Taxpayers and Administrators,* January 1998.

Q **265. What is the evidence for the high cost of complying with the U.S. tax code?**

A Estimates of cost of complying with the U.S. tax code range from $50 to $500 billion. One of the more often quoted estimates was made by the Tax Foundation, an advocate of tax simplification, which estimated, conservatively, that taxpayers would spend 5.3 billion hours complying with the 1996 federal tax laws. This estimate was based on the IRS estimate of the amount of time needed to keep tax records, read IRS instructions, and fill out the needed forms. A 1998 study by the accounting firm of Arthur D. Little arrived at nearly the same estimate of total hours, with a total cost of $224.7 billion (based on an hourly rate of $42.40). The hourly rate is considerably above the average U.S. wage, but it is at the low end of the hourly cost of professional tax preparation. It is worth adding that small businesses are relatively more disadvantaged by tax complexity and spend much higher percentages of their revenues complying than do large companies.

Q 266. What other expenses are incurred because of the tax code's complexity?

A Due to the complexity of the tax code, individuals and small businesses turn to professional help to file their returns. Thousands of tax accountants and lawyers deal with the complexities of the tax code on their behalf. On the government end, the Tax Foundation estimates that inflation-adjusted costs to administer the tax code increased 650 percent between 1955 and 1995, while government tax staff more than doubled from 63,712 to 136,155 over the same period. Society would only stand to benefit if the effort and talent of these tax professionals were employed in activities other than filling out tax returns.

Q 267. What is the evidence that the current tax system favors consumption over saving and investment?

A The current tax system taxes all forms of *income*—wage income, interest on savings, or capital gains—while some forms of *consumption* are encouraged by the tax system. The favorite personal deduction of all, the mortgage interest deduction, is based on consumption, that is, purchasing a house. Thus, some view this situation as punishing savings, while rewarding consumption. Both consuming and saving are necessary to an economy, but when saving is extremely low (even negative) as it is in the United States, the incentives created by the tax structure may be a good place to look for a solution. Policymakers' desire to stimulate saving is one of the motivations to reform the tax system.

Q 268. What are the counterarguments to criticisms of the current tax code?

A The main proponents of the current tax code point out that although the tax system is costly and complex, it is desirable for the government to inject social and other noneconomic priorities into the tax code. The complex system of credits and deductions, and even levels of eligibility within those credits and deductions, is the outcome of using the tax system as a tool to achieve social and economic objectives.

For example, the government currently encourages saving for retirement through the Individual Retirement Account (IRA), but wants to limit, as much as possible, the tax benefit to wealthier individuals. To do that, the government offers the $2,000 IRA deduction, but scales it back as the individual's income increases, or if the individual has another retirement plan. Combining the two goals of increased retirement saving and redistribution of income, within the same deduction, adds complexity to the tax code. Yet both the deductions and the progressive nature of the current tax code are popular. The same dual objectives apply to the child tax credit, child care expenses, capital gains rates, and other deductions. The government also encourages charitable contributions, small businesses, and higher education through tax deductions.

Q **269. What political reasons would block tax reform?**

A It is not clear whether Americans would want to do away with complexity and "intrusion" of the tax code if it also meant doing away with tax benefits in the form of personal deductions and credits. Any new tax reform would have to reduce, or at least not increase, their current tax liability in order to be widely accepted. With all the political hype surrounding the tax reform issue, it would probably take some time to convince people that a proposal was revenue neutral in order to gain sufficient support.

Q **270. Which economic considerations drive efforts to reform the tax code?**

A The primary goal of taxation is to generate revenue to pay for government. But there are many ways to tax to generate that revenue, and each way has a different economic effect. The guiding principles of designing a tax system are economic efficiency, simplicity, administrative ease, as well as equity within the same income bracket and between low to high brackets (referred to as horizontal and vertical equity, respectively, by economists). Another economic consideration of any new tax structure is whether the new tax code can and should be used for remedying market imperfections. For instance, some economists might want to grant investment tax credits to nonpolluting technologies, while others might want to reward saving by making interest tax free up to a certain amount. Still other economists eschew all of these interventions and believe that the market will make the best allocation between supply and demand, and that, in the end, it is best to keep the tax code as simple as possible.

One of the prominent themes is whether taxation should be based on income or consumption. Proponents of consumption taxes argue that income taxes tax people on what they contribute to society (labor and capital), while consumption taxes tax what people take out of society. In addition, income-based taxes influence people to work less. They also influence people to save less, invest less, innovate less, and result in lower living standards. Income-based taxes create a bias in favor of current consumption at the expense of saving and future consumption. The consumption tax, on the other hand, eliminates the distortion between present and future consumption by allowing the full return on saving and investment to be pocketed by the individual. It is important to add that even though economic theory supports the view that consumption taxes increase individuals' saving rates, the empirical evidence of that is not very strong.

The cost of actually complying with the tax code is also a serious consideration in determining which method of taxation is best. The more complex the tax code, the more hours it takes to implement it (for both taxpayers and tax collectors) and the more it costs. Economists who support maximizing efficiency would try to minimize the cost of tax compliance, subject to other tax code priorities.

Equity over time is also an important issue. For example, under the current income-based system, families that consume a lot early in life and less later, pay less lifetime taxes than a family that does the reverse. The reason is that the family that waits to consume a lot will typically have more income from savings and, therefore, pay more taxes. The investment allocation effects of the tax code are also important considerations. If tax policy tries to steer investment, for whatever reason (invigorate a depressed area, protect the environment), then it has to balance the costs and benefits of the distortions to "before and after tax" investment returns. Sometimes the complexity of regulations makes it difficult to make this estimate.

Q 271. Which value considerations drive tax code reform?

A Tax code reform is not just about generating the needed revenue in the most efficient way possible. Probably the most prominent nonefficiency-based feature of the tax code is the redistribution of income, achieved mainly through progressive tax rates in tandem with government outlays that favor those with the lowest incomes. Redistribution through progressive taxes means that the relatively well-off pay absolutely more, as well as a higher percentage of their income, compared with less well-off people. Differential tax rates are also used to penalize behavior unwanted by the policymakers and to reward desired behavior. This "carrot and stick" approach is used to favor what is viewed as economically superior as well as to promote certain values.

Under some of the less progressive consumption tax alternatives, wealth could accumulate quickly. According to recent estimates of the concentration of wealth in the United States, 1 percent of the population has 39 percent of total wealth. Tax proposals that would flatten the tax rates paid by individuals would mean lowering the tax rates on people with high income, and could further skew wealth distribution, and undermine support for the proposal. To mediate the potential effect of less progressive tax rates, many analysts argue that an effective inheritance tax would have to be maintained and strengthened.

(See 494 What has been the general trend in income distribution?)

Q 272. What are the major recent tax proposals?

A There was a surge in interest in tax reform in 1985 that led to some important reforms but fell short of a conversion to a new type of system. The flat tax was publicized by the efforts of two prominent Republicans: House majority leader Dick Armey in 1995 and presidential candidate Steve Forbes in 1996 and 2000.

Tax Proposal	Rate	Replaces	Exemptions
Flat income tax	20% (17% after 2 years)	Individual and corporate income tax, but not the payroll tax	Imports, first $17,000 plus $5,500 personal exemption
National sales tax	15%	Individual and corporate income, estate, and gift taxes	Uncertain, maybe food, medicine, education, and owner-occupied housing
VAT/individuals	5%	Nothing, levied for additional revenue for reducing the national debt and national health care insurance	Food, housing, medical care, exports, interest, etc.
VAT/business activities tax	14.5%	Corporate income tax and half of the OASDI[a] payroll tax	
Unlimited Savings Allowance (USA), or personal consumption tax	19–40% on individuals 11% on businesses	Individual and corporate income tax, and some of the payroll tax	Individuals

[a] Old Age, Survivors, and Disability Insurance (Social Security).

Q 273. Do any recent reform proposals resolve all major tax issues?

A The recent tax proposals leave many unresolved issues. Perhaps the largest issue is how state taxes would be levied. Currently, 37 state tax systems piggy-back on the federal tax system on individual taxes and 42 states follow the federal system on corporate taxes. Individuals calculate adjusted gross income on their federal return and use that number for their state return. If the federal system were changed to a value-added or national sales tax, how would states respond? Tax simplification might not be very effective unless state legislatures followed the federal government and adapted their tax system to the chosen alternative.

Another unresolved area is how to treat expenditures on education for tax purposes. Is education saving or consumption? The rental value of owner-occupied housing is another big component of taxes. In calculating GDP, national accounts specialists estimate the yearly value of living in one's own home. Is this a form of consumption that should be taxed? If the proposals are to be revenue neutral, what is taxed has to be firmly established, before the tax rate is set. There are also issues related to difficulties in making the change to a new system. How much difficulty would there be in changing tax systems? Maybe revenue would fall far short of needs.

Q 274. What are the estimated compliance costs for each alternative?

A For each alternative, the estimated compliance costs are

Type of tax	Costs ($ billions)	Source of estimate
VAT	$1.8 (administration)	GAO (1995)
	3.2 (other compliance)	
Flat tax	9.4	Tax Foundation (1996)
National sales tax	8.2	Tax Foundation (1996)
USA tax	36.0	Tax Foundation (1996)
Current income tax	224.7	Tax Foundation (1996)

Q 275. What is taxed and what is not under each proposal?

A The checkmarks in the following table indicate which items would be taxed under the various alternatives.

Component	National retail sales tax	Value-added tax	Flat tax	Personal consumption tax
Business level				
Included				
Sales of consumption goods and services	✓	✓	✓	
Sales of goods and services to other businesses, including investment goods		✓	✓	
Deducted				
Purchases of goods and services from businesses, including investment goods		✓	✓	
Wages			✓	
Individual level				
Included				
Wages			✓	✓
Cash flows received: interest and dividend income, funds from asset sales, withdrawals from accounts, borrowed funds				✓
Distributions from sole proprietorships, partnerships				✓
Deducted				
New saving: purchases of stock, bonds; deposits in accounts, repayment of debt				✓
Contributions to sole proprietorships, partnerships				✓

Source: Government Accounting Office, *Potential Impact of Alternative Taxes*, 1998, 63.

Q 276. What is a flat tax?

A A flat tax is a tax levied at the same percentage on all taxpayers, whether individuals or businesses. One publicized flat tax proposal (developed by Rep. Dick Armey and Sen. Richard Shelby in 1995) established the initial tax rate at 20 percent, falling to 17 percent over two to three years. The flat tax would eliminate almost all deductions and credits. As a consideration to lower-income earners, there is a personal exemption of $12,200 for a single person, $24,400 for a married couple, and $5,500 for each dependent child. A family of four would, therefore, pay no tax on the first $35,400, and 17 percent on all income above that amount. Personal exemptions would be indexed for (increased by the amount of) inflation. The flat tax would not replace Social Security and Medicare taxes, which would continue to be assessed at their current rate. The flat tax is divided into the Business Tax (BT) and the income tax. The BT is similar to the (Sales Subtraction) VAT except that the BT allows deductions for wages and contributions to employee retirement plans, and it taxes exports and not imports.

(See 282 What is the value-added tax?)

Q **277. What are the pros of the flat tax?**

A The flat tax would

- Simplify tax preparation—taxes could be filed on a single postcard form.
- Sharply reduce the role of the IRS.
- Reduce the cost of compliance from $224.7 billion currently to $9.4 billion per year.
- Eliminate double taxation of income by not taxing capital gains or dividends.
- Provide incentives to save by not taxing capital gains, dividends, or interest income.
- Provide a simpler concept of taxable income (defined as total income minus savings and investments, minus a threshold income).
- Exempt nearly half of all households from paying any federal income tax.
- Retain some progressivity by having large personal exemptions.

Q **278. What are the cons of the flat tax?**

A The flat tax would

- Be less progressive—the top marginal rate on the wealthiest taxpayers would be reduced from 39.6 to 17 percent.
- Be unnecessarily rigid (equal simplicity and greater progressivity could be achieved with multiple rates).
- Eliminate deductions for mortgage interest payments.
- Eliminate deductions for charitable donations.
- Prohibit corporations from deducting benefits, such as Social Security, health, or life insurance (wage and salary expenses could still be deducted).

- Prohibit corporations from deducting interest payments on debt.

- Provide no great advantage in simplicity to most taxpayers because about 70 percent of tax returns already include no itemized deductions or complicated forms.

- Have unforeseen consequences, such as expensive transitional costs, revenue shortfalls, excessive taxation, and a more skewed income distribution.

Q 279. What is a national retail sales tax?

A The national retail sales tax (NRST) is a tax on all goods and services purchased by the final consumer in the United States. It would eliminate all exemptions, deductions, and withholdings and would greatly reduce paperwork. It is very similar to the sales tax applied by most states throughout the country. In fact, one of the better-known versions of the national sales tax provides for individual states, rather than the IRS, to administer the tax. Food and medical supplies would most likely be exempt. This approach taxes what people spend rather than what they earn, under the premise of encouraging saving and investment.

Q 280. What are the pros of NRST?

A The NRST would

- Eliminate the income tax, tax forms, and, possibly, the IRS.
- Be familiar to consumers, who already pay state sales taxes.
- Tax all citizens at the same rate; those who spend more would be taxed more.
- Reduce the power of special interest groups seeking tax preferences.
- Provide greater incentives for saving and investment.
- Exempt no one, including illegal aliens, from the tax.
- Be extremely cost effective with no cost of compliance for consumers, and only $1 to $5 billion for businesses (about $220 billion less than total compliance costs of the current system).

Q 281. What are the cons of NRST?

A The NRST would

- Place a greater burden on businesses to collect and be liable for taxes.
- Be regressive, unless luxury goods are taxed at a higher rate, or other progressive compensation is also employed.

- Hurt the poor, unless food and medicine are exempted.

- Have a depressing effect on demand as people curtail their expenditures.

- Impose double taxation because taxes on business inputs could still comprise 25 to 33 percent of the national sales tax basis.

- Encourage tax evasion, as businesses and individuals would be tempted not to report transactions.

- Have unforeseen consequences, such as expensive transitional costs, revenue shortfalls, excessive taxation, and a more skewed income distribution.

Q 282. What is a value-added tax (VAT)?

A The value-added tax (VAT) is a tax that is applied to goods and services at each point of exchange, from the first stage of production, through final consumption. The tax is applied only to the value-added portion of each stage. The value-added portion is the difference between the sale price and the cost of the goods or services.

Q 283. How does the VAT work?

A The best known application of VAT is in Europe where the "invoice" method is used. Businesses pay the VAT on the full value of the item they buy, but later they get a refund for that amount of the tax.

The following is an example of a 10 percent VAT in a two-stage transaction:

1. A car manufacturer sells a car at $10,000 (to cover cost and profit) to a car dealership.

2. A 10 percent VAT, or $1,000, is added, and the dealer pays $11,000 for the car.

3. The dealer then adds $2,000 (to cover preparation, sales costs, and profit) to bring the cost of the car to $13,000.

4. The 10 percent VAT, or $200, is applied to the dealer's added value, raising the total price of the car to $13,200 for the final customer.

5. Total taxes paid are $1,200. Both the manufacturer and the dealer have passed their tax cost on to the next purchaser in the form of a higher price.

By examining where each of the three participants (manufacturer, dealer, and customer) stands at the end of the transactions shows how the whole tax is shifted to the final consumer:

1. The car manufacturer takes $1,000 in VAT from the dealer and passes it to the tax collector. Result: the manufacturer pays no out-of-pocket taxes.

2. The dealer pays $1,000 in taxes to the manufacturer but then sends an invoice to the tax collector for a $1,000 refund. The dealer also passes an additional $200 in VAT to the tax collector from the final consumer. Result: the dealer pays no out-of-pocket taxes.

3. The customer pays $1,200 more than the manufacturing and sales costs of the car. Result: the final customer effectively bears the whole tax ($1,200 out-of-pocket tax).

Q **284. What are the pros of the VAT?**

A The VAT would

- Be simple to administer and reduce the cost of compliance from $224.7 billion currently to about $5 billion.

- Reduce the size of the IRS, because no tax returns would be submitted by individuals.

- Provide incentives for saving.

- Tax imports but not exports.

- Follow familiar real-world examples, mainly from Europe, that would allow assessment of VAT's strengths and weaknesses.

Q **285. What are the cons of the VAT?**

A The VAT would

- Become cumbersome if differential rates, exemptions, and other special treatment for classes of taxpayers were allowed.

- Be regressive unless other measures are taken, such as levying VAT at higher rates on luxury goods such as yachts and jewelry, and/or exempting food and medicine.

- Have unforeseen consequences, such as expensive transitional costs, revenue shortfalls, excessive taxation, and a more skewed income distribution.

Q **286. What is the personal consumption tax?**

A The personal consumption tax, or unlimited saving account (USA) tax, is a combined progressive consumption tax on individuals, described as an income tax (IT), and a VAT on business activity (BT). The IT taxes individuals on income minus savings, or more specifically, on current income that is not invested in savings assets and on funds withdrawn from savings. The IT resembles the existing federal individual income tax because it allows deductions from reported gross income to arrive at adjusted gross income and additional deductions to arrive at taxable income. Many deductions are eliminated, but the savings deduction is added that converts the USA tax from an income to a consumption-based tax. Individuals would be able to take a tax credit for their share of FICA payroll tax.

For businesses, an 11 percent sales subtraction VAT is applied or a BT. That is, the BT is imposed on a business's gross profit, defined as the excess of taxable receipts over deductible amounts. Also, under the sales-subtraction method, the tax base is calculated from the purchase and sales data over a period of time, rather than on each sale, as in the credit subtraction type of VAT. The employer can claim a credit for the employer's share of the payroll tax. The BT taxes imports, but not exports.

Q 287. What are the pros of the personal consumption tax?

A The personal consumption tax would

- Be simple to administer, as it does away with depreciation schedules, calculating capital gains, and detailed record keeping.
- Reduce the cost of compliance from $224.7 billion currently to around $36 billion.
- Lend itself to progressivity because it is collected from the individual consumer and different rates and personal exemptions could be applied.
- Create incentives for saving and investment.
- Tax the purchases of illegal aliens.

Q 288. What are the cons of the personal consumption tax?

A The personal consumption tax would

- Place a heavy burden on businesses to be the tax collectors for society and be liable for tax revenue to the government.
- Set sales tax high in order to replace the income tax.
- Create incentives to circumvent the tax system through unreported transactions.
- Have unforeseen consequences, such as expensive transitional costs, revenue shortfalls, excessive taxation, and a more skewed income distribution.

Q **289. Which major individual changes to the current system have been proposed?**

A Besides entire new tax systems, some major changes to the current tax system have been proposed:

- Indexing business taxes to the rate of inflation, including indexing inventories, depreciation, income interest and expense, and capital gains. The effect of this change would most likely be to lower business taxes.

- Taxing business income only once by integrating corporate and individual income tax. Avoiding double taxation could be achieved by abolishing the corporate income tax, allowing a tax deduction for corporations for dividends paid, or by allowing individuals to deduct dividends from their taxable income.

- And the not so popular theme of broadening the tax base. Broadening could include taxing fringe benefits, taxing contributions to pension plans, taxing the imputed service value of owner occupied housing, and even taxing capital gains as they occur, not just when they are realized. In the latter case, the tax could be in the form of an interest charge estimated on the basis of the value of the deferred income.

Q **290. Is there any recent or pending tax reform legislation?**

A Congress votes on some form of tax cuts or tax increases nearly every year. However, Congress has not passed any substantial reform since 1986. Proposals involving the major tax alternatives discussed above have been debated for years, but none has mustered sufficient support to be brought to a vote.

Q **291. What is the process for changing the tax code?**

A Like every other piece of federal legislation, a bill to change the tax code must pass both houses of Congress by a simple majority vote and then be signed by the president.

MAINTAINING LOW INFLATION AND LOW UNEMPLOYMENT

Trying to achieve and keep unemployment and inflation low is a permanent goal of economic policy. This goal requires a continuous and difficult balancing act of fiscal and monetary policy, with a lot of cooperation from the business cycle and increases in productivity.

Q 292. What are the real costs of inflation?

A Inflation is not simply a rise in the level of prices matched by a simultaneous rise in nominal wages and interest rates that preserve real wages and returns. There is a delay during which wages, prices of goods, and interest rates adjust, which represents costs to the wage earner, consumer, and investor, respectively. Thus, real purchasing power and real return on investment can be, at least temporarily, eroded by inflation. Relative prices of goods and services, which signal to the economy how to allocate consumption and investment, also change, again, at least temporarily. All of this adjusting has economic costs. In a high inflation environment, it is difficult for people to accurately evaluate price information needed to make consumption and investment decisions. Because of the greater difficulty in processing information, mistakes are more frequent in allocating expenditures between today and tomorrow and between this product or that and additional real costs are incurred. Furthermore, during particularly high or unstable inflationary periods, investment is riskier and the investment level tends to shrink because a higher real return is required for the same level of investment. Therefore, keeping inflation as low as possible is one of the most important objectives of economic policy.

Q 293. How does the Federal Reserve try to keep inflation low?

A The role of the Federal Reserve (Fed) in changing the money supply is very important to the control of inflation. A faster growing money supply generally means higher inflation. This is because when there is more money in circulation chasing the same amount of goods, the prices of those goods rise. Inflation is kept down by keeping the growth of the money supply down. While the Fed cannot fully control the money supply, it can influence the money supply with three main tools: open market operations, regulating the discount rate, and regulating the required reserve rate. Through open market operations, the Fed reduces the money supply by selling the Fed's holdings of securities to the market, thereby taking money out of circulation. The Fed can also raise the discount rate to member banks, which is the rate at which member banks borrow from the Federal Reserve system. Raising this discount rate reduces the amount that member banks borrow. The required reserve rate is the percentage of deposits that banks must hold in cash. Raising the required reserve rate also takes money out of circulation, tightens credit, and effectively reduces the money supply.

(See 35 What is the Federal Reserve? 36 What is the money supply?)

Q 294. How can inflation and unemployment be kept low simultaneously?

A Keeping inflation and unemployment low is a true balancing act of monetary and fiscal policy. When the Fed reduces the money supply to keep inflation in check, there is the tendency for interest rates (and therefore the cost of investing) to go up, dampening economic activity. The difficult task for the Fed is to keep the money supply low enough to maintain a stable dollar and low inflation, but also provide enough money supply (that is, liquidity) to keep interest rates low enough to support investment sufficient for growth and high employment. In the late 1970s, the Federal Reserve policy was to pursue interest rate targets. The result was that the Fed increased the money supply to drive interest rates lower. But instead of interest rates moving down, inflation shot up, and it took a major recession in 1981–1982 and a minor one later in 1990–1991 to squeeze inflation out of the economy.

Figure 26 shows the trade-off between interest rates and inflation. Graph A shows how the interest rate is determined by the supply and demand for money. The vertical axis is the interest rate and the horizontal axis is the quantity of money supplied

Figure 26   How Money Supply Affects Interest Rates and Inflation

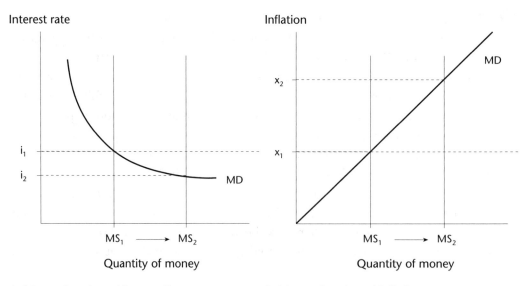

A. Money Supply and Interest Rates

B. Money Supply and Inflation

or demanded. The lines MS_1 (money supply) and MD (money demand) originally intersect at interest rate i_1. When the money supply is increased to MS_2 (the MS line shifted to the right), then the interest rate would fall to i_2. This occurrence would seem to be the desired goal of policymakers: just increase the money supply until the interest rate falls to a very low level, which would encourage investment. But Graph B, which shows how inflation is determined, reveals that increases in the money supply lead to increases in inflation (x_1 increasing to x_2).

In fiscal policy, the tools of spending and taxation also follow the tightwire act. Taxes can be reduced during slow growth or recessionary times in order to stimulate the economy and increase employment. At the same time, government spending is maintained even if a deficit is occurring so as not to undermine the stimulating effects of a tax cut. Stimulative fiscal policy is less risky in periods of economic slowdown, because inflation is usually not a threat. So, inflation can be kept low while unemployment also falls. In recent decades, government spending has not been viewed as the preeminent tool of fiscal stimulus as it was during the 1940s and 1950s. With the Kennedy tax cut of 1964, tax policy supplanted government spending as the preferred tool of fiscal stimulus. In the heyday of Keynesianism, it was thought that the government could actually spend its way out of a recession and on to full employment.

Because the economy grew steadily with low inflation while federal budget deficits turned to surpluses at the end of the 1990s, the government had the luxury of improving its long-term economic position by reducing debt and therefore the interest payments on the debt. It could hold in reserve the option of tax cuts, and did not need to make any major changes in monetary policy. These policy tools could be unsheathed at the appropriate time to avert unemployment or inflation.

(See 172 What and how much was the "Kennedy tax cut"?)

Q 295. Why does the unemployment rate not tell the whole story of employment?

A In the United States since 1960, the percentage of people in the workforce has risen from 59 to 67 percent. This percentage of the population in the workforce is called the participation rate. This increasing participation rate means that to keep the unemployment rate from rising, the U.S. economy has had to employ the extra 8 percent of the population (mostly women) who want to work. So, to capture the net increase in jobs, it is necessary to look at *the growth of employment* in addition to the unemployment rate.

(See 23 What has been the overall trend in employment from 1946 to 1999?)

296. Is there a trade-off between inflation and unemployment?

A One of the great pillars of Keynesian economics was the inverse correlation between inflation and unemployment: high employment meant high inflation, and low inflation meant low employment. Since World War II, however, this correlation (illustrated by the Phillips Curve) has been true about as often as it has not been. During this period there have been many years of both low inflation and low unemployment, as well as high unemployment and high inflation. It is true that some of the forces that contribute to high employment also contribute to high inflation, as would be the case with rapid money supply growth. But other phenomena, such as an increase in productivity, have thwarted the Phillips Curve relationship by making simultaneous low unemployment and low inflation possible. In addition, external events such as the oil shock in 1973 helped create high unemployment and recession simultaneously with high inflation.

Q **297. What is NAIRU?**

A An updated concept of the inflation/unemployment trade-off is the nonaccelerating inflation rate of unemployment (NAIRU). NAIRU states that as unemployment falls to below its natural level (which is somewhere between 5.5 and 7 percent), inflation must accelerate to maintain unemployment below its natural level. (In 1998, the average unemployment rate was only 4.5 percent while inflation was only 1.6 percent.) The reason is that the only way additional workers will take jobs is if inflation is higher than they expect. In this way, workers are *fooled into thinking* that their real wages are higher than they are and are lured into accepting jobs. Eventually workers figure out that their wages are actually behind inflation and cease to work at the available jobs. The only way to get them back on the job is to cause even higher rates of unexpected inflation. Hence, inflation accelerates. The lowest unemployment rate that can be maintained without accelerating inflation is called NAIRU.

Q **298. Which policy tools have the Federal Reserve, the president, and Congress employed to achieve the combination of low unemployment and inflation?**

A The period of 1983–1990 was a period of low inflation expansion. In 1992, the economy was in a low inflation recovery that by 1995 had become another expansion with even lower inflation. So, from 1983 to 2000, the United States enjoyed economic growth with low inflation, interrupted only by the mild, if prolonged, 1990–1991 recession. It is not clear how much if anything Presidents Reagan, Bush, or Clinton had to do with these results. Much of the growth, low inflation, and low unemployment since 1992 have been attributed to the spate of corporate restructurings in the 1980s that continued into the 1990s, benefits from deregulation, the peace dividend from the end of the cold war, the loss of OPEC's power to keep oil prices high, and other productivity increases. At a minimum, it can be said that that policymakers did nothing to hinder these favorable economic events. During the earlier expansion of 1983–1990, the main policy measures instituted were the large tax cut implemented in 1982–1984, significant tax reform in 1986, and tight monetary policy under Federal Reserve Chairman Paul Volcker in the early 1980s. In the later expansion of 1992–2000, the two main components of policy were the two budget deals of 1990 and 1993, and the continuity of careful monetary policy under Federal Reserve Chairman Alan Greenspan. The 1990 and 1993 budget deals had a fair amount in common: moderate tax increases, combined with spending controls. The two budget/tax deals, combined with a growing economy, were particularly effective in eliminating the federal deficit, in the midst of low inflation and unemployment.

(See 199 What were the elements of the Tax Reform Act of 1986? 203 How did President Bush violate his "no new taxes" campaign pledge? 388 What are the long-term effects of restructuring on corporation? 631 What spending adjustments did Clinton make to help eliminate federal budget deficits?)

Q 299. Can government policies maintain this combination of low inflation and low unemployment indefinitely?

A It is unlikely that this combination can be maintained indefinitely. Although increasing globalization is probably more supportive of low inflation and low unemployment, regional economic and financial crises can be transmitted quickly across borders. In the 1990s, the Asian financial crisis, followed by the Russian and Brazilian crises, were thought to be the first major threats to continued low unemployment and inflation. However, the Asian crisis bottomed out quickly during 1998–1999, barely affecting the U.S. economy. The country's three major economic indicators—GDP, inflation, and unemployment—continued to show a nation in good economic health, awaiting the next global threat or swing in the business cycle.

SAVING AND INVESTMENT RATES

Investment is necessary to generate income for the future. Saving—the sacrifice of consumption today for income tomorrow—provides the resources required for investment.

Therefore, saving and investment are closely linked keys to economic growth. The financial markets provide the necessary intermediation by receiving funds from those who save and lending the funds to those who invest. If saving is so important to investment, and investment is so important to the economic future, then why does the United States save so little? What policies could improve saving and investment performance? To answer these questions, some background on the different types of saving and investment are presented along with discussion on how the two behave.

Q 300. Why is it important to have at least a certain level of investment and saving?

A Investment is the basis for future income. Without new net investment every year, the capital stock (the machinery, factories, infrastructure, and research and development that labor has to work with) slowly melts away. Overall productivity, especially labor productivity, falls and the economy shrinks. In principle, if saving drops, then investment will also drop. Investment can be higher than saving only if there is a capital inflow from abroad. Capital inflow accounted for 2 percent of U.S. investment in the 1980s.

Q 301. Is there an optimal rate of investment and saving?

A The optimal rate of saving and investment would be the amount that maximizes consumption for all generations. If saving rates are too low, then either interest rates rise because of the scarcity of funds for investment, which, in theory, would bring saving and investment into equilibrium at a lower level or capital must be imported from foreign savers.

Figure 27 illustrates the relationship of interest rates to saving (and investment). Saving is positively related to interest rates while Investment is negatively related. As interest rates move higher, the saving rate moves higher; when interest rates move lower, the saving rate moves lower. The inverse is true for investment rates. Point A is the interest rate where saving and investment are equal. A study done by the International Monetary Fund concluded that U.S. saving during 1986–1990 was half of the optimal amount. The saving rate has fallen since then.

Q 302. What factors influence saving and investment?

A Saving is a deferring of consumption to make additional resources available to produce more consumables in the future through investment. Factors that affect how

Figure 27   Relationship of Interest Rates to Savings (and Investment)

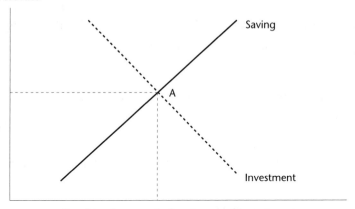

much to save or consume now have to do with how much people make, what they will need to support their standard of living, and their reward for saving (the return, or interest rate). Investment is influenced by the investor's expectations of the return on investment compared with the "opportunity cost" of the capital needed to invest.

Q **303. What is the opportunity cost of capital?**

A The opportunity cost of capital is an economists' term meaning the return that investors would earn had they invested in the next best activity. For example, a group of investors is considering the best place to invest $10 million: in a cement-making plant or a software company. After reviewing the data for expected returns over the lives of the two investments, the group agrees that expected returns are 14 percent per year for the software company and 11 percent for the cement company. The investors decide to invest in the software company, and their opportunity cost of capital is equal to the return on the next best investment, which is the cement company, or 11 percent. Opportunity cost can also be simply the interest rate charged by the bank on the funds borrowed for investment.

Q **304. What is the permanent income hypothesis?**

A The permanent income hypothesis is a theory of consumption, and therefore saving behavior developed by Milton Friedman, Nobel Prize winning economist from the

Chicago School of Economics. The theory states that households have expectations about their incomes over their lifetimes and adjust their consumption to those expectations. Under this hypothesis, fluctuations in how much people make tend not to affect consumption patterns. If there is a surge in income, then it is saved. If there is a shortfall in income, then households dip into their savings. This theory suggests that interest rates play a very minor role in determining saving.

Q 305. What did John Maynard Keynes mean by animal spirits?

A Animal spirits was Keynes's convention for describing the forces that sometimes drive entrepreneurs to invest and to innovate. Keynes felt that it was too limited to explain investment behavior through the interest rate, or the marginal efficiency of capital.

(See 152 Who was John Maynard Keynes and what was his influence on U.S. economic policy?)

Q 306. Do interest rates really matter to saving and investment?

A If Friedman's permanent income hypothesis and Keynes's animal spirits hold true, then interest rates do not greatly affect saving and investment. Data show that the correlation is weak between savings and interest rates, but stronger between investment and interest rates. Economic theory states that interest rates have an effect on saving that is opposite to their effect on investment. Low interest rates encourage investment, but give a lower return to saving. Because the saving-interest rate link is weaker, it is easier to promote greater investment with lower interest rates than it is to stimulate saving with higher interest rates. Therefore, economic policy usually seeks to keep interest rates low.

(See 301 Is there an optimal rate of investment and saving? 302 What factors influence saving and investment?)

Q 307. What else drives investment?

A Firms do not invest only on the basis of impulse, or interest rates, but on a set of prevailing conditions and expectations as well. Firms invest when they are operating at a high capacity and if they expect demand to remain high.

Q **308. How do saving and investment rates of today compare with those of the previous five decades?**

A Personal saving rates have dropped into nothing and even turned negative for part of 1999. Gross private investment rates have held fairly steadily. The difference between gross private saving and gross private investment has been made up with an inflow of foreign funds. The following table charts the saving and investment rates from the 1950s through the 1990s.

Year	Gross private saving as % of GDP	Personal saving as % of disposable income	Gross private domestic investment as % of GDP
1950–1959	15.0%	7.7%	15.2%
1960–1969	17.0	8.3	15.5
1970–1979	17.9	9.4	16.7
1980–1989	19.5	9.4	16.9
1990–1998	17.5	6.8	15.5
1999	14.9	2.4	17.5

Q **309. Why has personal saving collapsed?**

A Americans, who for decades have been less thrifty than their European and Japanese counterparts, became even more consumption-minded in the 1990s. Why? It is not because Americans can afford to save less, because studies show that Americans save too little and start saving too late for their retirement. It could not be because of increasing inequality of income and wealth, because increasing inequality, which has been the trend, would contribute to higher saving. Wealthy people save a higher percentage of their income than less wealthy people, so concentration of income among a smaller percentage of the population would raise saving, at least on a national level. The increasing concentration of wealth in the United States has been overwhelmed by the abysmal saving rates of much of the population. One might speculate that the increasing ease of purchasing with credit cards, as well as higher credit limits, coupled with persuasive, saturation advertising and many Americans' "live for now" philosophy are key factors.

Another explanation has to do with the saving measure itself. The saving measure does not take into account Americans' increased stock market or real estate wealth.

This increase has a wealth effect that emboldens people to consume more. They consume everything they earn and more, reasoning that they can just cash in some stock if they get into financial trouble.

(See 335 What is the controversy about the standard saving rate measure?)

Q 310. How do U.S. gross saving and personal saving rates compare with those of other countries?

A The United States is one of the least thrifty among industrialized nations, as the following table illustrates:

Country	Gross national saving as % of GDP[a]	Household saving as % of disposable income[b]
Japan	31.7%	13.6%
Germany	20.7	11.0
Italy	20.4	11.5
France	20.0	14.1
Canada	18.4	1.2
United States	17.4	0.5
Great Britain	14.9	7.8

[a] 1997 data.
[b] 1998 data.

Source: *OECD Economic Outlook,* June 1999.

Q 311. How does the Federal Reserve affect saving and investment?

A The Fed is directly interested in maintaining low inflation as well as low interest rates in order to support investment. Through its major tools of buying and selling government securities (open market operations), changing the discount rate on funds lent to member banks, and changing the required reserve rate, the Fed exerts its influence on interest rates and inflation and, by extension, saving and investment.

(See 48 What is the effect of interest rates on saving, investment, and growth? 294 How can inflation and unemployment be kept low simultaneously?)

Q 312. Which other policy measures can raise saving and investment rates?

A Changing the tax code to encourage saving could offer one way of increasing the saving rate. Most of the major proposed alternatives to the current tax code, including the unlimited savings allowance (USA) tax, would tax consumption, but not saving or income from saving. Proponents of these alternatives cite increased saving as a major advantage in a country where personal saving rates have actually become negative. However, empirical evidence for such an advantage is not strong. Tax incentives for investment should be used carefully because they often encourage marginal or even nonviable investments. The Individual Retirement Account (IRA) has been a popular vehicle for many taxpayers. However, it is not clear that the availability of IRAs has actually induced Americans to save more than they otherwise would have through other vehicles.

(See 286 What is the personal consumption tax?)

THE NATIONAL DEBT

Until the late 1990s, it appeared that the national debt was going to continue to soar and limit the maneuverability of U.S. economic policy. Higher and higher percentages of the federal budget would be spent on servicing the debt. Because of this trend, policymakers would not be able to allow interest rates to rise to stave off inflation, because a substantial increase in interest rates would force debt service higher, further limiting flexibility on fiscal policy. Recent trends in the budget balance appear to have changed that situation, or have they?

Q 313. How does the national debt matter to the U.S. economy?

A Some economists maintain that the size of the national debt is not relevant to economic well-being. They argue that the government has a need for a certain amount of money for its activities, and that the government can secure that money in a number of ways: taxation, borrowing, and printing money. Each way has its costs and limits. Both taxation and government borrowing diminish resources available to the private sector. Printing money causes inflation. According to some economists, the effect on economic performance is the same whether the government raises revenue by taxing or borrowing. The existence of high debt simply means that the government had to tax less, which is good.

    The more conventional view is that there exists a debt level above which the economy is damaged through higher interest rates and the public sector crowding out of the private sector in the capital markets. In addition, a higher share of the annual federal budget must be spent on interest on the debt (debt service), leaving less flexibility to either increase or reduce government spending. A high debt with its high interest payments also means a worsening of the income distribution. Interest payments come from relatively poorer taxpayers and are transferred to relatively richer debt holders (owners of Treasury bills).

Q **314. How high can the national debt go before it adversely affects the economy?**

A It is difficult to say exactly, but when the national debt reaches 45 percent of GDP, the economy and the budget seem to feel the burden. Debt as a percentage of GDP reached a post–World War II low in 1981 of 32.5 percent (it had been below 36 percent for most of the 1970s). It reached a 40-year peak of 67.3 percent in 1996. During its upward trend in the 1980s and 1990s, interest payments usurped a greater and greater share of the budget. As the debt percentage of GDP passed 40 percent in 1983, interest payments rose to 11.1 percent. When debt rose to 45 percent of GDP in 1986, interest payments climbed to 13.7 percent. These levels of interest payments require more budget resources than policymakers would like because these high levels reduce policy flexibility and have the potential for becoming much worse if interest rates begin to rise.

Q **315. Is the current level of national debt too high?**

A Yes. The debt in 1999 stood at 61.5 percent of GDP. The interest payments on the debt were $230 billion or 13.5 percent of the budget in 1999, down from a high of 15.4 percent in 1996. Until 1996, the gross debt was still rising as a percent of GDP, meaning it was becoming both absolutely and relatively a greater burden on the economy. If the debt were, say, 40 percent of GDP, and the rate paid on the debt were 5 percent, then interest payments on the debt would be about 10 percent of the budget. With the vast majority of the debt having term of less than five years, any surge in interest rates would make interest payments balloon.

(See 317 What is the term structure of the national debt and why is it important?)

Q **316. What types of securities does the government sell to make up the national debt?**

A Sixty percent of federal government debt is marketable debt, which consists entirely of various types of financial instruments issued by the Treasury Department. Nonmarketable securities account for 40 percent of federal debt, most of which is Treasury Special Issues and other paper issued to trust funds.

(See 318 Who owns the national debt and how much is owned by foreigners?)

Interest-bearing Public Debt Securities by Type of Obligation

Type of Obligation	Amount ($ billions)	% of total
Marketable	$3,331.0	60%
Treasury bills	*637.6*	*12*
Treasury notes	*2,009.1*	*36*
Treasury bonds	*610.4*	*11*
Indexed Treasury notes & bonds	*75.8*	*1*
Nonmarketable	2,187.7	40
U.S. savings securities	*180.8*	*3*
Foreign series	*35.1*	*1*
Government account series	1,777.3	32
Other	194.4	4
Total interest-bearing securities	$5,518.7	100

Sources: *Economic Report of the President,* 1999; U.S. Treasury Department.

317. What is the term structure of the national debt and why is it important?

The longer the term of the maturity of the national debt, the less risk there is from short-term interest rate fluctuations. The level of exposure in 1998 was significant because 72 percent of the debt had a maturity of 5 years or less. Thus, if interest rates were to shoot up in the near future, then interest payments would soar, and substantially diminish budget flexibility. The term structure applies to only the privately held portion of the debt, which stood at $2.9 trillion in 1998. The average maturity of the privately held portion was 5 years and 8 months in 1998, compared to 6 years, 1 month in 1990 and 3 years, 9 months in 1980. The current average maturity is much higher than it was in the 1970s and close to what it was in the 1980s.

Term Structure of the Privately Held Federal Debt ($ billions)

Maturity class	Amount	% of total
Within 1 year	$ 940.57	33
1 to 5 years	1,105.18	39

Term Structure of the Privately Held Federal Debt ($ billions) (Continued)

Maturity class	Amount	% of total
5 to 10 years	$ 319.33	11%
10 to 20 years	157.35	6
20 years or more	334.21	12
Total outstanding	$2,856.64	100

Sources: *Economic Report of the President,* 1999; U.S. Treasury Department.

Q 318. Who owns the national debt and how much is owned by foreigners?

A Again this is the portion of the debt owned by private investors, so it excludes the debt held in government accounts. Most percentages did not change much between 1992 and 1998. The exceptions are the drop in state and local accounts, and Other ownership, and the rise in foreign ownership. Foreigners owned 37 percent or $1.2 trillion of the privately held debt in 1998.

Estimated Ownership of Public Debt Securities by Private Investors

Investor	Amount in 1992		Amount in 1998	
	($ billions)	% of total	($ billions)	% of total
Commercial banks	$ 294.4	10%	$ 260.0	8%
Nonbank investors	2,545.5	90	3,041.0	92
Individuals	289.2	10	352.3	11
Savings bonds	157.3	6	186.0	6
Other securities	131.9	5	166.4	5
Insurance companies	197.5	7	188.0	6
Money market funds	79.7	3	84.2	3
Corporations	192.5	7	271.4	8
State/local governments	566.0	20	469.0	14
Foreign & international	549.7	19	1,217.2	37
Other investors	670.9	24	458.9	14
Total	$2,839.9	100	$3,301.0	100

Sources: *Economic Report of the President,* 1999; U.S. Treasury Department.

319. Which federal agency is responsible for tracking the national debt?

The Treasury Department has primary responsibility for the debt, because it must service the debt and tally the surpluses and deficits, which pay down and build up the debt. The Office of Management and Budget, under the auspices of the White House, tracks the debt in order to help the president present a detailed federal budget to Congress every February. It is Congress that takes the president's proposed federal budget and approves the budget (subject to the president's final signature). Congress also must track the debt. The Congressional Budget Office is the most accurate congressional source of information on the budget and the debt.

320. How does U.S. debt compare to the debt of other countries?

Surprisingly, the United States is not as mired in debt as most other industrialized countries. The Organization for Economic Cooperation and Development (OECD) has estimated general government gross liabilities. These numbers do not match exactly with gross federal or publicly held debt, because they have been adjusted to be consistent with the different way other countries calculate debt.

Industrial Countries Gross Government Liabilities as a Percent of GDP (Selected Years)

Country	1982	1992	1998
United States	40.5%	61.9%	56.7%
Japan	56.6	59.8	97.3
Germany	39.0	44.4	63.1
France	34.2	45.5	66.5
Italy	65.8	118.3	119.9
Great Britain	53.9	46.9	56.6
Canada	49.0	86.1	89.8
Average	46.0	62.5	71.5

Source: *OECD Economic Outlook,* June 1999.

321. Is the United States a net debtor to the rest of the world?

Foreigners do own more U.S. assets than Americans own foreign assets. America turned from a net creditor to a net debtor nation in 1987. In that year, both foreigners and Americans owned about $1.8 trillion of each other's assets.

322. Is the debtor status of the United States a problem?

A It is not a major problem, nor is it necessarily a sign of economic weakness. Because foreigners hold U.S. assets and U.S. dollars, foreigners can enjoy consuming U.S. goods. That advantage to foreigners is also an advantage to the U.S. economy because foreigners have to give business to the U.S. economy to obtain those goods. Secondly, foreigners own only about 10 percent of the total value of domestic assets in the United States. Moreover, foreigners own only about half a trillion dollars more of U.S. assets than Americans do of theirs, which is only one-fortieth, 2.5 percent, of the total value of assets in the United States.

Q **323. Will the debt become a larger or smaller problem for the U.S. economy in the next decade?**

A The United States began to solve its debt problem only after deficits fell sharply at the end of the 1990s. Only in 1997 did the debt begin to shrink as a percent of GDP. To achieve a more manageable level of gross federal debt of 40 to 45 percent, or less, of GDP, it would probably take five to ten years of continued, recession-free, economic growth. Government borrowing from the trust funds (Social Security, transportation, etc.) will continue to grow both absolutely and as a share of the gross federal debt. Therefore, it would probably be better if the debt could even be reduced to the 35 to 40 percent range. The further reduction would create an added buffer for government finances in the event of a recession.

THE PITFALLS OF ECONOMIC INDICATORS

Economic indicators, popularized in the media, seem to drive economic policy. For example, more than a trillion dollars in entitlement programs are adjusted every year by the consumer price index (CPI), the government's index that measures consumer prices. But these indicators, which U.S. policymakers rely on to set the nation's most important economic goals and measure its progress, are not infallible, and they have limitations. Unfortunately, weaknesses in indicators often go unremedied. Many policymakers seem to sidestep the faults of the indicators at the expense of economic policy. However, it is critical that policymakers and the general public not be misled by what an economic indicator represents so that they pursue the right economic goals.

324. Which indicators have raised controversy in their use and interpretation?

A All economic indicators generate some controversy as economists interpret their meaning differently or argue whether they are the best indicators for certain purposes. Probably the most intense controversy is over the consumer price index (CPI), the most widely used indicator of inflation. Other indicators that are controversial include the gross domestic product (GDP), the Census Bureau measures of the population below the poverty line, and the saving rates (as calculated by the National Income and Product Accounts (NIPA) of the Department of Commerce). The intensity of the controversy depends on whether program benefits are affected and the degree to which policies are based on the indicator.

Q 325. What is the central controversy over the Consumer Price Index (CPI)?

A To adjust benefits according to the cost of living, the question is: "What percent increase in income will consumers need to be just as well off with the new set of prices as the old?" The controversy is whether the CPI answers this question accurately. Does it measure inflation accurately? If the CPI overstates inflation, as is widely accepted, then many programs have been giving beneficiaries overly generous cost-of-living (COLA) increases, and taxpayers have been getting tax cuts when tax brackets are indexed to the CPI.

Q 326. What is the case that the CPI overstates inflation?

A In 1996, a commission led by Michael Boskin, the Stanford economist and former Chairman of the Council of Economic Advisers under President Bush, issued a report concluding that the CPI overstates inflation by 1.1 percent on average every year and has done so since 1978. The report attributes 0.5 percent of the overstatement to the fact that the CPI does not take fully into account the flexibility of consumers to adjust to price changes, or to economize. For example, if the price of a watermelon increases from $4 to $6 in one month, the CPI is calculated with the assumption that the consumer will continue to buy the same amount of watermelon (the CPI uses expenditure weights that are fixed for five years). In reality, the consumer will likely substitute cantaloupes or some other fruit that did not increase as much in price. The specific omissions of the consumer's ability to economize are: (1) ignoring the consumer's ability to buy lower-priced substitutes; (2) ignoring the rise of discount superstores (prices for the CPI are usually collected at higher-price outlets); and (3) collecting data only during the week, when sales usually occur on the weekend. The Congressional Budget Office (CBO) quotes Bureau of Labor Statistics (the agency that produces the CPI) analysis that suggests an overstatement of between 0.2 and 0.8 percent annually.

The second component of overstatement is that the CPI does not take into account *quality improvements* in the products it tracks, and that consumers generally get better and better service from the products they buy. The CPI just measures the change in the price of the product, but not the change in the quality of service, or output, it provides. On quality improvements, the CPI is estimated to overstate inflation by about 0.6 percent each year. New products are not introduced into the CPI until they are well established in the market. For example, VCRs, computers, and microwave ovens were not included until a decade after they were on the market and their prices had already fallen precipitously. Cellular phones were not included until 1998 when there were more than 50 million users.

Likewise, statistics do not keep up in the areas of health care. The CPI will capture the change in per day cost of a hospital room, or the annual salary of a cardiologist, but not the fact that heart attack treatment is more successful. The CPI also does not register quality gains in the form of improved products, or in the distribution network of products. The CPI does not capture the fact that people are enjoying a better living for the money, not the same living for the money. Clearly, prices should be adjusted for changes in quality as well.

Q 327. What are the counterarguments to the view that the CPI overstates inflation?

A The arguments that the CPI understates inflation are considerably weaker than the notions that it overstates inflation. The use of outdated population weights (needed to calculate a total, combined CPI for all areas in the United States) means that higher than average prices in fast-growing areas are underweighted. This means that the CPI would undervalue the importance of higher prices that tend to prevail in fast-growth areas. Some cost increases are not tracked by the CPI. The increase in cost of a car by the addition of mandatory safety equipment is not counted by the CPI, because the safety equipment is treated as a separate product, without necessarily increasing the base cost of making a car. Quality declines in services, like quality improvements, are also not considered in the CPI, but indirectly increase the cost of living. However, on balance, the effects of quality losses are almost certainly far outweighed by the effects of quality improvements on the cost of living over time.

Q 328. Does the cost of living rise at the same rate for everyone?

A Inflation faced by one segment of society is not the same for others. The specific spending patterns of the elderly, for example, are different from the rest of the population, with a higher percentage of the elderly's income going to health care. The cost of health care also tends to increase faster than the prices of other goods and services. On the other hand, the elderly often own their homes and are not subject to rent inflation. Nor do the elderly have expenses related to children, such as education and toys. So policymakers should take into account the specific consumption patterns of affected groups when making adjustments to the COLA.

Q 329. What is at stake in reducing the inflation adjustment of the CPI?

A A lot of money. Over 20 years, the compounded effect of a 1.1 percent COLA change would amount to a 25 percent overall change. Taxes would be higher because the income thresholds at each higher tax rate would increase more slowly. So, to reduce the inflation measure is to give the government more tax revenue. Reducing the CPI adjustment of tax brackets by 0.5 percent is estimated by the CBO to produce $9 billion more in federal revenue in the year 2000. Because the CPI measure of inflation is the index by which the government also adjusts most benefit programs, reducing it by the amount estimated by the Boskin Commission would mean lower future benefits payments from Social Security (which accounts for three-quarters of indexed federal outlays) and other benefits programs.

With this adjustment on the spending side, the CBO estimates lower government spending of $13 billion in Fiscal Year 2000. This adjustment has been considered an important step in the long-term solvency of Social Security. Keeping the COLA based on the current CPI will mean higher deficits (lower surpluses), higher debt, and greater difficulty in funding programs such as Social Security and Medicare. Although the economic evidence is strong for the overstatement, adjusting the COLA to reflect economic realities will be extremely tough politically. Those that would stand to lose—including seniors and labor unions—are mobilized to resist what most economists agree is good sense.

Q 330. Why is the gross domestic product (GDP) a controversial indicator?

A Most people, including policymakers, view GDP as the preeminent indicator of economic performance and standard of living. Many believe that as long as the GDP grows at a reasonable rate (after adjusting it for inflation) then not much else matters. The controversy over gauging the health of a nation by GDP is that the indicator does not always accurately reflect the standard of living. It does not take into account other aspects, such as the well-being, fulfillment, or happiness of the population. It is a measure of production in a country in a given year. Its increase does not always mean an increase in the living standard.

Undesirable events can spark GDP growth. For example, a hurricane that damages property and leaves people homeless clearly reduces the living standard of the hurricane victims. But the hurricane also stimulates growth of GDP by creating the need to rebuild buildings and infrastructure. After rebuilding, GDP is up, but the living standard is about the same. Increases in crime also increase the cost of the criminal justice system—including the cost of more police, courts, and prisons. With crime, GDP increases due to increased spending, but society is actually worse off.

(See 8 Is GDP the best indicator of a nation's economic performance?)

Q 331. Then why is GDP a useful measure?

A GDP is a valuable measure of economic *activity*. Even if undesirable events precipitated a series of actions that increased GDP, the economy still had to carry out those economic activities. So, GDP is a good and comprehensive measure of the economy's ability to produce. On that score, it is the best indicator around.

Q 332. What are the other limitations of GDP?

A Another problem with GDP is that some of the production measured might not, itself, be desirable. Does a strip mall that replaces a park or a grove of trees represent an improvement in economic well-being? To some people, it is an improvement in that it brings commercial opportunity. Other people may view the strip mall as destructive of the quiet, the fresh air, and lower traffic volume of the "unimproved land." GDP also could be said to have some of the limitations of the CPI in that it does not take any account of improvement in the quality, convenience, or reliability of the goods and services provided. In economists' terms, GDP does not capture increases and decreases in consumer surplus. GDP places no value on leisure or aesthetics. And GDP does not account for depletion of natural resources, which is a reduction in economic wealth.

(See 342 What is the economic value of innovations?)

Q 333. How can these omissions of GDP be rectified?

A In 1994 the Bureau of Economic Analysis (BEA), where the GDP is calculated, began a pilot program to track the depletion of U.S. natural resources such as minerals and oil. Green accounting, as it was referred to, attempted to develop a framework that (1) examined the rate natural resources were being used up; (2) assessed what share of GDP owed specifically to the exploitation of natural resources; (3) determined what was the share of expenditures by governments, households, and businesses for maintaining and restoring the environment; and (4) estimated the costs of environmental degradation to other economic activities such as fish harvests and lower timber yields. Although this program did not move beyond the planning stage in 1994, the idea of charting interactions of the economy with the environment is still being considered.

GDP could also be expanded to incorporate more well-being measures, such as leisure and aesthetics. Leisure could be fairly easy to account for, because the Department of Commerce accounts for the number of hours worked in the United States. The Bureau of Labor Statistics keeps track of unemployment so that statisticians would know whether the "leisure" was voluntary or because of unemployment. Aesthetics would be a harder, far more subjective realm to quantify. However, some type of measurement on the cleanliness of air and water could provide a meaningful basis for adjusting GDP.

An independent source calculated an alternative welfare measure called the genuine progress indicator (GPI) which added the value of household- and volunteer-produced goods and services to GDP, but subtracted such items as crime-related costs, resource depletion, loss of leisure, and others from GDP. The result of the GPI was that the standard of living actually declined by 45 percent from 1970 to 1995, as opposed to rising by 65 percent as indicated by GDP per capita.

(See 523 Is the exploitation of federal lands priced at fair market value?)

Q 334. Why do policymakers want to measure saving?

A Policymakers are concerned about saving, because, in the long run, saving finances the investment that the economy relies on for growth, whether the investment is in capital stock, research and development, or education.

(See 300 Why is it important to have at least a certain level of investment and saving?)

Q 335. What is the controversy about the standard saving rate measure?

A The standard saving rate most often reported is measured in the National Income and Product Accounts (NIPA) by the BEA of the Department of Commerce. NIPA provides several saving rates, including gross saving, gross private saving, and personal saving. Gross saving includes saving by the government. For 30 years after 1969, the federal government did not save, that is, it ran deficits. In the late 1990s, the federal government actually began to save money. However, because the government saves money through excess taxes over expenditures, it becomes more difficult for the private sector to save. Government surpluses do add to national saving, but considerably less than the amount of the surplus, because some of the potential private sector saving is taken in taxes.

Personal saving is how much individuals save from their after-tax income. In the 1980s and 1990s, at the same time the stock market appreciated rapidly, personal saving gradually declined and approached zero by the end of the 1990s. With such an increase in wealth, how could saving be negative? First, the NIPA saving rates do not include changes in asset value and, therefore, do not include stock market appreciation in the calculation of savings. If stock appreciation were included in saving, then the rate would be much higher. Second, with stock prices increasing so rapidly, people feel wealthy enough to spend all, or more than all, of their current income. The latter is possible by taking on, for example, additional consumer debt.

(See 55 What are the main measures of saving? 304 What is the permanent income hypothesis?)

Q 336. What else does the saving rate exclude?

A It does not include real estate appreciation, unless the real estate is sold and the realized appreciation is saved. Therefore, the NIPA savings concept captures the share of income that is not spent, but not all increases in wealth.

Q 337. Are these exclusions of the NIPA a big problem?

A The fact that the saving measures account only for saving out of current income and not changes in asset values should be clearly understood. Although saving rates have been declining for years and are of genuine concern, keying in on NIPA personal saving rates might lead policymakers to overrespond with measures to increase saving. Still, national saving needs to be at a level sufficient to fund investment in a growing economy. For the individual, it is also risky to depend too heavily on increasing personal wealth through the stock market. A downturn in the stock market could result in a spate of personal bankruptcies among those who are overextended with consumer debt.

(See 309 Why has personal saving collapsed?)

Q 338. Why has controversy arisen around the main poverty indicator?

A No matter how much the economy grows or how generous the government safety net becomes, it seems impossible to bring the poverty level below 12 percent of the population. The controversy is whether poverty can ever be eradicated.

Q 339. What are the major criticisms of the poverty indicator?

A The indicator that tracks the percent of the population below the poverty line excludes noncash transfers such as food stamps, discounts, and free programs. It also excludes the favorable tax treatment to the poor afforded by a progressive tax code. Lastly, it measures the intermediate indicator, that is, income, rather than the final indicator, actual consumption, which is the real measure of whether people are living in poverty.

The result is that the percent of the population below the poverty line may be overestimated and may lead many to the conclusion that economic growth and antipoverty programs have not reduced the level of poverty in the last quarter century.

(See 480 Measurement Issue No. 1: Should income include noncash benefits? 481 Measurement Issue No. 2: Does the poverty threshold take into account taxes? 482 Measurement Issue No. 3: Which is more important to measuring poverty, how much cash a person receives, or how much he consumes?)

Q 340. Can government statistics be fixed?

A Improving economic statistics faces strong conceptual and political challenges. On the political side, entrenched interests have prevented changes to the CPI. Strong credible political leadership is necessary to fight for changes where powerful interests defend their benefits. On the conceptual side, as the United States increasingly becomes a service economy, with more companies contributing service output, collecting accurate data becomes harder than in a product-oriented economy. This difficulty is reflected across national accounts and trade data. The incorporation of environmental effects into national accounts will also take a long-term concerted effort, one that is currently in limbo.

Q 341. How reliable are economic projections?

A Forecasts of future economic activity are probably the most inaccurate economic measurement of all. The following example of deficit projections illustrates just how inaccurate they can be.

Budget Balance Projections for the Year 2003

Date of projection	Amount ($ billions)
1993 (January)	-$650
1993 (September)	-359
1994 (January)	-324
1999 (January)	209

Source: Congressional Budget Office.

The conclusion from these budget projections is that just about any projection greater than two years into the future may well be worthless.

(See 243 How do budget projections affect plans for the Social Security trust fund?)

PRIVATE SECTOR ISSUES

TECHNOLOGICAL ADVANCES AND ECONOMIC PROGRESS

It is incorrect to think that economic policies are the only ingredient in economic well-being; there are many other factors. Students learn from economic textbooks that the three components of production are land, labor, and capital. What affects these factors, affects economic well-being. Better education and health of the general population, as well as increased capital, improve labor productivity. Better natural resource management improves land productivity. Technological advances improve capital productivity. If one factor is improved, the productivity of all factors of production is improved. Technology improves the standard of living by helping workers perform old and new tasks faster and better. The time and energy saved by workers can be redirected to leisure, or toward more work and earning more money. This section examines the economic value of technology, some of the major recent technological developments, the process for achieving these developments, and the policies that are most favorable to technological development.

Figure 28 expresses technological advance in economic terms. It depicts the famous guns or butter trade-off. Because there is a finite supply of inputs—labor, capital, and nat-

Figure 28   Production Possibility Frontier and Technological innovation

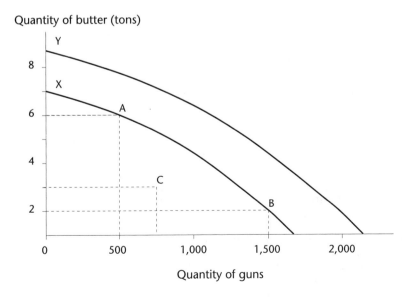

ural resources—the more guns produced, the less butter, and vice-versa. Points on the curve, or frontier, represent the maximum production given the available resources in the economy. Therefore, all points on the curve are also the most efficient use of the resources. Point A represents 6 tons of butter and 500 guns; Point B represents 2 tons of butter and 1,500 guns. The interior point C (3 tons of butter and 750 guns) represents an inefficient point. Inefficiency could be caused by, for example, gun makers who are not working at optimal levels, or poorly fed cows that cannot produce enough milk, or improperly maintained equipment in either production process. At full efficiency, the economy is capable of producing any combination of guns and butter along the curve X. If there is a technological innovation, for example, an improved milking machine (for butter), or a more efficient assembly line (for guns), then more of both can be produced. The effect of this innovation is shown by a shift to the new curve Y.

Q 342. What is the economic value of innovations?

A Any measure of the economic value of innovation is probably an underestimate. How can one measure the value of laser eye surgery that saves people from poor vision or blindness? Economics seldom measures the full value of something, only what people actually pay for it. The *consumer surplus* is the difference between the full value and what people pay, and is not accounted for in the GDP. Economists have estimated the value of innovation in terms of its contribution to GDP by subtracting the effects of all inputs, such as increases in education and capital, and calculating what is left. This residual can be measured as a percentage of the increase in the standard of living over a period of time.

So how much does an improved standard of living owe to innovation? The answer is, conservatively, about half of it. The following table compares the GDP per capita in 1948 with that in 1998, adjusted for inflation:

Year	GDP ($ billions)	Population (millions)	GDP/capita ($ thousands)
1948	$1,491.0	146.63	$10,168
1998	7,551.9	270.55	27,913

The standard of living in 1998, measured by GDP per capita, is $27,913, or 2.75 times higher than 50 years ago. This is a conservative estimate because many economists believe that the current measure of inflation (CPI) has been overstating inflation by about 1 percent annually. If this overstatement is factored in, then the standard of living of 1998 reaches 4.5 times its 1948 level. About half of this improvement can be explained by increased capital expenditure and education, with innovation accounting for the other half, or 2.25 times the 1948 level. The standard of living is also enhanced by the fact that people are working fewer hours than 50 years ago, which affords them the benefit of more leisure time. The consumer surplus, that is, the benefits that consumers do not pay for, has probably expanded and would mean that its omission would underestimate the actual standard of living by an increasing amount.

The other factors that contribute to higher output (improved standard of living) are the raw level of effort (labor), the consumption of natural resources, greater capital input (achieved through saving), and education. These factors have much stricter limitations unlike innovation. For example, working more yields higher income, but also less leisure, which can detract from the living standard. Second, most natural resources are finite and their exploitation becomes increasingly expensive and difficult to sustain. Capital investment above a percentage of GDP also becomes unfeasible. Education plays a role as well but is limited by individuals' avility to absorb additional education.

(See 326 What is the case that the CPI overstates inflation?)

Q **343. If technological innovation produces half of the economic gains in society, and education, natural resources, and capital produce the other half, then what good is economic policy?**

A Of course, economic policies alone do not produce anything. However, the right economic policies accommodate the gains from technology, while the wrong economic policies depress those gains. The right economic policies help create incentives for technological improvements and efficiency that lead to economic well-being. For example, sound monetary policies, which keep inflation and interest rates low enough to encourage long-term investment, including research and development (R&D), create an economic environment that encourages the development of new products and production methods. Perhaps more important are the perceived entrepreneurial payoffs that a free market system offers to those who develop new technologies.

Q **344. Is it therefore easy to justify the development of technology on financial grounds?**

A No. Technological innovation often cannot be justified using standard cost-benefit analysis. Either the time to achieve new innovation is too long or the prospects of success too uncertain. Benefits often have to be exaggerated to get the necessary financial backing to develop the technology. For example, large companies tend to have considerable trouble achieving a second big innovation. (The first innovation having turned the companies from small to big.) Once large, the companies employ critical, analytical staffs who usually recommend that the company steer away from innovation, because the cost-benefit numbers just do not support it.

Q 345. Is technological development always a good thing?

A It may always be good to have the *choice* of whether to use a particular technology, but many technologies have serious negative side effects. Technological development is almost synonymous with growth. Just as growth naturally takes a toll on the environment, technologies often damage the environment through pollution or unsustainable exploitation. Sometimes the damage is greater than the benefits, such as with the building material asbestos and the insecticide DDT. The GDP per capita does not fully measure these negatives and sometimes counts them as positives. Overreliance on potential technological breakthroughs to solve a growing problem, whether global warming, traffic congestion, or epidemic diseases, to the exclusion of preventative measures, is risky. Thus, preventative measures may be the best course, while technological solutions are sought.

(See 330 Why is the gross domestic product (GDP) a controversial indicator?)

Q 346. Why is breakthrough or basic research not enough?

A After a breakthrough occurs or basic research is complete, product developers still have to spend time and money to make a product that people can use and want to buy—by making and testing prototypes, and designing and marketing an attractive product. These steps in product development are also called downstream activities. The ability to take a brilliant idea and manufacture it affordably is necessary for the innovation to have an economic impact.

Q 347. What are some different types of technical innovations?

A Innovations are often thought of as useful gadgets like lawn mowers and fax machines. But innovations also include improvements to existing products such as increasing the reliability and fuel efficiency of automobiles, and improving the speed and capacity of computers. Improved techniques, such as those used in surgery, are considered as innovations. Innovations can also be found in improving a process, such as finding a better way of restructuring a corporation; creating new investment instruments, such as using asset-backed securities, junk bonds, and securitized mortgages; and discovering new ways of doing business in deregulated industry.

MAJOR INNOVATIONS OF THE TWENTIETH CENTURY

Q **348. What are some of the top innovations in medicine?**

A Some of the top innovations in medicine are

Innovation/discovery	Year	Inventors
Gene theory of heredity	1910	Thomas Morgan
Penicillin	1928	Alexander Fleming
Oral contraceptive pill	1951	Gregory Pincus/Min Chuch Chang/ John Rock/Carl Djerassi
Deoxyribonucleic acid (DNA)	1953	Francis Crick/James Watson
Polio vaccine	1955/1957	Albert Sabin/Jonas Salk
Test-tube human fertilization	1978	Patrick Steptoe/Robert Edwards
Magnetic resonance imaging (MRI)	1978	Raymond V. Damadian
Cloning of an adult animal	1997	Ian Wilmut
Viagra	1997	Pfizer

Q **349. What are some of the top innovations in office and information technology?**

A Some of the top innovations in office and information technology are

Innovation/discovery	Year	Inventors
Photocopier	1938	Chester Carlson
Electronic computer	1943	T. H. Flowers/M. Newman/ A. Turing
Modem	1958	Bell Laboratories
Internet	1969	Defense Dept. (ARPA)
Microcomputer (first marketed)	1975	Altair 8800
Worldwide Web (and browser)	1990	Tim Berners-Lee

350. What are some of the top innovations in industry?

Some of the top innovations in industry are

Invention/discovery	Year	Inventors
Nylon and neoprene	1932	Wallace Carothers/Arnold Collins
Teflon	1938	Roy Plunkett
Radar	1940	Robert Page
Transistor	1948	William Shockley/ John Bardeen/Walter Brattain
Fiber optics	1955	Narinder S. Kapany
Communications satellite	1958	SCORE
Laser	1958	Charles A. Townes/Arthur L. Schawlow/ Gordon Gould

Q **351. What are some of the top innovations in agriculture?**

A Some of the top innovations in agriculture are

Invention/discovery	Year	Inventors
Gas-powered tractor	1904	Benjamin Holt
Seed hybridization (miracle wheat and corn)	1946	Borlaug
Taxol (anticancer drug from yew tree)	1971	USDA/National Cancer Institute
Genetically altered potato	1995	Various scientists

Q **352. What are some of the top innovations in entertainment and the household?**

A Some of the top innovations in entertainment and the household are

Invention/discovery	Year	Inventors
Brassiere	1914	Mary Phelps Jacob
Domestic refrigerator	1918	Nathaniel Wales/E. J. Copeland
Television	1926	John Logie Baird/C.F. Jenkins/ D. Mihaly/Philo Farnsworth

Invention/discovery	Year	Inventors
Frozen food	1929	Clarence Birdseye
Tupperware	1945	Earl W. Tupper
Velcro	1948	Georges de Mestral
Video game	1972	Noland Bushnel
Video tape players	1975	Sony/Matsushita/JVC
Compact disc players	1984	Sony/Fujitsu/Philips

PROCESSES OF U.S. TECHNOLOGICAL ADVANCES

Q 353. What are some of the paths that innovations have taken?

A The striking feature of technological breakthrough is the unpredictable, haphazard, sometimes sloppy way it occurs. Scientists often have no idea, even at the time of the breakthrough, what the commercial application of a new discovery might be. The breakthrough itself may be unintended. History has shown that it often takes 25 to 30 years after a major breakthrough for usable products to be developed. Thereafter, incremental improvements roll on, as in the case of computers, which have steadily improved performance since the late 1940s. The examples of the radio, telephone, transistors, and lasers illustrate the ad hoc nature of the paths of innovation.

The telephone was thought of as a business instrument like a telegraph to exchange very specific messages. In fact, when the patent for the telephone was applied for, it was described as "improvements in telegraphy." Alexander Graham Bell had no conception of the use of the telephone for exchanging information on matters of routine, everyday life, much less of its role as the infrastructure of the Internet.

The radio, developed by the Italian inventor Marconi, was to be used only for communications normally satisfied by wire, in point-to-point communication, but where wire was impossible, such as over water. Only when David Sarnoff saw a broader application of broadcasting information, music, and entertainment to thousands of listeners did the technology really have an impact on the quality of life.

The transistor was made public in 1948 primarily to improve hearing aids. Later, transistors were critical to the development of solid-state appliances and computers. The first transistor radios were one-fifth the weight and one-third the cost of vacuum tube radios. The replacement of vacuum tubes with transistors in radios and computers greatly improved their usefulness and marketability.

The applications of lasers were even more unanticipated. Lasers are a narrow beam of light that is emitted by using light to stimulate the emission of more light of the same wavelength and phase by excited atoms or molecules. Lasers were discovered in

SIGNIFICANT EVENTS IN THE DEVELOPMENT OF THE COMPUTER

Year	Discovery	Significance
1679	Binary theorem	Expresses all numbers as 1 or 0, on or off
1805	Punch card (for loom)	Converts numbers to sets of instructions (for weaving)
1906	Vacuum tube	Marks beginning of electronics
1910–1913	Symbolic logic	Expresses logical concepts as numbers
1918	Programming/feedback (for aircraft gunnery)	Marks beginning of programming
1946	First operational computer (ENIAC)	Launches information age
1948	Transistor	Replaces vacuum tubes
1956	Transistor-based computer	Reduces computer size
1958	Integrated circuit	Combines transistors, capacitors, and resistors on a silicon substrate
1971	Large-scale integration	Miniaturizes thousands of transistors on a silicon chip only 0.2 inches square
1972	8-bit microprocessor	Places 5,000 transistors on one chip
1985	32-bit microprocessor	Places 275,000 transistors on one chip
1995	64-bit microprocessor	Places 5.5 million transistors on one chip

1958 as a purely scientific discovery. The application of lasers revolutionized not only surgery, navigation, and military technology, but also manufacturing in making precision cuts and compact disc music reproduction and telecommunications. In 1966, a transatlantic cable carried 138 calls simultaneously. Using laser technology, in 1988, the first fiber-optic cable carried 40,000 calls. Today that technology has improved so that 1.5 million calls can be processed. Yet, early laser developers were hesitant to apply for a patent because no one believed that lasers had any application for telecommunications.

Innovations include the discovery of totally unanticipated benefits of mature products as well. The drug *spironolactone* was used for decades as a treatment for water retention. The 40-year-old drug was recently (1999) tested for its ability to treat congestive heart failure, a debilitating syndrome in which the heart becomes unable to pump blood effectively. Doctors were shocked at the drug's potency against this heart disease that kills a quarter million Americans every year. The discovery of this unexpected benefit of spironolactone will save billions of dollars in reduced hospital expenditures and tens of thousands of lives every year. Incidentally, this savings is why this discovery about spironolactone will probably reduce rather than raise GDP, despite its pronounced positive effects on human well-being.

(See 332 What are the other limitations of GDP?)

Q **354. If a U.S. company invented transistors, then why did the Japanese companies achieve greater profits from the use of transistors in their products?**

A One reason for this occurrence is something that business management guru Peter Drucker calls "entrepreneurial judo." It shows the importance of the interface between scientific breakthroughs and sound economic strategy. Drucker cites five bad habits that expose (in this case, American) companies to the entrepreneurial judo of newcomers and imitators that want to move in and take over products:

1. Believing that something is not good unless it is developed within the same industry or country. (Transistors were developed at Bell research labs, not by the electronic industry.)
2. Targeting the high-profit customers only, or "skimming the cream." (Xerox erred when it originally did this with its copiers.)
3. Believing that quality is what the supplier puts into it, not what the customer gets out of it. (Vacuum tubes took skill to manufacture, while transistors were cheap and mass produced, although they provided better sound.)
4. Charging a premium price (as a way of connoting quality).
5. Maximizing rather than optimizing a product. (Xerox did not customize copiers to the particular market—it produced an expensive one-size-fits-all copier that was too expensive for smaller offices.)

When innovative companies develop these types of bad habits, other firms are able to capitalize on and develop inventions that they did not develop by being much more responsive to market conditions and requirements.

Q 355. What are the different types of research and development?

A Research and development (R&D) can be broken down into three categories: (1) scientific discovery or basic research; (2) applied research (research leading to a useful product); and (3) development (the design and manufacture, at least of a prototype, of the product). Of all research in the United States in 1996, 63 percent was for development, 21 percent was applied research, and 16 was basic research. Industry conducted 73 percent of all research; universities and colleges, 15 percent; government, 9 percent; and other nonprofit institutions, 3 percent.

Q 356. How much does the government spend on R&D and where does it spend it?

A In 1998, the government spent more than $75 billion on R&D: about $43.3 billion on product development, $14.9 billion on basic research, $14.5 billion on applied research, and $1 billion on equipment. This federal share of R&D accounts for about one-third of the total national R&D.

Defense R&D accounted for $37.8 billion in 1998, about half of the federal government's R&D budget. The defense share has decreased since the 1960s. In 1960 the federal government spent $6.1 billion on defense R&D, 80.3 percent of the government's R&D budget.

Top Recipient Federal Agencies of R&D Budget in 1998

Agency	Amount ($ billions)
Defense Department	$37.8
Health and Human Services Department	12.7
NASA	10.3
Energy Department	6.7
National Science Foundation	2.3
Agriculture Department	1.5
Other	4.0
Total	$75.3

Q **357. What are the present-day business realities that hinder advancements of technology?**

A The following business realities can hinder technological advancement:

- Good products are the enemies of the better products. It is hard to abandon a product that is successful for a product that may be better. That is why, for example, it was hard for many people to switch from DOS to Windows, from rotary cord phones to the touchtone cordless phones, and from the English measurement system to the metric system.

- Innovation is destructive. For example, switching from manual to automated processes can eliminate jobs (such as when automatic elevators replaced elevator operators or when robots replace assembly-line workers). Following the same principle, super stores may be more convenient and cheaper for shoppers, but they also can put little competing stores out of business.

- Cost-benefit analysis can be rigid in valuing potential benefits. Few pursuits of technological discovery can be justified by a reasonable prediction of future benefits.

Q **358. What are the business attitudes that work to the furtherance of technology?**

A The following business attitudes can assist technological advancement:

- Maintaining self-delusion by ignoring the financial facts.
- Overselling and exaggerating the benefits to potential investors.
- Taking risks.
- Cultivating the ability to visualize the innovation and its future benefits.

Q **359. What is the institutional framework for technological development?**

A Innovations come from several main sources: universities supported by private and government grants, private laboratories funded by corporate budgets, and the military, funded by the federal government. The federal government spends about $75 billion on R&D annually, which is filtered through various agencies, mainly defense, and on to universities, private laboratories, and contractors. About half of federal R&D makes it to manufacturing industries.

(See 356 How much does the government spend on R&D and where does it spend it?)

Percentage Distribution of R&D Funding by Industrial Sector

Sector	Federal R&D funds	Industry's R&D funds	Sector's share of total R&D funds
Aerospace	17.4%	6.9%	24.3%
Electrical machinery and communications	6.1	10.1	15.2
Machinery	1.9	13.1	15.0
Chemicals	0.2	10.5	10.7
Autos and other transport	1.5	9.4	10.9
Other	1.2	13.0	14.2
Total manufacturing	28.3	63.0	91.4
Nonmanufacturing	5.5	3.2	8.7
Total	33.9	66.2	100.0

Source: *Beyond Spin-Off,* Battelle 1990.

Q **360. How have military considerations led to the development of technology?**

A Periodically, external events accelerate the advance of technology. At the peak of the cold war, the Soviet Union's successful orbit of the first satellite, *Sputnik,* brought on widespread fear that the United States was vulnerable militarily and falling behind in technology. This perception spurred additional funding for R&D and science instruction in high schools and universities.

Competition within the military branches also produced innovation. The navy's quest for missiles that could be launched from submarines led to the development of Polaris solid fuel missiles. Solid fuel rockets have huge advantages over liquid fuel ones. Liquid fuel rockets cannot be fueled until launch, while solid fuel rockets can be fueled and stored, even on a ship.

However, the military approach to technological development is not really viable from a commercial point of view. Commercial competitive success requires concentrated attention to downstream activities such as production engineering and manufacturing. Commercial spinoffs from military R&D must bridge the gap between technical novelty originating in big national projects like aerospace planes, supercomputers, and moon voyages, and equally challenging, but less visible, tasks of designing consumer products, improving their quality, and cutting costs.

(See 362 What is the difference between civilian and military development of technology?)

Q 361. How is defense industry R&D related to industrial applications?

A There are a variety of ways in which defense and commercial industries benefit from each other's R&D. Sometimes a military product that has commercial applications is converted directly to commercial use. This is called the "classic spinoff." The microwave oven and the Internet are two such items that originated in the defense industry. Another way of sharing benefits is through shared infrastructure, as in the cases of nuclear power and satellite communications. Defense agencies also support generic research that has led to the development of "dual-use" products, such as lasers and artificial intelligence. There is also a reverse relationship where commercial industry develops products first that benefit the military later, such as improved semiconductors.

Q 362. What is the difference between the civilian and military approach to development of technology?

A Although each benefits from the other's technological development, military and civilian approaches to technology are very different. The civilian approach is driven very much by the demands of the marketplace and is characterized by small, but frequent, improvements in existing products. The military, by contrast, is directed by military requirements and aims at big improvements, such as entire new weapons systems. Civilian technological development places a premium on minimum manufacturing cost and maximum quality and is geared to high-volume production. The military is much less concerned with cost compared with functional performance and usually expects limited production volume. Finally, in the civilian sector, R&D tends to be closely integrated with production and customer service to guarantee responsiveness to market needs and to minimize cost, whereas military R&D is usually separately contracted from the production process.

Q 363. Why is the United States the world leader in developing new technology?

A The United States is the world leader in developing new technology because it operates on a larger economic scale, has a higher degree of competition, maintains a highly skilled and well-educated workforce, and offers free market incentives to innovate. R&D expenditures in the United States are about the same percentage of GDP (2.7 percent) as other higher spending countries such as Germany (2.8 percent) and Japan (2.6 percent).

Q **364. How is technological improvement evident in today's economic growth?**

A By 1999, the United States had recorded an eight-year economic expansion, approaching full employment without a resurgence of inflation. Federal Reserve Chairman Alan Greenspan acknowledged that this noninflationary expansion was partly due to increased productivity made possible by the use of new technology. For example, greater use of the Internet has helped companies process orders faster and thereby trim costly inventories.

Q **365. Why should the government invest in R&D?**

A In economic theory, the government has a role in promoting the production of "public goods." Public goods are goods that have a high value to society but do not offer sufficient financial return to producers to make them. R&D has characteristics of a public good in that it is necessary for technological advance (meaning a high "social return"), but the market will not carry out enough of it (because of a low "private return").

Q **366. Is there a particular strategy that the United States could follow for developing new technologies?**

A Technological historians tend to agree that the government should resist aggressively championing particular technologies. It is better to allow for a deliberately diversified research portfolio. As one technologist put it, "Open as many windows as possible to let the private sector explore what can only be faintly viewed from those windows." Directed research has proven wasteful in the past as in the cases of synthetic fuels, the artificial heart, and parts of the space program.

Q **367. How can the government best support private-sector investment in R&D?**

A No one method has emerged as the most cost-effective way of encouraging private-sector R&D. Besides direct funding of R&D, offering tax-based subsidies would seem to be the more market-oriented method: private-sector firms are apt to use credits where the private return is the highest. It is always difficult or expensive for the government to make the private sector do something. Could the government target the tax breaks to specific R&D? Theoretically, the government could offer tax breaks, but special interests and bureaucrats exert a lot of pressure toward suboptimal directions.

The National Bureau of Economic Research (NBER) concluded that one dollar of tax credit induced a one-dollar increase in R&D, demonstrating that tax credits were not a potent incentive to encourage R&D. The government will continue to use both direct financing and tax credits to encourage R&D, but the current trend is toward the greater use of tax credits.

Q 368. How do policies affecting technology development differ from conventional policies that "optimize"?

A Given the accidental nature of many technological discoveries, rigid specifications of the desired product should be avoided because they might prevent development of an equally, or more desirable, product. In deciding which technology path to promote, it is better to practice with several approaches than to rely on a cost-benefit analysis (as in the case of conventional optimizing policies) because there are too many uncertainties. Later, when uncertainties are reduced, a path might be chosen using cost-benefit analysis.

Q 369. What are some areas of innovation that could produce the most substantial gains in the United States?

A Some aspects of the American lifestyle are particularly unenviable. For example, Americans seem to be stuck in traffic far more often than prosperous citizens should be. Innovations in transportation might, therefore, have some handsome pay-offs. However, a solution to traffic congestion might not necessarily involve a scientific breakthrough but rather a more modest, but still ingenious, type of urban planning, or higher-density living, that allows people to reach their destinations without sitting in traffic jams. Or the innovation might be reducing the requirement to travel to the workplace, allowing some or all work to be done at home.

Another area of potentially high pay-offs for innovation is in housing construction, where advances have come slowly during the previous decades. Construction of houses that have lower maintenance and have lower utility costs are probably well within the capabilities of today's builders and architects. Superior house technology has existed for 50 years. For example, the Dymaxian house, a circular house conceived by Buckminster Fuller in 1948, has maximum construction strength, acoustics, and fuel efficiency, and can be made very cheaply. However, this type of house has not caught the interest of builders nor of the market in general.

Q 370. Which other innovations are available now but have not been successful in the mass market?

A Modern-day innovations that have yet to become successful include electric cars, which are too slow and require heavy, expensive batteries; solar panels, which are expensive and generate a limited amount of energy; and passive solar houses, which have not made inroads into the planned communities that dominate new construction in the United States.

CORPORATE RESTRUCTURING: STOCKHOLDER GREED OR COMPETITIVE NECESSITY?

Corporate restructuring is not new. Corporate restructuring—in the form of downsizing, reorganizations, and mergers and acquisitions—has occurred in this country as long as there have been companies. However, corporate restructuring seemed to accelerate in the 1980s as management and corporate directors discovered that restructuring had much greater potential to improve corporate performance and increase share prices. Corporate restructuring continued into the 1990s and increasingly affected white-collar workers. A portion of the prosperity of the 1990s and beyond has been attributed to corporate restructuring that began in the 1980s.

Q 371. What is corporate restructuring?

A Corporate restructuring is a major cost reduction and reorganization of the operations of a corporation. This reorganization could mean closing operations in certain geographic locations, closing or selling off businesses within the corporation, changing management, and so on. Corporate restructuring is usually carried out under pressure to increase a corporation's stock price. Restructuring almost always means downsizing the workforce, outsourcing functions once performed by in-house employees, and using contingent workers (independent contractors and temps).

Q 372. What are the different types of corporate restructuring?

A Corporations have devised a number of ways to restructure:

- **Divestiture:** selling a portion of the firm to an outside party, usually for cash or marketable securities.
- **Equity carve-out:** selling a subsidiary to outsiders. New equity is issued to a new stockholder base, and a new legal entity is created.

- **Spin-off:** creating a new entity (a separate company run by separate management). This is done by distributing new shares to existing stockholders according to each's share of ownership in the company (a pro-rata basis), so there is no cash infusion into the parent corporation and the stockholder base is the same.

- **Split-off:** trading a division of the parent company to some of the stockholders in exchange for their shares in the parent company.

- **Split-up:** breaking up the entire company and replacing it with a number of newly formed companies. It is equivalent to a number of spin-offs.

Q 373. Why do corporations restructure?

A A better question might be, "Why did corporations not discover the benefits of restructuring earlier?" The most widely known reason for restructuring is that stockholders discovered that companies could produce the same amount with less, especially less people. Wall Street rewards companies, and top executives receive generous stock price–based compensation packages, as stock prices rise. With increasing globalization, restructuring also became essential to competitive survival.

Q 374. What is the process for restructuring?

A In deciding whether to restructure, the management of a corporation first conducts exhaustive financial analysis of all of the alternatives, specifically: (1) estimating the after-tax cash flows of the division to be divested or spun off in relation to those of the parent company; (2) estimating the present value of the division; and (3) subtracting market value of the division's liabilities. If the present value of the after-tax cash flows exceed the divestiture proceeds, then the parent company generally does not go forward with the restructuring. If not, then a restructuring plan is formulated and presented for shareholder approval. After attaining approval, new shares of a spin-off are registered with the Securities and Exchange Commission (SEC). The division is then separated from the parent according to an established timetable.

Q 375. Why was there a surge of corporate restructuring in the 1980s?

A One factor was the deregulation of the airline, trucking, telecommunications, and banking industries that began in the late 1970s and increased rapidly in the 1980s. Prior to deregulation, there was less incentive for these industries to boost productivity. With free competition replacing regulation, companies were forced to lower costs while maintaining service.

376. Did corporate restructuring ruin U.S. manufacturing?

A Actually, several formerly prosperous U.S. manufacturing industries were already in decline before the surge in corporate restructuring in the 1980s. Jobs in textiles, shoe making, and steel were already heading overseas in the 1960s and 1970s to take advantage of lower wage rates and benefits, and lenient environmental controls. The absolute number employed in manufacturing has remained constant in the United States during the last three or four decades, although manufacturing's share of total employed dropped sharply.

Employment in Manufacturing (millions)

Year	Number of employees
1950	15.2
1960	16.8
1970	19.4
1980	20.3
1985	19.2
1990	19.1
1995	18.5
1998	18.7

Sources: Office of Management and Budget; Bureau of Labor Statistics.

Q **377. How many people were downsized during the 1980s? The 1990s?**

A Surprisingly, no comprehensive, reliable statistics are kept on the number of workers downsized, although some data are collected for ad hoc surveys. Downsizing was on the increase by the end of the 1990s, despite the strong overall job market. Still, as the economic expansion of the 1990s lengthened, relatively fewer firms that laid off workers actually reduced their *total* employment.

Staff Cuts Announced by U.S. Companies

Year	Number of employees
1989	111,000
1990	316,000
1991	555,000
1992	500,000

Staff Cuts Announced by U.S. Companies

Year	Number of employees
1993	615,000
1994	516,000
1995	440,000
1996	477,000
1997	434,000
1998	677,000

Source: *The Challenger Employment Report.*

Q 378. How did corporate restructuring of the 1990s differ from that of the 1980s?

A Early in the 1980s, manufacturers were doing most of the restructuring through downsizing and other means. Mainly blue-collar workers were affected. In the 1990s, downsizing began to affect white-collar workers in greater numbers, especially in banking, retail trade, and telecommunications. Another difference between the two decades is that in the 1990s corporations outsourced jobs, such as office cleaning, accounting, security, and computer operations at a higher percentage (14 percent) than in the 1980s (5 percent).

Q 379. Is corporate restructuring a shortsighted way to hike stock prices to benefit the major stockholders?

A No doubt, basing compensation of top executives on stock prices increases the zeal for restructuring. Still, the benefits of corporate restructuring are real. Not only have stock prices continued to rise (to more than 10 times the level of 1982 by the end of the 1990s), but companies are more productive. One question that lingers is whether a company's lower commitment to its employees by restructuring has a negative effect on worker loyalty and performance.

Q 380. What has been the net effect of corporate restructuring on employment?

A Although downsizing was significant throughout the 1980s and 1990s, net employment increased, indicating that workers found jobs elsewhere and did not remain unemployed for long.

Q 381. Has corporate restructuring shifted people out of high-paying jobs and into low-paying ones?

A In the 1980s and 1990s the increase in real compensation for the labor force, on the whole, was fairly sluggish. For all economic sectors combined, however, compensation nearly kept pace with productivity. Thus, what some people call the "McDonald's effect," or the shifting of workers into lower-paying service jobs, is not reflected in the data. However, wages have stagnated within the lower-skilled occupations.

(See 531 What are the costs of globalization?)

Q 382. Why has growth in the median wage been slow during recent decades?

A One reason that the growth in the median wage has been slow is that the percentage of total compensation that workers receive in the form of nonwage benefits—such as health care, time off, and pensions—has been rising. Nonwage benefits grew from 19 percent of payroll costs in 1951, to 42 percent of payroll costs by the mid-1990s. The growth in nonwage benefits has the additional benefit to workers because this type of compensation generally is not taxed. So workers have gained a tax advantage. However, wage stagnation is real and is not only the result of downsizing, but also of intensifying international competition where lower-skilled jobs are sent overseas.

(See 532 Should unskilled workers be compensated when their livelihoods are affected by globalization?)

Q 383. Have corporate profits soared due to restructuring?

A Corporate profits have not soared recently, but they have improved. In 1995, after-tax corporate profits averaged about 4.5 percent, twice as high as in 1980 and a third higher than in 1990. Corporate profits were, however, still lower than in the 1960s, when corporations routinely earned between 5 and 7 percent after taxes. Much of the improvement is because corporations have lower debt-servicing costs, because of lower interest rates and less need to borrow. Corporate interest payments fell from $147.5 billion in 1990 to only $88.5 billion in 1996. Corporations borrow less because improved computers and overnight delivery service allow them to keep inventories low. The inventory-to-sales ratio in manufacturing fell from 1.95 in 1982 to 1.34 by 1995. This improved inventory management also reduces economic volatility. The lower corporate and federal deficits have meant that the because the United States can spend less on financing corporate and federal debt in the form of corporate bonds and Treasury bills, they can spend more on stocks, driving up stock prices.

Q 384. Why are chief executives paid so much?

A Shareholders like to see higher share prices. Boards of directors are elected by shareholders. The executives negotiate with the boards, which approve their compensation packages. Naturally, the boards that represent stockholders want to link executive pay to stock price performance. In other words, high executive compensation is achieved through negotiation, just as it is with premium sports stars. Star basketball players who can fill the stands can command hundred-million-dollar contracts. While high executive pay is understandable from an economic point of view, it is sometimes poor public relations for many CEOs who earn more than 100 times that of the average worker in their companies.

Q 385. What is reengineering?

A "Reengineering" is a restructuring buzzword that refers to improving the bottom line by changing business processes. Reengineering most commonly takes place in the areas of filling orders (the customer supply chain), product development, selling, and customer service. Reengineering is just one small aspect of corporate restructuring and depends upon improvements in information technology.

Q 386. Is it possible that too many people will be laid off?

A Not really. When companies produce the same products with fewer people, they can charge less for goods. Consumers can then buy what they could before and have money left over to buy something in addition. Consumers' purchases of other goods and services (with the leftover money) create demand in new areas. Cheaper airline tickets allow people to spend more money (since Americans do not seem inclined to save) on cars, houses, education, or even more trips, which, in turn, employs people in these areas. It is here that the downsized workers can be absorbed, while consumers reap greater benefits through lower prices and wider choices of things to buy.

387. Has downsizing gone too far?

This question can be better answered if rephrased another way. If the United States had undergone less downsizing in the 1980s and 1990s, who would be filling the new jobs people now occupy? With the United States at or near full employment (by the end of 1999), it is clear that corporate downsizing only accommodated the evolutionary course of the economy. Still, the volatility of employment, the shuffling of people between jobs, and the uncertainty that restructuring brings have created a sense of insecurity.

388. What are the long-term effects of restructuring on corporations?

In economics, nothing happens in isolation. Corporate restructuring, spurred by deregulation and reinforced with heavy investment in information technology, has resulted in increases in production per unit of inputs (improved productivity). In the service sector, productivity began to increase in the 1990s, from a relatively low 0.7 percent annually in the 1980s, to about 1.5 percent. As other industries discover the benefits of "restructuring," productivity could be on an upward trend for quite a few years.

389. What are the long-term effects of restructuring on society and on labor?

As downsizing has become a permanent feature of American industry, total unemployment in the 1990s fell to its lowest level in 30 years. Still, the increases in productivity have not been passed on to many employees in the form of higher compensation. The segments of the labor force that benefit the least are those blue-collar workers who do not have college degrees who lose high-paying jobs. Managers also find it difficult, with less pay and promotion possibilities to offer, to win the loyalty of their workers. Some companies try to compensate with additional education and training opportunities. During the 1990s, the average work week for factory workers actually increased, halting a downward trend that began in 1850. Critics of corporate restructuring claim that corporations view employees as costs to be cut rather than assets to be developed. It is true that wages and benefits make an inviting target for cost-cutters because they comprise 70 percent of the costs of a typical enterprise.

Q 390. Are Americans convinced that corporate restructuring is a good thing?

A Publicity surrounding the downsizing in the 1980s was more negative than reports on recent reductions. Society appears to have weathered the initial shock of the downsizings in the 1980s, and now the consensus appears to be that restructuring that includes downsizing does not necessarily mean a reduction in total employment. Of course, the economic boom of the 1980s and 1990s was helpful in building this consensus.

REGULATION AND DEREGULATION

Regulation is a wild card in the free market economy. Through regulation, government has the power to prevent or undo what the free market has done. Sometimes the regulatory action of the government is for the better, but sometimes it is not. Economists continually examine the costs and benefits of government regulation and refine its measurement.

The issue of deregulation is not new, but it is still very current. Deregulation of major U.S. industries in the transportation, finance, energy, and communications sectors began in the mid-1970s, when economic analysis demonstrated that the costs of strict regulation exceeded the benefits. Analysts attribute much of the economic expansions of the 1980s and 1990s to deregulation. However, with the caution borne out of unforeseen transition costs, deregulation has been a very slow, ongoing process.

GENERAL REGULATION

Q 391. Do we need regulation?

A Although the market economy does a great job of turning resources into the goods and services that Americans enjoy, the free market often produces results that society does not want. For example, unregulated industry could emit much larger amounts of pollution into the air and water, which would diminish the environment's productivity as well as aesthetic beauty. Pulp and paper, and oil refining require the heaviest pollution abatement. Without the regulation of pollution, consumers might have low-priced paper and oil, but they would be living in a polluted environment. Safety is another area where society depends on regulations, whether it is on-the-job safety, or disclosure of the risks of using consumer products.

Q **392. Who regulates?**

A Federal, state, and local governments all regulate to a certain extent. Because regulations require legal authority, only government entities can issue regulations. Regulations come into existence through passage of enforceable laws.

Q **393. Is there reliable and comprehensive data to assess the total costs and benefits of regulation?**

A Not really. Most estimates on the total costs and benefits of regulation rely on many simplifying assumptions. With all the assumptions, there are many places where estimates can diverge. Not surprisingly, the costs and benefits of regulation are affected by people's sympathies for and against regulation.

Q **394. What are these estimated costs and benefits of regulation?**

A Estimates of the cost and benefits of regulation have to be qualified. The Office of Management and Budget (OMB) estimates in the table below, for example, do not include any regulations that have less than $100 million in associated costs nor any indirect costs of regulation. The analysts that produced the OMB estimate still

Estimates of the Annual Costs and Benefits of Regulation for 1997 ($ billions)

Category	Benefits	OMB cost estimate	Independent cost estimate
Environmental	$162	$144	$185
Other social	136	54	62
Economic		71	
Efficiency			81
Transfer			148
Paperwork/disclosure			10
Process			232
Total	$298	$279	$708

Sources: Office and Management and Budget.

believe that both costs and benefits are overstated. Economic (efficiency) costs in the table refer to the loss of production caused by the added costs of regulation. Transfer costs are payments from one group in society to another, like higher prices paid by consumers to farmers because of imposed production quotas. Process costs are simplar to paperwork/disclosure costs in that both capture aspects of the administrative burden of requlation. The process cost estimate is much higher than the paperwork cost estimate because it includes costs of compliance with tax regulations.

It is clear from the table how divergent estimates can be. OMB criticizes the private industry estimate for including an estimate of compliance cost that includes U.S. tax regulations. Even with that adjustment, however, the other cost estimate would be twice that of OMB. It is worth noting that the cost estimate here of complying with the tax code is very close to that used by proponents of tax reform.

Q **395. Should the cost of compliance with the tax code be included as a cost of regulation?**

A The cost of tax code compliance raises the somewhat different issue of tax reform. On a fundamental level, the government's intervention through the tax code is similar to its regulations because both are trying to steer economic behavior. Regulations tend to try to reduce the negative effects of free market activity. For example, some tax code provisions attempt to reduce skewed income distribution that is also a result of free market activity.

DEREGULATION

Q **396. What is deregulation?**

A Deregulation can be defined as the elimination or reduction of restrictions by government on the pricing, entry, and exit decisions of firms. Entry and exist decisions refer to firms' assessment of whether they should be active in an industry or not. If an industry is heavily regulated, then there may be substantial added costs for new firms to enter that industry.

Q **397. When did the recent move toward deregulation start in the United States?**

A The first U.S. industry to be deregulated was the airline industry. in the 1970s. Liberalization of fares, entry, and exit began when the Civil Aeronautics Board first encouraged discount fares and was completed in 1983.

Q **398. Why does deregulation take so long?**

A There are two components to deregulation: dismantling the regulatory regime in place and adjustment by industry to the new competitive environment. Management practices become ingrained in the very culture of the industry. Tearing down barriers to efficiency and becoming alert to opportunities for technological advancements and to new markets seem to require a phasing out of the old guard in favor of the new. Deregulators also want to proceed gingerly because they want to minimize unforeseen adverse consequences of deregulating large industries. So the deregulation itself proceeds gradually.

Q **399. What is the current status of deregulation?**

A The following lists the current status of regulatory reforms in selected industries.

• **Airlines:** pricing, entry, and exit have been fully deregulated.

• **Trucking:** interstate and intrastate rates, entry, and exit have been fully deregulated.

• **Railroads:** most rates, including contract rates, have been deregulated, but "tariff" rates for certain commodities are still subject to maximum rate "guidelines."

• **Banks:** ceilings on interest rates (except for demand deposits) have been eliminated by deregulation. Congress has authorized banks to engage in interstate banking. Thrift institutions have been allowed into consumer and business lending, while affiliates of banks have been permitted some degree of securities underwriting.

• **Natural gas:** prices at the wellhead have been fully deregulated. Independent shippers now have access to pipelines at rates regulated by the Federal Energy Regulatory Commission. By obtaining "interruptible" service (that is, a pipeline owner can stop service to a customer when demand is high under conditions specified by a contract), shippers can obtain discounts from these rates. Shippers can also sell their surplus pipeline capacity to other entities. This competitive reselling has also led to rates below the tariff rates. Finally, market-based or negotiated rates for pipeline storage service, hub service, and even transportation services are being allowed.

Q 400. Has deregulation improved efficiency?

A Yes, in most instances deregulation has improved efficiency. Data suggest that deregulation has helped industries improve productivity and reduce operating costs in the range of 25 to 75 percent. The following provides a summary of major efficiency gains by industry.

- **Airlines:** airlines have increased the average percentage of occupied seats from roughly 52 percent the decade preceding deregulation to roughly 62 percent since deregulation. Real costs have declined at least 25 percent since deregulation. Industry profits have been very volatile during deregulation, although higher, on average, than they would have been under regulation.

- **Trucking:** carriers have substantially reduced their empty miles since deregulation. Operating costs have fallen between 35 and 75 percent (for different parts of the industry), but operating profits are slightly lower than they would have been under regulation.

- **Railroads:** railroads have abandoned one-third of their track miles since deregulation. Real operating costs have fallen 60 percent, and rail profits are much higher than they would have been under regulation.

- **Banking:** real cost of an electronic deposit has fallen 80 percent since deregulation. Operating costs have declined 8 percent because of branch deregulation. Recent industry returns on equity exceed those just before deregulation.

- **Natural gas:** pipeline capacity has been much more efficiently utilized during peak and off-peak periods since deregulation. Real operating and maintenance expenses in transmission and distribution have fallen roughly 35 percent.

(See 403 What other industries could benefit from further deregulation?)

Q 401. Have consumers benefited from deregulation?

A Much of the increased performance has benefited consumers, because industry profit, except in the case of railroads, has not increased significantly. Higher profits for railroads were actually a positive development because railroads desperately needed to generate profits since they were faltering badly in the 1970s. In fact, there were widespread doubts that railroads could ever survive in a liberalized market. The following provides a summary of improvements by industry.

- **Airlines:** average fares are roughly 33 percent lower in real terms since deregulation, and the number of available flights has improved significantly.

- **Trucking:** service times have improved significantly, and average rates have declined between 35 and 75 percent.

- **Railroads:** average rates have declined more than 50 percent in real terms since deregulation; variation in transit time has fallen at least 20 percent.

- **Banking:** consumers have benefited from higher interest rates on savings, better opportunities to manage risk, increased availability of automated teller machines, and more banking locations.

- **Natural gas:** average prices for residential customers have declined at least 30 percent in real terms since deregulation, and average prices for commercial and industrial customers have declined even more than 30 percent. In addition, service has been more reliable as shortages have been almost completely eliminated.

But deregulation can also go awry as in the case of the deregulation of the savings and loan institutions in the 1980s, whose total federal bail-out is estimated at about $500 billion. (See box on page 192.)

(See 196 How did the savings and loan crisis of the 1980s materialize?)

Q 402. What has been the effect of deregulation on labor?

A Predictably, when efficiency rises, labor gets squeezed. While the overall efficiency and consumer gains from deregulation are substantial, there is evidence that from 1973 to 1996 the earnings of workers declined in real terms. On the other hand, unemployment fell greatly over that same period. The four industries studied in the table below all had substantial increases in the number employed, which rose by half during the period.

Unionization, Employment, and Labor Earnings in Transportation and Telecommunications Industries

Industry	1973	1978	1983	1988	1991	1996
Trucking						
Union membership rate	49%	46%	38%	25%	25%	23%
Workforce size (thousands)	997	1,111	1,117	1,544	1,617	1,907
Weekly earnings[a]	$499	$491	$404	$ 386	$405	$353

Unionization, Employment, and Labor Earnings in Transportation and
Telecommunications Industries

Industry	1973	1978	1983	1988	1991	1996
Railroads						
Union membership rate	83%	79%	83%	81%	78%	74%
Workforce size (thousands)	587	580	428	363	286	282
Weekly earnings[a]	$475	$491	$507	$490	$494	$470
Airlines						
Union membership rate	46%	45%	43%	42%	37%	36%
Workforce size (thousands)	368	465	464	683	696	800
Weekly earnings[a]	$499	$498	$455	$420	$443	$435
Telecommunications						
Union membership rate	59%	55%	55%	44%	42%	29%
Workforce size (thousands)	949	1,075	1,060	1,114	1,107	1,126
Weekly earnings[a]	$399	$442	$457	$447	$458	$488
All other industries						
Union membership rate	23%	22%	19%	16%	15%	11%
Workforce size (thousands)	72,619	81,737	85,220	97,704	99,080	107,844
Weekly earnings[a]	$399	$363	$301	$310	$322	$334

[a] In 1983–1984 dollars.
Source: "Deregulation and the Labor Market," *Journal of Economic Perspectives,*
Summer 1998, 111–130.

Q **403. What other industries could benefit from further deregulation?**

A The three most often-cited industries that could benefit from further deregulation
are telecommunications, cable television, and electricity. Some deregulation has
already begun in these industries: cable television was deregulated in 1984 and rereg-
ulated in 1992; the AT&T monopoly was broken up in 1984 as the first step in dereg-

THE SAVINGS AND LOAN CRISIS

The defaults by savings and loan associations (S&Ls) in the 1980s were one of the most devastating collapses ever in the U.S. financial sector. They are also an excellent real world example of the economic harm that could occur when deregulation is pursued without the proper safeguards.

Prior to the 1980s, S&Ls, or thrifts, were kind of sleepy financial institutions that depended almost entirely on financing home mortgages. The length of maturity of their assets (generally 30-year mortgages) made thrifts vulnerable to high interest rates. In the 1970s when interest rates climbed into double digits, many S&Ls were squeezed as depositors fled thrifts in search of higher payoffs in money market mutual funds. In response to the crisis, the government deregulated thrifts in the early 1980s. The main components of deregulation allowed thrifts to (1) offer adjustable rate mortgages; (2) add credit cards and consumer loans (up to 30 percent of their assets); (3) add commercial real estate loans (up to 40 percent of their assets); and (4) eliminate interest rate ceilings.

Yet as thrifts entered new loan markets, the remaining thrift regulatory system was still geared to the safe world of home mortgages. Thrifts did not have to follow the financial reporting requirements, tighter scrutiny, and higher net worth standards required for banks. Thrifts were also not required to pay insurance premiums for any extra risk they took with their loans. Thrift executives, who faced downsizing or liquidation, were encouraged to seek out high-return, but risky loans.

As the groundwork for crisis was laid, government policies made the situation worse by (1) reducing net worth standards for S&Ls from 5 percent of liabilities to 3 percent; (2) basing net worth on book value rather than market values, which exaggerated net worth; (3) giving thrifts access to promissory notes to help them reach the meager net worth levels; (4) allowing thrifts to spread loan losses over a 10-year period; and (5) not increasing the field force of examiners and supervisors.

Although the net worth of thrifts increased dramatically in the mid-1980s, the bubble burst when oil and real estate prices, which many thrifts had gambled on, declined in the southwestern United States. Perhaps the most poignant example of this decline was the Houston real estate market with its empty skyscrapers and auctions of buildings at cents on the dollar. Most of the burden of the S&L cleanup fell on the Bush administration. The Resolution Trust Corporation (RTC) was set up to manage the liquidations of troubled thrifts. The cleanup is still ongoing and has now been taken over by the successor to the RTC, the Office of Thrift Supervision. The price tag on the S&L resolution has been estimated at $500 billion.

ulating telecommunications; pilot programs in deregulating electricity have already begun in several states. These industries were once thought to be "natural monopolies," and unable to benefit from deregulation. A natural monopoly is one whose unit costs of production continue to fall until the company is large enough to efficiently serve the entire market. In such industries, entry by other companies into the market is not only difficult, it is inefficient and almost impossible. Technological changes, such as digital transmission over fiber optics or the electromagnetic spectrum, mean that competition is increasingly possible in telecommunications and cable television. The small-scale efficiency of electricity generated from combined cycle gas turbines has opened this sector to competition as well.

Q 404. How might competition be affected in these industries by deregulation?

A With deregulation, the potential for cross-industry competition is high. For instance, the local telephone providers (Bell operating companies), independent companies, small rural companies, and long-distance phone companies—such as AT&T, MCI, and Sprint—could vie for each other's markets. Cellular and wireless companies, cable TV companies, and electric utilities, that own fiber-optic cable networks, might also enter local and long-distance markets.

Q 405. Is the company Microsoft a natural monopoly?

A Microsoft might be viewed as a natural monopoly, but mostly in a marketing sense. It is the cost of *not* buying Microsoft products that the market tries to avoid. It is customers' fear of not complying with the industry standard, supplied only by Microsoft, that gives the company its advantage, and not the ever-lower cost of production that is the main advantage of the conventional natural monopoly.

Q 406. What are the key success factors for deregulation?

A The key components of successful deregulation are competitive access, "stranded assets," and universal service. Competitive access means that new companies must have the option of interconnecting with existing networks so that their initial investment is not too high a barrier to entry into the market. The sticking point is determining what the new entrants should pay for the use of the network.

Stranded assets refers to the handicap that existing firms claim because regulators encouraged them to invest in uneconomic assets, such as nuclear power. To pave the way for deregulation, the authorities devise ways to help telecommunication and electric companies recoup the disadvantage so that they will be on an even playing field with new entrants that have more efficient technologies.

Universal service (that is, serving areas that are uneconomic to serve) has been a difficult issue for deregulation. The best approach is the one that is least costly, least distortive of incentives, and tailored to the industry and the area needing service.

Q 407. What other areas of society could benefit from deregulation in the future?

A Currently regulated areas that could probably gain significantly from deregulation include ocean transport, urban transport, and education.

THE COSTS OF CIVIL LITIGATION

The cases of the $4.9 billion award against General Motors for failure to install an inexpensive safety device, and the $2 million award against McDonald's to a person who spilled coffee in her lap, make great news stories. What is the economic impact of all the huge damage awards and settlements? Who is paying for them and are they justified? Is the practice of tort law a benefit to the economy by giving consumers a weapon to force corporations to be more responsible, or is it an abuse of the system by trial lawyers who rake in huge fees and settlements at the expense of companies that basically produce good, reliable products? These questions are not limited to product liability, from which the above examples come, but also include medical malpractice, sex, race, and age discrimination suits, automobile accidents, and more.

Q 408. What is a tort?

A A tort is an injury or a wrong. Legally, a tort is "a breach of duty imposed by law (rather than by contract) that gives a right of action for damages."

Q 409. Why is there a clamor for tort reform?

A There is a popular belief that the legal system has been taken over by unscrupulous and greedy lawyers who engage in excessive litigation that exacts an enormous economic cost from society. Some damage awards have attracted huge media attention, such as the celebrated McDonald's coffee-spilling case, or the breast implant suits that bankrupted the manufacturer (Dow-Corning, a billion-dollar company) even in the absence of a scientific link between the implants and the claimed tort. A common but unsubstantiated estimate of tort actions is $300 billion annually, about 3 percent of GDP. It is not clear whether this number is the total of all initial compensatory and punitive damage awards, legal costs, indirect costs to companies, out-of-court settlements, or a combination thereof. Insurance companies are probably the most cohesive group calling for tort reform.

Q 410. What do opponents of tort reform say?

A Opponents of tort reform commonly argue that there is no tort crisis, and they cite the rarity of the award of punitive damages, which are the component of damages that drives awards into the millions of dollars and higher. Opponents challenge the $300 billion total tort cost figure cited above as unfounded, but they do not appear to have a broadly agreed figure of their own. Tort reform opponents agree that an empirical study of the incidence and size of punitive damages is needed to provide judges and juries with a yardstick to evaluate competing claims.

There is not much attention to the costs of the entire tort process beyond those related to punitive damages. Nor is there much attempt to evaluate the costs associated with out-of-court settlements where the majority of cases are resolved. Opponents of tort reform gain strength, however, from two studies, one by the Rand Corporation and one by the General Accounting Office, that conclude that punitive damage awards are rare and are usually scaled back considerably from the original jury awards that are reported in the media. The McDonald's case cited above was reportedly settled out of court for substantially less than the initial award after going through various appeals. The Association of American Trial Lawyers is probably the most powerful group opposing tort reform.

Q 411. What are some of the more celebrated product liability tort cases?

A Some celebrated product liability cases in the 1980s and 1990s are

Product	Defendant
Dalkon Shield (an intrauterine device)	A. H. Robbins
Breast implants	Dow Corning
Overly hot coffee	McDonald's
Exploding gas tanks (Pinto models)	Ford Motor
Asbestos	Monsanto/Johns-Manville
Y2K compliance liability	Any noncompliant company

Q 412. What are the major trends in legal costs?

A Reliable data on how much is spent on legal services of all types are difficult, and sometimes impossible, to find. In 1996 the Census Bureau estimated total national cost of legal services at $124.6 billion, an increase of 28 percent over 1990 and 136 percent over 1985 ($52.8 billion in nominal growth). These numbers presumably include both criminal and civil legal expenses, but exclude costs for courts, law enforcement, corrections, and any damage awards. Figures from 1992 place total employment in legal services at 923,617 with a payroll of $39 billion. This estimate seems quite low given that the number of licensed lawyers exceeded 1 million in 1999.

(See 416. How many lawyers are licensed in the United States today?)

Q 413. Which category of legal expense has risen the most?

A Lamentably, there is no comprehensive reliable breakdown, even between civil and criminal expenses. A reasonable number could be derived, but would require piecing together information from each of the 50 states.

Q 414. What are the direct and indirect costs of tort litigation?

A The total cost of tort litigation, which would guide the decision of whether or not to pursue tort reform, has not been quantified. Such an estimate would need to include both direct and indirect costs. Costs would include actual damage awards paid, as well as all legal costs associated with settling cases, including lawyers' fees from filing the case through final appeal for both plaintiff and defendant lawyers, all court costs, and value of time of the litigants. Another category of direct cost is rather dark and mysterious, that is the cost of out-of-court settlements. This category may well constitute the bulk of tort associated costs and to omit it would skew the issue in favor of tort reform opponents. The problem is that out-of-court settlements are almost always secret, sealed by the court at the request of the defendant with the apparent motive of not unleashing hoards of similar suits.

Indirect costs include the added cost to the defendant of doing business after the suit (if the decision affected business practices), after accounting for possible consumer benefits, such as better safety. An example is the cost of medical malpractice insurance that physicians must carry to continue to practice. One U.S. senator who supports tort reform cited specific price *increases* as a result of the "litigation tax": (1) $24 for an 8-foot ladder, (2) $3,000 for a pacemaker, and (3) $170 for a motorized-wheelchair. (Specific support for these numbers was not offered in the congressional hearing transcript.)

Q 415. How long does it take to settle tort cases?

A The average length of time to decide a case in court varies by tort. The following are representative examples from tort cases in Georgia:

Type	Months
All torts	19.3
Auto accidents	16.7
Medical malpractice	26.4
Product liability	25.0

Q 416. How many lawyers are licensed in the United States today?

A According to the American Bar Association (ABA), the number of licensed lawyers passed a milestone in 1999. There are now more than one million licensed lawyers in the United States.

Q 417. How fast is the number of lawyers growing?

A The number of lawyers doubled from 1980 to 2000. The growth has been 3.5 times the rate of growth of the general population over these twenty years (ABA):

Year	Number of lawyers
1979	498,249
1985	653,686
1990	755,694
1995	896,140
1999	1,000,440

Q 418. How many people graduate from law school each year?

A There is a strong upward trend in the law school graduation rate. The growth in the number of degrees increased at more than 4 percent per year or four times the population growth rate. Even more remarkable is the entry of women into the profession, increasing from only 5.4 percent in 1970 to nearly half of all lawyers by 1994.

	1970	1994
Number of law degrees earned	14,916	40,044
Percent of graduates who are women	5.4%	43.0%
Number of law schools	145	185

Source: U.S. Center for Education Statistics.

Q 419. How do lawyers' compensation compare with that of other professions?

A Lawyers' compensation exceeds that of most all other occupations except that of physicians. Lawyers' compensation covers a wide range according to whether lawyers practice in the public or private sector and their geographical locations. In 1997, entry-level salaries for federal government attorneys were as low as $40,000 with the mid-range at $75,000 to $80,000. In the private sector, median-base corporate salaries were $105,000, but these salaries increased substantially with bonuses. In some prestigious law firms, salaries for first-year associates sometimes exceeded $100,000 per year, while starting salaries for chemical engineers with a master's degree were about $45,000. The nationwide average annual salary for family physicians was $140,000 (1996). Teachers' nationwide median salary was $35,800 (1995). Unskilled workers earned considerably less. For example, construction workers earned about $21,000.

Q 420. Are there benefits from the practice of tort law?

A In addition to plaintiffs who are actually awarded damages from negligent companies, there are positive effects of greater public safety and corporate responsibility. The following lists safety steps taken after verdicts against manufacturers in various cases:

Product	Defect	Steps taken
Natural gas line	Malodorant was not placed in newly constructed gas line.	Malodorant added.
Revolver	Accidental discharge occurred after dropping gun.	Redesigned.
CJ-7 Jeep	Inadequate rollover protection.	Redesigned, new warning added.
Toyota Corolla	Gas tank placement caused fuel-integrity problems.	Redesigned.

Product	Defect	Steps taken
Seven-Up bottles	Hundreds of blow-off cap injuries	Warnings changed.
Dalkon Shield	Inadequate testing and design resulted in injuries by users.	Taken off market.
Power lines	Uninsulated power lines caused hundreds of electrocutions.	Multimillion dollar safety campaign.

Q 421. Is tort reform needed?

A It is difficult to say whether tort reform is necessary, because no comprehensive economic analysis has been done of the full economic effects of the practice of tort law, on either the cost or the benefit side. However, the proliferation of tort cases, the exorbitant costs of medical malpractice, and the large unknown of out-of-court settlements argue strongly for an immediate, nonpartisan assessment of the full direct and indirect costs and benefits of torts in the United States. The decision whether and how to proceed with tort reform could be made based on the resulting recommendations.

CORPORATE WELFARE

It seems only fair that if welfare to the poor is scrutinized so closely, especially since the 1996 welfare reform legislation, then favors to corporations should also be examined. Such federal handouts have come to be known as "corporate welfare." Some corporate welfare has a purpose, just like federal tax provisions that try to promote or penalize individuals' behavior. Some is pure waste. Corporate welfare is substantial, but how does it compare with social welfare? It may depend on how it is counted.

Q 422. What is corporate welfare?

A Broadly defined, corporate welfare is any government spending, tax break, subsidy, or other favor to the private sector as an inducement to carry out some project or action desired by the government. The clearest form of corporate welfare is the direct government expenditure to a single corporation, or a class of corporations, to carry out something that would not, or might not, be carried out otherwise.

Q 423. How does corporate welfare differ from social welfare?

A In social welfare, an individual receives benefits for what he or she *is*. In most cases this means being poor, as defined by eligibility criteria. Corporate welfare is given for what the corporation *does*. Social welfare is given in the form of transfer payments, food stamps, discounts, and low tax or tax-free income. Corporate welfare, which is generally in the form of inducements or agreements between business and the government, may not really be welfare in the strictest sense.

Q 424. What are the types of corporate welfare?

A Corporate welfare can be given in many forms: cash; government contracts; complementary investments to help reduce the cost of setting up operations in an area, such as government-financed roads for sports stadiums; and tax breaks to invest in certain technologies, or to not relocate operations. Increasingly companies are discovering that they are in a position to exact better terms from the government for doing business in that jurisdiction. As a result, state and local governments find themselves in bidding wars to attract and keep corporations.

Q 425. How much corporate welfare does the federal government give?

A On the spending side, it is estimated that the federal government puts out between $60 to $70 billion annually on programs that provide subsidies to businesses. In 1997 the libertarian Cato Institute identified the top 55 most serious examples of corporate welfare as totaling $38.2 billion. A more complete list identified by the Cato Institute identified a total of $87.3 billion in business subsidies in 129 programs. Of that amount, $17.6 billion came from the Agriculture Department ($9.8 billion from the Commodity Credit Corporation fund—farm subsidies), $13.6 billion from the Transportation Department ($8.7 billion from the Federal Aviation Administration), and $13.5 billion from the Defense Department (much of it from procurement of various weapons systems including $1.8 billion for the B-2 bomber).

Q 426. What else can be considered corporate welfare?

A Corporate welfare also comes in the form of tax breaks. But to get the tax breaks, firms have to do more of the government's bidding, and the incentives become harder to label as "welfare." Tax breaks are therefore usually not included in estimates of corporate welfare.

Q **427. Is there more corporate or social welfare?**

A In terms of pure spending, there is probably substantially more social welfare than corporate welfare. Social welfare well exceeds $200 billion annually. Opponents of corporate welfare estimate that corporate welfare is close to $87 billion. If the tax breaks for corporate activities that are unnecessary are added, then it is possible that corporate welfare might be comparable to, or even exceed, social welfare. An estimate of the tax side of corporate welfare is needed to answer the question definitively.

(See 483 What are the government's major antipoverty programs?)

Q **428. Is there any change on the horizon for corporate welfare?**

A There is no great change looming for corporate welfare. In 1995, Congress went on the attack and reduced corporate welfare by about 15 percent. The zeal of this attack subsided, although the president and Congress pledged to continue fighting corporate welfare.

SOCIAL AND ENVIRONMENTAL ISSUES

HEALTH CARE COSTS, REFORM PROPOSALS, AND MEDICARE

National health care expenditures, at more than $1 trillion annually, account for nearly one-seventh of the total GDP. This makes health care one of the largest sectors in the U.S. economy, third in size behind the food and housing sectors. Governmental policies that affect how health care is provided and distributed and that restructure the relationships between providers, patients, and insurers naturally qualify as a high-priority economic issue.

Q **429. How much do Americans spend on health care annually?**

A For decades, U.S. expenditures on health care have been growing faster than GDP, and, therefore, have been growing as a percent of GDP. In 1960, total national health expenditures were $26.9 billion ($127.1 billion adjusted for inflation using 1992 dollars), or about 5.1 percent of GDP. By 1997, that share had grown to $1,084.4 billion ($947.3 billion inflation-adjusted) or 13.5 percent.

Q **430. What are the major areas of health care spending?**

A The following table lists how much was spent in various health areas in 1997 along with the percentage of the total:

Category	Amount ($ billions)	Percentage
Hospital care	$371.1	34.0%
Physicians' services	217.6	19.9
Nursing home care	82.8	7.6
Prescription drugs	59.4	6.3
Dental services	50.6	4.6
Program administration and net cost of private insurance	50.0	4.6
Government public health activities	38.5	3.5
Research	18.0	1.6
Construction	16.9	1.5
Medical equipment (durable)	13.9	1.3
Other	173.6	15.0
Total	$1,092.4	100.0

Source: Health Care Financing Administration.

Q 431. How have total national health care expenditures grown during the previous decades?

A From 1960 to 1998, the average annual growth rate for health care expenditures was 5.4 percent (adjusted for inflation). The following table breaks down the annual growth rate by decade:

1960–1969	7.4%
1969–1979	5.2%
1979–1989	5.3%
1989–1998	3.7%

Q 432. How have expenditures on hospital care grown during the previous decades?

A From 1960 to 1998, the average annual growth rate for hospital care expenditures was 5.3 percent (adjusted for inflation), about the same rate of growth as all health care expenditures. The following table breaks down the annual growth rate by decade:

1960–1969	8.2%
1969–1979	6.1%
1979–1989	4.3%
1989–1998	2.6%

Q 433. How have expenditures on physicians' services grown during the previous decades?

A From 1960 to 1998, the average annual growth rate for expenditures on physicians' services was 5.3 percent (adjusted for inflation), again, about the same growth rate as overall health care expenditures. The following table breaks down that annual growth rate by decade:

1960–1969	6.8%
1969–1979	4.9%
1979–1989	6.8%
1989–1998	2.8%

Q 434. How have expenditures on dental services grown during the previous decades?

A From 1960 to 1998, the average annual growth rate for expenditures on dental services was 4.2 percent (adjusted for inflation). The following table breaks down that annual growth rate by decade:

1960–1969	6.0%
1969–1979	3.7%
1979–1989	3.7%
1989–1998	3.6%

Q 435. How have expenditures on prescription drugs grown during the previous decades?

A From 1960 to 1998, the average annual growth rate for expenditures on prescription drugs was 4.3 percent (adjusted for inflation). The following table breaks down that annual growth rate by decade:

1960–1969	4.9%
1969–1979	0.5%
1979–1989	5.8%
1989–1998	6.0%

Q 436. How have expenditures on nursing home care grown during the previous decades?

A From 1960 to 1998, the average annual growth rate for expenditures on nursing home care was 7.7 percent (adjusted for inflation), making it the fastest growing category of health care costs. The following table breaks down that annual growth rate by decade:

1960–1969	13.6%
1969–1979	7.7%
1979–1989	5.4%
1989–1998	4.3%

Q **437. How have expenditures on medical equipment grown during the previous decades?**

A From 1960 to 1998, the average annual growth rate for expenditures on medical equipment was 3.7 percent (adjusted for inflation), making it the slowest growing category of health care expenses. The following table breaks down that annual growth rate by decade:

1960–1969	6.3%
1969–1979	2.3%
1979–1989	4.6%
1989–1998	1.4%

Q **438. Has the expansion of health maintenance organizations affected growth in health care costs?**

A There has been at least a temporary leveling off in the growth of health care expenditures in the 1990s that has coincided with an increase enrollment in health maintenance organizations (HMOs) from 13.4 percent of the population in 1990 to 25.2 percent in 1997. During the 1970s and 1980s, the growth of national health expenditures grew at 5.3 percent. This rate of growth continued until 1992, then dropped for four straight years to only 1.4 percent in 1996. The growth edged back up to 2.4 percent in 1997 and 4.1 percent in 1998. During the 1990s, the growth in real health expenditures averaged 3.7 percent compared with 5.4 percent from 1960 to 1998.

Q **439. How has the government's share of health expenditures changed since the 1960s?**

A The government's share of health care spending rose from one out of four dollars spent in 1961 to one out of every two spent in 1998. The following table shows percentages of government health care expenditures of total health expenditures for selected years:

	Total health care spending ($ billions)	Government health care spending ($ billions)	Government's share of total (percentage)
1960	$26.9	$6.6	24.8%
1970	73.2	27.7	37.8

	Total health care spending ($ billions)	Government health care spending ($ billions)	Government's share of total (percentage)
1981	$ 247.3	$104.8	42.4%
1990	699.5	284.4	40.7
1998	1,146.8	540.4	47.1

Source: Health Care Financing Administration.

Q 440. What were the major elements of President Clinton's "Health Security Act" of 1993?

A There were four major elements of President Clinton's health care reform plan: (1) community rating of premiums; (2) competition within a budget; (3) employer mandates; and (4) universal coverage. Under his plan, the cost of coverage would have been paid mainly by companies with the government subsidizing coverage for the unemployed or those who worked for small firms. Private insurance companies would sell coverage as before, except for three things: (1) companies would have to assemble a list of standard benefits; (2) they would have to offer this set of benefits to everyone at the same price; and (3) the annual increase in insurance premiums would be limited by the federal government. The third item is what President Clinton referred to as competition "within a budget." The plans that insurers would offer could include several options, including fee for service plans that allowed customers to go to the doctor of their choice.

Q 441. What is community rating of premiums?

A "Community rating of premiums" means that everyone is charged the same premium regardless of health status. Premiums do not reflect individuals' particular health risks.

Q 442. How would the proposed system have been financed?

A According to the Clinton administration, the additional federal costs of the proposed system would have been financed from the following sources: (1) reducing the growth in Medicare expenditures; (2) folding the acute care portion of Medicaid into the overall health care system; (3) folding federal workers into the overall health care system; (4) reducing the rate of growth of health insurance costs, which are a tax-free benefit, thus freeing money (from employers) to provide additional taxable wages; and (5) setting higher "sin" taxes. (It was never specified which products would have been taxed or by how much.)

Q 443. What other health care reform plans were debated in 1993 and 1994?

A During the national debate on health care, several other health care reform plans were proposed:

• **"Single payer" plan:** the government would make all medical payments financed through a medical tax that would replace current insurance payments (a Canadian-style system supported by some Democrats in Congress.).

• **New tax breaks:** employees would receive tax breaks to purchase insurance (favored by Republicans in Congress).

• **Medical savings accounts:** employees would set up tax-free accounts to pay medical bills (favored by Republicans in Congress).

• **"Play-or-pay" plan:** companies would be required either to buy health insurance for their workers, or pay into a public fund that would insure workers not covered by their companies. People not working would not be insured (supported by many Democrats).

Q 444. How do medical savings accounts work?

A For medical savings accounts, employers would make annual deposits into accounts out of which employees would pay medical bills. Employees would keep whatever money they did not spend. Depending on how these accounts are set up, deposits are tax free and unspent funds increase free of taxes over an individual's lifetime. Individuals exercise the cost-control function, because they decide when and where to purchase medical services.

Q 445. What is COBRA?

A COBRA stands for the Consolidated Budget Reconciliation Act that Congress passed in 1985. COBRA permits individuals leaving a company of 20 or more employees to retain their health insurance for up to 18 months by paying 102 percent of the premium that their employer had been paying. COBRA was the basis for portability of health insurance until the 1996 Health Act.

(See 447 What is the Health Insurance Portability and Accountability Act of 1996?)

Q **446. What happened to President Clinton's "Health Security Act"?**

A Political support waned for the bill, and prior to the 1994 elections the bill was abandoned without being brought to a vote in Congress.

(See 206 Why did President Clinton's health care plan of 1993 fail?)

Q **447. What are the provisions of the Health Insurance Portability and Accountability Act of 1996?**

A The Health Insurance Portability and Accountability Act of 1996 prevents the loss of health insurance resulting from job changes, guarantees health insurance access, and guarantees health insurance renewability. On an experimental basis, the act allowed medical savings accounts. The act also contains severe penalties for defrauding health care benefit programs or making false representations in connection with delivery of health care services. Some opponents of these provisions voiced concern that authorizations for medical treatment that were later deemed unnecessary by government reviewers could be the basis for criminal prosecution of physicians. Another provision, the health information system, empowers the government to collect detailed information on medical records of individuals to establish a national database.

Q **448. What are the major government health programs?**

A Medicare and Medicaid are the major national health and medical insurance programs. Medicare, which spends about $200 billion annually, covers the aged and disabled who are insured under the Social Security program. Medicaid, which spends more than $100 billion in federal money alone, covers eligible persons with limited financial resources. The Medicaid program is funded jointly by the federal government and the states but it is administered solely by the states. Medicaid's outlays are more than $165 billion per year for both federal and state portions.

Q **449. What agency manages the federal health programs?**

A The Health Care Financing Administration (HCFA), a division of the Health and Human Services Department, manages both Medicare and Medicaid. HCFA also administers the Child Health Insurance program. More than 74 million Americans are covered by the three health programs.

Q 450. What are the two parts of Medicare?

A Medicare consists of Hospital Insurance (HI-Part A) and Supplementary Medical Insurance (SMI-Part B). HI covers hospital, nursing home, home health, and hospice care. SMI helps pay for physician, outpatient, and home health care.

Q 451. When did Medicare and Medicaid start?

A Title XVIII of the Social Security Act, entitled "Health Insurance for the Aged and Disabled," authorizing the Medicare program, became law on July 30, 1965, during President Lyndon Johnson's administration. Medicare was tied to popular Social Security amendments that included a substantial benefits increase, which helped win congressional votes for its passage. Medicaid was also passed in 1965 as Title XIX of the Social Security Act.

Q 452. How big are Medicare and Medicaid?

A In 1999 Medicare paid out $190 billion in benefits, or 11 percent of all federal outlays. There were 147 million U.S. workers (96% of employed workers) who contributed to the program via payroll taxes. There were 39 million Medicare beneficiaries (14 percent of the U.S. population). Medicaid paid out $165 billion in benefits or 9 percent of all federal outlays. There were 36 million Medicaid beneficiaries (13% of the population).

Q 453. What is the Medicare trust fund?

A The Medicare trust fund operates similarly to the Social Security trust fund but is administered by the Health Care Financing Administration. The Medicare trust fund also consists of two separate funds corresponding to its two main programs: the Hospital Insurance Fund (HIF), the larger of the two, and the Supplementary Medical Fund (SMF).

(See 450 What are the two parts of Medicare?)

Q 454. How is Medicare funded?

A The Medicare-HIF is funded out of payroll taxes, while the Medicare-SMF is funded out of premiums paid by beneficiaries and contributions from the federal government. The tax rate for Medicare-HIF for both employers and employees has remained at 1.45 percent (or a combined total of 2.9 percent) since 1986. The amount of income that can be taxed for Medicare-HIF, unlike that for Social Security, has no ceiling. Medicare and Social Security taxes combined total 7.65 percent each for the employer and employee (or a combined total of 15.3 percent). A self-employed person pays both the employer and employee shares. SMI is funded by general federal revenues, and the premiums paid by participants. The latter accounts for 25 percent of program costs.

Q 455. How is the HI trust fund holding up?

A Not very well, in fact it is in much deeper trouble than the Social Security trust fund. The Medicare trustees expect the HIF trust fund to be exhausted by 2008 (based on a 1998 forecast). The trustees also estimate the average 75-year (a time horizon that actuaries use) deficit to be 39 percent of program costs. The HIF trust fund is already being drawn down (annual outlays exceed annual income), meaning that some non-payroll taxation is already devoted to redemption of government securities held in the trust fund's portfolio.

Q 456. What can be done to keep the Medicare trust fund solvent?

A The Medicare trust fund could be stabilized by either cutting benefits, increasing payroll taxes, or devising new and clever ways to deliver health care services more cheaply. Fixing the Medicare trust fund is a politically divisive issue whose fundamental solution has been put off, no doubt increasing the cost of remedying the imbalance between revenues and expenditures in the future.

Q 457. What are the projected health care expenditures to the year 2007?

A The HCFA projects federal health care spending to accelerate again, and to double to $2.1 trillion by 2007, a 6.8 percent annual increase from 1997 to 2007.

THE ECONOMY AND ENVIRONMENTAL PROTECTION

The economy and the environment are deeply intertwined. Natural resources constitute much of the wealth of the United States, and are one reason why the nation became a world power. However, the exploitation of these resources by a growing human population has significant negative impacts on the environment. Government regulation is needed to complement the free market system to protect the environment. Without regulation, society as a whole, and not the actual polluter, would pay the cost for the prevention and/or remedy of environmental degradation or, as economists say, "externalities."

For example, pollution from a lead smelter damages health and "costs" the community, but it is not a direct cost to the smelter as labor or raw materials are. Since pollution without regulation would be "cost-free," producers would have no incentive to control the pollution. The challenge to policymakers is to reduce the negative effect on the environment of population and economic development without strangling the economy. How should economists evaluate the cost of environmental controls, as well as their benefits, in terms of achieving sustainable resource exploitation as well as taking into account benefits like better health and a higher quality of life?

Q 458. What are the types of environmental protection?

A Environmental protection encompasses a wide range of actions including "end of pipe" pollution removal by industry, pollution prevention, treatment of municipal wastewater and drinking water, disposal of municipal garbage, cleanup of contaminated sites, and control of "non-point source" pollution. Pollution is often categorized by the media (air, water, or solid waste), or the source of the pollution. A "point source" refers to a single, identifiable source of pollution, like the smokestack of a factory. A "mobile source" refers to pollution from vehicles. "Non-point source" refers to ubiquitous pollution that cannot be traced back to a single source. Different types of pollution are often connected. For example, exhausts from automobiles (air pollution) that settle on land become non-point source water pollution when rainwater washes it off into surface water.

Q 459. What is the cost of environmental protection?

A Estimating the cost of environmental protection is very complex and includes the cost of government expenditures, private sector compliance, legal expenses, and financial impacts on economic production. There is no single information source that compiles all of these costs. Direct compliance costs for pollution abatement (that is, the cost of capital equipment and labor needed to comply with environmental regulations) are the easiest costs to measure. The difficulty of estimating even these costs is reflected by the wide range of values from different sources. For example, during debate of the Clean Air Act Amendments in 1990, the Bush administration estimated that the annual costs of the proposal in the first decade of the twenty-first century would be $25 billion. An industry-sponsored estimate concluded that the cost would be closer to $100 billion.

Cost of Pollution Abatement and Control ($ millions of real dollars)

	1972	1982	1992	1994
Pollution abatement				
Business	$34,586	$42,776	$ 65,925	$ 72,157
Government	10,653	15,757	26,639	29,606
Personal consumption	4,180	9,649	7,897	9,204
Regulation and monitoring	1,161	1,897	2,604	2,168
Research and development	2,743	2,295	1,561	1,927
Total	$52,813	$72,191	$104,626	$115,133

Sources: Bureau of Economic Analysis; Bureau of the Census.

Figure 29   Cost of Pollution Control, 1972–1994

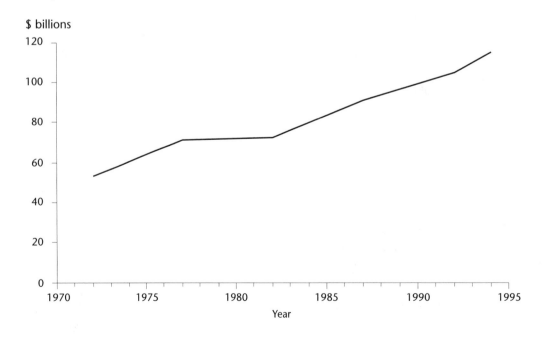

Until 1994, when budget cuts ended the collection of cost data, the Census Bureau (CB) was the best source of information for the cost of pollution control. The CB estimated that direct compliance costs for controlling pollution in 1994 were $115 billion. Ninety-five percent of the cost was direct spending on pollution abatement, that is, the direct reduction of pollutant releases (preventing the generation of pollution, recycling, or treating pollution). Other costs in the CB figure were for regulation and monitoring by the government (2 percent), and research and development by government and industry (2 percent).

In 1990, the Environmental Protection Agency (EPA) compiled perhaps the most comprehensive report on the cost of pollution control ever, *The Cost of Clean*, and estimated that by the late 1990s, the annual cost of environmental protection in the United States would be more than $150 billion. This estimate is larger than CB numbers because EPA annualized investment outlays (with a 7 percent discount rate) instead of simply reporting the annual expenditures like the CB. EPA also included additional programs, such as drinking water, pesticides regulation, non-point source control, and Superfund.

The Office of Management and Budget (OMB) estimated that in 1997, regulatory compliance with environmental regulations would cost $144 billion. The report noted that this figure may overstate the cost because of the rising baseline for comparison. This means that if all regulations disappeared today, few companies would stop controlling substances like asbestos, lead dust, or benzene, for fear of unleashing a spate of lawsuits. OMB concluded that if the amount spent on pollution control likely to continue without regulations was not counted, then the 1997 cost of environmental regulation would fall to $93 billion. On the other hand, OMB's cost excludes the indirect costs of pollution control, such as the decreased productivity of industry.

(See 467 Are there other noneconomic approaches to regulation? 470 What are the trends in the cost of pollution control?)

Q 460. How much of the U.S. GDP is spent on pollution control?

A According to the Census Bureau, from the mid-1970s to 1994, the United States consistently spent between 1.7 to 1.8 percent of the GDP on pollution control. EPA estimates that in 1972, when new major environmental regulations were first implemented, pollution control cost 1.5 percent of GDP. According to EPA estimates for the late 1990s, the cost of pollution control is closer to 2 percent of GDP. Thus, there has been a modestly increasing trend of spending on pollution control.

461. What is the economic cost of global climate change in the United States?

A Climate change refers to the warming of earth's climate caused by an increase in greenhouse gases (that retain heat in the earth's atmosphere). Since the issue made headlines in the late 1980s there has been considerable controversy about the degree of change (or if there is any change), the effects of change, and whether change can be attributed to humans.

The cost of climate change to the economy can be estimated only under strong assumptions that drastically simplify reality. Qualitatively, economic costs from a warming climate could include extreme weather (more frequent and extreme floods, storms, tornadoes, droughts), health effects (heat-related deaths, increased smog, and changes in the spread and pattern of infectious disease), agriculture changes (altered growing seasons, water availability, pests), rise in sea level (projected increase ranging from 6 to 37 inches causing coastal flooding and inundation of coastal areas), water availability (changes to the water cycle), and ecosystem damage (shifts of growing zones, loss of species). Some impacts, like faster crop growth or farming in areas that are currently not suitable for agriculture, may even be economically beneficial.

Because of the unknowns involved, estimating a meaningful cost associated with a warmer climate is very difficult. The Intergovernmental Panel on Climate Change (IPCC)—a panel of 2,000 climate scientists from around the world—estimates that the total annual damage may be from 1 to 1.5 percent of GDP for industrial economies, such as the United States, with substantially higher costs for some countries such as island nations that are more open to flooding from the rise in sea level.

The benefits of avoiding potential environmental damage from global warming need to be weighed against the cost of reducing greenhouse gases to slow future warming. Estimates for this cost vary tremendously and extremes are often along industry and environmentalist advocate lines. In 1997, the United States agreed to the Kyoto Protocol, an international agreement struck by 159 nations in Kyoto, Japan. Under the Protocol, the United States must reduce emissions by seven percent under 1990 levels over a five-year period. (U.S. ratification of the treaty must have Senate approval and the treaty must have at least 55 countries sign to enter into force.) The Clinton administration estimates that compliance with Kyoto will add $70 to $110 to an average family's annual energy bill by 2010.

Estimates are only as accurate as the assumptions are realistic and no one really knows the impact that complying with Kyoto will have on the U.S. economy. One study by the World Resources Institute found, depending on the economic assumptions, that the economic effect of reducing greenhouse gases in the United States could range from a nine-percent decrease in GDP to a two-percent increase. Some of the major variables affecting the estimates are: the extent of substitution among energy sources, improvement in energy efficiency, rate of technological innovation, availability and cost of nonfossil energy sources, international cooperation, the approach used to decrease emissions including treatment of carbon tax revenues, and the economic benefits of reduced fossil fuel emissions. Resources for the Future economists estimate that the economic benefits of pollution reduction, primarily related to health, would offset around 30 percent of the cost of reduction.

Q 462. What are the major environmental statutes and when were they enacted?

A Major environmental statutes during the previous decades include the following (most of which have undergone significant amendment since the original enactment):

Rivers and Harbors Act	1899
Federal Insecticide, Fungicide, and Rodenticide Act (FIFRA)	1947
National Historic Preservation Act (NHPA)	1966
Clean Air Act (CAA)	1963
National Environmental Policy Act (NEPA)	1970
Clean Water Act (CWA)	1972
Ocean Dumping Act	1972
Marine Mammal Protection Act	1972
Coastal Zone Management Act (CZMA)	1972
Endangered Species Act	1973
Safe Drinking Water Act (SDWA)	1974
Toxic Substances Control Act (TSCA)	1976
Resource Conservation and Recovery Act (RCRA)	1976
Federal Land Policy and Management Act (FLPMA)	1976
Surface Mining Control and Reclamation Act (SMCRA)	1977
Comprehensive Environmental Response, Compensation, and Liability Act (CERCLA or Superfund)	1980
Emergency Planning and Community Right-to-Know Act (EPCRA)—amendment to CERCLA	1986
Pollution Prevention Act (PPA)	1990
Oil Pollution Act (OPA)	1990

Q **463. What are the major government agencies concerned with the environment?**

A The major government agency responsible for the control of pollution is the Environmental Protection Agency (EPA). This agency was created in 1970 by combining existing programs that were scattered in six different agencies. Other federal agencies involved in environmental programs include the Department of Energy (clean up of contaminated nuclear weapons manufacturing sites), the Department of Agriculture (non-point source control), the Army Corps of Engineers (wetlands), Department of Health and Human Services, the National Aeronautics and Space Administration, the Department of the Interior (Endangered Species Act, public lands), the Department of Commerce, and the Executive Office of the President (Council on Environmental Quality, the Office of Management and Budget, and the Office of Science and Technology Policy). State pollution control agencies have major responsibility for the implementation of federal environmental statutes.

Q **464. How much pollution is acceptable?**

A From a regulatory standpoint, the answer to what is allowable depends on the specific law. Some of the major environmental laws allow no pollution at all. One goal of the 1972 Clean Water Act Amendments was the end of all discharges. Other laws, like the 1970 Clean Air Act Amendments, set very stringent limits based on health effects. While zero pollution is a laudable goal, it is not always realistic, given current technological, economic, and social constraints. The cost for zero emissions may be astronomical and even physically impossible to achieve.

What level of pollution allows a sustainable use of resources and a healthy quality of life? A realistic, frequently used approach is to balance the risk associated with pollution, or the benefits of control, against the cost. The goal is to achieve the greatest good for the lowest price. Some environmental laws, like FIFRA and TSCA, require this approach. In addition, presidential executive orders have periodically required the analysis of costs and benefits in the development of regulations. According to a study by the think tank, Resources for the Future, the EPA appears to have been informally weighing costs and benefits when setting pollution limits, regardless of the direction given by the legislation.

Cost-benefit analysis is the methodology used to determine the point at which the marginal cost of more pollution abatement equals the marginal benefits of the environmental improvement (where spending more on controlling pollution does not result in a significant improvement of the environment). This methodology is often criticized for scientific uncertainties, data limitations, and disagreements about techniques.

One requirement of cost-benefit analysis is that the data must be converted to a common unit, dollars. However, many feel that cost-benefit analysis that uses dollar units is inadequate to value such things as the continued existence of a species of animal or plant, or clear sunsets at the Grand Canyon.

A related tool for setting environmental protection goals is risk assessment, which is the estimation of the probability of some harm occurring. Risk assessment is a broad approach that is based on multiple sciences (toxicology, biology, chemistry, and statistics), utilizes different methodologies (from the lab to the field), and is used to assess different types of risks: short-term health risks such as food poisoning, long-term risks like cancer, and even the ecological risk from global warming. One weakness of risk assessment is that, unlike cost-benefit analysis, it does not provide a decision rule, that is, clear criteria that dictate one decision or another. In cost-benefit analysis, an action is not carried out if costs exceed benefits. Another weakness of risk assessment is that it is not really a science, but was developed as a policy instrument. The combination of science with assumptions (how much dirt would a child playing at a toxic waste site eat) results in a controversial method that is faulted both by industry for exaggerating risk and by environmental advocates for underestimating risk.

Q 465. What are "command and control" regulations?

A In "command and control," such as employed by the EPA, regulators specify detailed rules, backed by public hearings and court review, that industry must comply with or face penalties. Command and control can include permits with set limits on releases, required reports, and mandating the use of specific technology. Command and control is criticized for being inflexible and thus not always controlling pollution as well or in the most economically effective way.

Q 466. Are there other economic approaches to regulation?

A Yes, increasingly regulators try to use incentives or market-based mechanisms to achieve results. The theory is that the "market" can achieve the greatest reduction of pollution for the lowest cost. Tradable emissions permits are the primary market tool that has been used to date. This approach has been successful under certain conditions in certain industries.

Tradable sulfur dioxide permits are an example of a successful market-based approach. In 1990, under the Clean Air Act, electricity generators were allowed to trade the permits that were required for each ton of sulfur dioxide that was emitted. Thus, a plant with high compliance costs could purchase permits from a firm with lower costs and release more sulfur dioxide. Since the increased emissions from the high-cost plant are balanced by fewer emissions from the lower-cost firm, the overall goals are achieved. Under this program, acid rain deposition has been reduced by 50 percent.

The EPA is currently piloting permit trading for the discharge of wastewater and estimates that the potential cost savings may range from $611 million up to $5.6 billion. Several demonstration projects using effluent trading are under way, but the approach has not yet been widely implemented.

Permit trading works for pollution affecting a regional or global area, but not for pollution that stays in a small area, like the hazardous air pollutant benzene, which creates local "hot spots" and significant local problems. The approach is also limited to a system that can be monitored for a reasonable cost.

Q 467. Are there other noneconomic approaches to regulation?

A Yes, liability law, which is often used in conjunction with command and control, is the other basic form of regulation used to control pollution. Liability-based laws make a polluter financially responsible for the social cost of pollution. For example, the Superfund law requires companies to pay for the cleanup of hazardous waste sites. Superfund has been criticized as an overly bureaucratic program whose cleanups have been slow and expensive. This reputation may be more the result of legal aspects such as poorly defined cleanup objectives than its liability scheme. The organization Resources for the Future estimates that changing the responsibility for cleanups from responsible parties to the public sector would increase the total cost of site cleanup by $3.4 billion annually. The liability approach can be more flexible and cost effective than command and control because firms make their own decisions on how to reduce pollution. Such a law can also make companies reduce pollution to avoid future liability. The weaknesses in this approach are that the law only applies after the pollution has been released and fails completely if the company is bankrupt or does not have the money to comply. An alternate approach is financial responsibility which requires potentially polluting businesses such as landfills to demonstrate sufficient resources to pay for environmental damages.

Q 468. Would environmental taxes help curb pollution?

A From time to time the idea of taxing pollution is put forth as a control strategy. Such a tax might correct the "market failure" that occurs when pollution that damages public resources is paid for by society rather than the individual polluter. When a fac-

Figure 30   Share of Pollution Control Spending by Sector

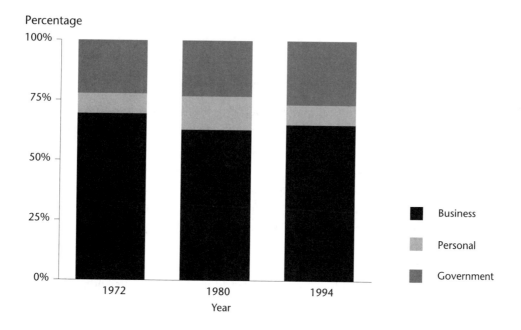

Source: U.S. Commerce Department, Bureau of Economic Analysis.

tory pollutes or individuals drive vehicles with excessive exhausts, the community pays the cost of damage to the environment. Without imposing a direct cost for the activity, there is little incentive to minimize the pollution. Thus the market fails to put a "price" on the pollution or the use of the environmental resource, such as clean air and water. A tax would make the polluter pay. However, such taxes are currently very unpopular with targeted groups, and politically unfeasible.

Q 469. Who pays for pollution control?

A According to the Census Bureau figures, business pays the majority (65 percent) of pollution abatement costs. Federal, state, and local government spending for pollution control (27 percent) includes the cost of wastewater treatment, construction of wastewater treatment plants and sewer systems, and solid waste disposal. The cost of pollution control for individuals (8 percent) was estimated for the cost of motor vehicle emission devices such as the catalytic converter (that increase the price of automobiles and decrease mileage). See Figure 30.

Legislation can alter who pays for pollution control. For example, the Clean Water Act changed the allocation of spending between federal and local governments on the construction and upgrading of municipal wastewater treatment plants. In the early 1970s, federal and state governments contributed 80 percent of the funds for the protection of water, but, by the mid-1990s, local governments were paying 90 percent of the cost.

Q **470. What are the trends in the cost of pollution control?**

A Generally, the trend in pollution control spending has been close to that of average GDP growth. Pollution control spending increased by an average annual real rate of 3.6 percent from 1972 to 1994. Spending remained between 1.7 and 1.8 percent of GDP from the mid-1970s to 1994.

Costs for air, water, and solid waste pollution control have different growth rates. For example, the cost of air pollution control increased faster than other pollution control expenditures from 1972 to 1980 because of new requirements for vehicle emission control devices. But after 1980, spending for air pollution control grew more slowly. The area that has grown the fastest is the cost of the disposal of solid waste. Spending trends could change significantly in the future depending on what laws that are passed.

Average Annual Rates of Change for Pollution Abatement and Control Spending

	1972–1994	1972–1980	1980–1994
Pollution abatement and control	3.6%	4.5%	3.1%
By type			
Air	2.7	5.0	1.5
Water	2.6	4.1	1.7
Solid waste	6.3	4.7	7.2
Other/unallocated	-6.8	2.9	-12.0

Note: "Other" includes nonmanufacturing business and government spending for abatement and control of noise, radiation, and pesticide pollution.

Q **471. Are there other business costs associated with pollution control?**

A Yes, there are also indirect costs associated with spending on the environment. When businesses spend money on pollution control, they have less to spend elsewhere, such as for producing more products. Thus, spending money on environmental protection can cause higher prices and reduced production. While there is agreement that indirect costs exist, there is no consensus on the magnitude of the costs. The Census Bureau estimated that spending on pollution control reduces production by 3.2 percent for oil refineries, 5.3 percent for paper mills, and 7.6 percent for steel mills. (These industries all have greater pollution abatement costs than manufacturing in general.) Some researchers estimate that for every dollar spent by a company on environmental protection, there is an indirect increase of total production costs of $12. But other economists believe that such studies overstate the actual economic cost of pollution control and find that $1 spent on pollution abatement raises total production costs by less than $1.

Q **472. What other costs are associated with protecting the environment?**

A The cost of other elements of environmental protection are even more difficult to measure than the cost of pollution control and there are no recent comprehensive estimates. Besides direct costs there are opportunity costs, such as reduced economic rents, altered development plans, lost wages, and lower agricultural production. The Endangered Species Act is a controversial law and estimates of costs associated with species protection range from several thousand to billions of dollars. Federal and state agencies spent approximately $26.4 million to protect the Northern Spotted Owl between 1989 and 1991. According to the Bonneville Power Administration, in 1994, salmon conservation cost the company $300 million in lost power revenues (about one percent of 1994 revenues). Loss of economic benefits of this magnitude might be expected to impact the states where the endangered species live but no such correlation has been found.

Other costs may not be routinely included with estimates of environmental protection because they are not covered under the regulatory umbrella. For example, the United States spends anywhere from hundreds of millions to billions of dollars each year fighting introduced or exotic species of bugs, animals, and plants. Nonnative species, whether introduced on purpose, such as the Australian pine that was imported for roadside planting in Florida, or accidentally, like the Eurasian zebra mussels that clog pipes in cooling systems, can devastate farms and forests, block waterways, foul lakes and ponds, impair human health, and destroy native species. It is estimated that every year about a fourth of the U.S. agricultural GDP is lost to foreign plant pests and related control costs. For example, more than $50 billion has been spent on the boll weevil since it arrived from Mexico in the 1890s, $110 million was spent controlling leafy spurge in 1990, and every year it costs $100 million to keep waterways clear of Sri Lankan hydrilla and the Central American water hyacinth.

Q 473. What are the economic benefits of environmental protection?

A One of the more comprehensive efforts to quantifying the benefits from environmental protection is a 1991 paper published in the *Yale Journal on Regulation* by Robert Hahn and John Hird. According to the paper, in 1988, the cost of environmental regulation ranged from $55.7 to $77.6 billion, but the value of benefits was $16.5 to $135.8 billion, with a best-guess estimate of $58.4 billion. EPA has calculated that the health benefits of the Clean Air Act from 1970–1990 were $22.2 trillion, compared with compliance expenditures during the twenty-year period of $0.5 trillion. Thus, the EPA estimates that the United States received $45 in health benefits for each $1 spent to control pollution.

There are also unexpected benefits of environmental protection. One study of home prices found higher values for the homes in counties with greater regulation of suspended particulates and therefore, improved air quality. For each one-unit reduction in suspended particulates, home values were higher by 0.7 to 1.5 percent. Nonpoint source pollution control measures may also add to home prices.

The National Association of Home Builders estimates that the value of homes close to water increases up to 28 percent. When runoff is controlled by a permanent wet pond or constructed wetland that looks like a natural system or is used for recreation (walking trails, picnic areas, boating), surrounding property values increase. In a Salt Lake City subdivision of single-family homes, lots that surrounded a constructed wetland sold for up to 30 percent more than lots with no water view. Waterside lots in a Wichita, Kansas development near a wetland (that was enhanced instead of filled as originally planned) sold for premiums of up to 150 percent.

Q 474. What are the general benefits of environmental regulation?

A The primary benefits of environmental regulation include protecting the health of individuals; maintaining healthy and productive ecosystems, such as wetlands, lakes, and rivers as well as farm land; protecting the durability of buildings and other materials; and sustaining aesthetic beauty. Maybe the best way to measure benefits is to look at what happens without regulation. Countries in central and eastern Europe, where for many years the enforcement of environmental regulations was virtually nonexistent, provide a model. A 1995 World Bank study found ample evidence of health problems associated with pollution that included increased newborn mortality rates from respiratory causes (five to eight times higher in more polluted areas); reduced IQ in children; chronic bronchitis rates three times higher than less polluted areas; stunted development in children including decreased height, weight, and chest expansion; increased death from asthma; and higher rates of cancer, including lung and stomach cancer. (For example, in one village, stomach cancer death rates were 65 percent higher in a village with high rates of nitrate in the drinking water.)

Q 475. Has all this spending on pollution control worked?

A The short answer is yes, the air and water in the United States are cleaner. (A river has not caught fire since 1969, when the industrial waste in Cleveland's Cuyahoga River burned for 20 minutes.) Since 1970, emissions of most major air pollutants have decreased (at the same time U.S. population increased 31 percent and the GDP grew 114 percent). Acid rain is also less of a problem. In 1996, the sulfate level in rainfall (which indicates acidity) was 10 to 25 percent less that it would have been had the trend from 1983 to 1994 continued.

Water quality has also improved since the Clean Water Act was enacted in 1972. Two-thirds of surveyed waters are safe for fishing and swimming, compared to one third in the early 1970s; topsoil loss due to runoff has been reduced by one billion tons annually; and the rate of wetlands losses slowed from 460,000 acres annually during the mid-1950s to the mid-1970s, to 70,000 to 90,000 acres between 1982 and 1992 on nonfederal land.

Major Air Pollutants—Emission Trends, 1970–1995

Carbon monoxide	-28%
Lead	-98
Particulate matter	-79
Sulfur dioxide	-41
Nitrogen oxides	+ 6
Volatile organic compounds	-25

Source: U.S. Environmental Protection Agency.

But pollution control can only go so far. Despite the gains of the previous twenty years, serious problems remain. Although water quality is better today, the EPA found in 1998 that more than 350 beaches (out of 1,403 surveyed) issued an advisory or were closed because of contaminated water and 40 percent of waters that were surveyed in 1996 were too polluted for swimming and fishing. Air pollution, too, remains a problem in many areas. In 1997, at least 107 million people lived in areas with unhealthy air and the Natural Resources Defense Council estimates that particulate air pollution may cause approximately 64,000 premature deaths in the United States from cardiopulmonary disease. The real issues for the future are the underlying causes of pollution: population, technology, land use and lifestyle, and policies affecting areas such as energy, agriculture, and transportation, which must be resolved in order to protect the environment.

One of the difficulties for the future is that easier problems have been addressed, such as the control of point sources like smokestacks, leaving the more difficult ones, like non-point source pollution, to solve. For example, in the Chesapeake Bay watershed, the water quality of the Potomac River has greatly improved and fish no longer suffocate in the summer from lack of oxygen. However, the Chesapeake Bay remains threatened and current improvements are likely to be overwhelmed by pollution, such as runoff and automobile exhaust, caused by agriculture and increased development in the area. Other problems are only now being recognized, like indoor air quality. In the 90 percent of time that Americans are indoors, they are exposed to contaminants like radon, tobacco smoke, biological contaminants (bacteria, molds, viruses), carbon monoxide, formaldehyde (wood products), pesticides, and volatile organic compounds (paint, cleaning products, cosmetics). Often the indoor air has higher concentrations of pollutants than outside air, even in industrial areas. Another recent worry are endocrine disrupters. These chemicals, including some pesticides, disrupt endocrine systems and have the potential to cause problems such as infertility and breast and prostate cancer.

Q **476. What is "sprawl" and what are its negative effects?**

A Sprawl is the land use pattern of low-density development. For example, the population of metro Cleveland declined 11 percent, but used 33 percent more land. The population of the Portland urban region doubled from 1940 to 1970, but four times the amount of land was used. The concern about sprawl is that this pattern of development will undermine environmental improvements made in the last 25 years because of pollution from increased driving, loss of natural areas, and the increase of impervious surfaces. In the 1980s in Oregon, the number of vehicle miles traveled increased eight times faster than the population and in the United States as a whole the number of vehicle miles traveled between 1969 and 1989 increased by 98.4 percent. The increased driving has a significant impact since vehicles are a major cause of air and water pollution.

Aside from environmental problems, low-density development is a heavy cost to local communities. One study found that less dense developments built away from existing infrastructure cost $43,381 per home for streets, utilities, and schools while closer-in development cost $11,597 per home for the same services. Another estimate found that in Eugene, Oregon, there was a $2,000 impact fee for new homes while the actual cost of public infrastructure was more than $20,000 for each house. A number of government policies either directly or indirectly contribute to this pattern of land use including highway construction, mortgage policies, flood plain insurance, property tax systems, tax preferences for employer-provided parking and not for mass transit, and the tax treatment of home sales and mortgage interest.

Q 477. Are there other damaging environmental practices that are subsidized?

A Yes, there are a number of subsidies that support environmentally damaging practices. For example, the price of sugar in the United States is double the world price because of the sugar import control program. The high price subsidizes existing sugar cane plantations that damage the environmentally sensitive Everglades. The tax code also contains a number of exceptions that promote harmful practices. For example, oil and gas producers receive a number of tax preferences that most other businesses do not, including extra write-offs for oil and gas depletion, preferential tax treatment of royalty income, and exemptions from passive loss write-offs. Friends of the Earth (an environmental advocacy group) estimates that over five years these subsidies cost taxpayers over $10 billion. In addition, such preferential treatment makes renewable energy sources like solar and wind even less competitive with fossil fuels.

Q 478. Is there really a trade-off between jobs and the environment?

A Although perhaps counterintuitive, the general consensus among economists is that environmental regulations have not caused significant job loss in this country, nor adversely affected competitiveness as measured by net exports or trade flows. Individual jobs and plants may be affected, but when viewed on an industry-wide basis, few jobs are lost due to increased environmental regulation. According to data from Department of Labor, Bureau of Labor Statistics Bulletins, environmental and safety regulations caused only a fraction of one percent of layoffs between 1987 and 1990. Environmental and safety regulations were the cause of 4 out of 2,546 layoff events in this period. The same figures show that workers were 500 times more likely to be laid off because of seasonal and other work slow-downs and contract completions than because of environmental or safety regulation. There has been a modest negative impact on productivity; however, positive feedback effects from environmental improvements are not counted.

Air quality regulations in the Los Angeles area are some of the most stringent in the nation and heavily regulated oil refineries face high pollution abatement costs. Yet researchers found no evidence of decreased labor demand, plant exit, or plants not moving to the area when Los Angeles area refineries were compared with plants in less regulated areas.

One study that compared environmental spending (used as a proxy for regulation) against employment levels for four heavily regulated industries—pulp and paper, plastics, petroleum, and steel—found that job loss resulting from spending on environmental protection was insignificant. According to the study, there was an average loss of 0.95 jobs for every $1 million in spending on environmental control. If this estimate is applied to all 632,000 jobs lost in the manufacturing sector (all industries) from 1984 to 1994, then environmental spending may have caused the loss of 4,700 jobs or seven-tenths of one percent of all jobs lost. (This calculation is based on an increase of environmental spending during that period as reported by the Department of Commerce of $4.9 billion in 1987 dollars.)

POVERTY AND INCOME AND WEALTH DISTRIBUTION

Most economic questions directly concern production and consumption. But another aspect is the distribution of production and consumption across the population. The main goal of economics is to maximize production and consumption, but economists also grapple with the question of why a percentage of the population is unable to meet its own basic needs. Social scientists search for social and cultural explanations, but the economists' task is to measure distribution and to propose measures to alleviate poverty. These measures include creating more wealth and economic opportunities, as well as ways to distribute the income, wealth, and opportunity that have been generated. Of income and wealth, income is the more immediate concern, because day to day and week to week, families need a minimum level of income to purchase basic needs. Uneven income distribution leads to even more uneven wealth distribution. Because wealth distribution is a cumulative measure and can become skewed much faster than income distribution, economists also monitor the dimensions of wealth distribution.

Q **479. Why is poverty an important economic issue?**

A Poverty is an important issue, because it highlights the conflict between two main economic goals: equity and efficiency. The level of poverty has a heavy impact on fiscal costs and social stability and is an important part of the issue of distribution of income and wealth. The poverty level in society is also important because of the economic production that is lost because people are poor. The government has waged a continuous battle against poverty. The federal government's $200 to $300 billion annual transfer payments to the poor are evidence of the government's priority of addressing poverty. These transfer payments are only the short-term part of the battle to alleviate poverty. The government also carries out a wide variety of programs to attack poverty at its sources by funding programs that address children's health, education and nutrition, job training, and workfare. The arguments that carry the most political weight in the fight against poverty are those based on compassion, fairness, and equity. Other economic arguments, such as the cost of these poverty programs and the loss of production from the nonworking poor, must also be considered.

Given the amount spent on government programs and the economic expansion of the 1990s, one would have expected poverty to decline significantly during that decade. However, poverty remains above the level of 25 years ago. This observation raises questions of the effectiveness of the antipoverty programs, the inclusiveness of the economic expansion of the 1990s, and even the reliability of the measurement of poverty.

(See 79 How does the government define poverty?)

Q 480. Poverty measurement issue no. 1: Should income include noncash benefits?

A The federal government measures the amount of poverty in the United States by estimating the income needed to meet the basic human needs and then counting the number of families whose income is less than that. The issue is whether the exclusion of noncash benefits in the determination of the poverty level yields a misleading estimate of poverty. Whether or not to include noncash benefits depends on whether the aim is to evaluate how many poor people still need to be rescued from poverty after government help. If so, then social program policymakers must determine who, after all poverty alleviating inputs are accounted for, including income and social programs, is still left out. This goal argues for the inclusion of noncash benefits in families' total income. On the other hand, economists find it useful to estimate total poverty without any benefits, cash or noncash. This way, they can estimate the full need for jobs and wage increases for poor and borderline poor labor such that they no longer require economic assistance, cash or noncash.

481. Poverty measurement issue no. 2: Does the poverty threshold take taxes into account?

A An important weakness of the poverty line indicator from both an economic and social point of view is that it is based on pretax income. Thus, tax breaks for the poor are not directly reflected in the poverty line data. Increasing progressivity of the tax structure through lowering the effective rates on the poor, if they pay any taxes in the first place, should also have a poverty-reducing impact, which is not captured by the poverty line indicator. The Census Bureau, which collects the poverty line statistic, also points out that respondents tend to underreport their income. Probably the main reason for underreporting is that many of the programs of which the respondents are beneficiaries are means-tested and the respondents obviously do not want to disqualify themselves.

Q **482. Poverty measurement issue no. 3: Which is more important to measuring poverty, how much cash a person receives, or how much he or she consumes?**

A Economists tend to rely on intermediate indicators like income and production to know what is happening in the economy. But it is final indicators, like consumption, that tell what the ultimate economic benefit really is. In determining whether a person is poor or not, measuring a person's consumption, rather than income, can make a big difference in concluding whether he or she is poor. A person may be poor in terms of income, but not in terms of consumption. The consumption measure has advantages. First, it takes into account the noncash payments by the government to poor people. Second, it deals with part of the problem of the CPI's overestimation of the inflation rate in adjusting threshold income levels. If the CPI overestimates inflation, as is widely believed, then the poverty threshold will keep moving higher and higher in real terms, making it more difficult to reduce the poverty line statistic. Third, because it is a final, not intermediate indicator of actual well-being, a consumption-based measure would eliminate those from the poverty estimate that had incomes below the poverty line but were actually consuming goods and services above poverty level. Use of the consumption measure of poverty shows that poverty has fallen considerably from the all-time low in 1973 of 11.1 percent (the Census Bureau's income-based poverty measure), to about half that low currently. Opponents of consumption-based estimates maintain that poverty has persisted and at higher levels since the 1970s. They cite reduced opportunities for low wage and unskilled labor as the main cause.

(See 325 What is the central controversy over the consumer price index? 490 Why has poverty been so stubborn to reduce over the previous 25 years?)

Q 483. What are the government's major antipoverty programs?

A The government implements a variety of programs for the poor or near poor. Although Social Security is not an antipoverty program per se, the Census Bureau cites the program as having the largest antipoverty impact of any government program. A conservative estimate would have 20 percent of Social Security payments going to the poor. Antipoverty programs account for approximately $231 billion or 13.6 percent of the federal budget. The share of the budget increases to 18.2 percent if the 20 percent antipoverty portion of Social Security is added.

Major Federal Antipoverty Program Outlays, 1999

Spending Program	($ billions)	Share of federal budget
Unemployment compensation	$21.4	1.3%
Food and nutrition assistance	28.7	1.7
Supplementary security income	28.2	1.7
Family and other support assistance	19.2	1.1
Earned income tax credit	25.6	1.5
Medicaid	108.0	6.3
Total	$231.1	13.6
Social Security	$390.0	4.5[a]

[a] Estimated 20 percent of Social Security outlays going to poor.
Source: Office of Management and Budget.

Q 484. How many Americans live below the poverty line?

A The most recent estimate by the Bureau of the Census, which maintains the poverty line data, is that 34 million people or 12.7 percent of the U.S. population live in poverty (1998). Within this group, there are gradations of poverty ranging from those who are barely not making it, to the deep poverty of the truly destitute, such as the homeless.

Q 485. What is the double cost of poverty?

A The double cost of poverty is the cost of safety net payments required to maintain the minimum basic needs for poor individuals and families, plus the loss of their economic contribution to society because they are poor.

Q **486. Why is poverty difficult to solve from an economic, as opposed to a social or cultural, standpoint?**

A Poverty can be self-perpetuating not only within a single lifetime, but also from generation to generation. The distribution of income and wealth correlate closely with the inputs needed to maintain that level of wealth. Clearly, having a lower stake in economic progress plays out in decisions and expectations parents have for their children's development. The educational input to young children, and in more extreme cases, nutrition and health, are dependent on the level of wealth. So poverty, like wealth, becomes self-perpetuating.

Q **487. What is the "trickle down" theory?**

A The "trickle down" theory contends that economic policies that increase resources for the relatively wealthy (such as through tax breaks) result in savings and investment that increase general economic growth and then raise the wealth of the poor (largely through employment creation). The trickle down theory received widespread notice during the 1980s when the Reagan administration pursued tax cuts as the way to help the poor.

Q **488. What is the evidence for and against the "trickle down" theory?**

A The trickle down theory has been very difficult to prove or disprove. Economists do know that, in the long run, national savings must be sufficient to support investment, and wealthier people do have higher savings rates. However, it is not at all clear that trickle down policies are an effective way to decrease poverty. It is clear that poverty falls when the economy grows. A comparison of long-term GDP growth and the population below the poverty line shows that periods of economic growth coincide with declines in the percentage below the poverty line and recessions coincide with upswings or less rapid reductions in poverty. For example, a surge in poverty occurred under the Reagan administration during the deep 1981–1982 recession, when unemployment topped 10 percent and real GDP dropped by almost 2 percent. After the recession, the share of the population below the poverty line decreased from 15.2 in 1983 to 12.8 percent in 1989. The antipoverty effects of economic growth under Reagan apparently overcame the effects of cuts in social spending. So it can be said with a reasonable degree of confidence that "a rising tide raises all boats." This relationship of growth to poverty reduction is consistent with, but still different from, the trickle down theory.

Q **489. Have poverty programs been successful?**

A Social programs appear to have contributed to poverty reduction. The Great Society measures of President Johnson coincided with a rapid downward trend in poverty, far ahead of the rates achieved under Presidents Kennedy, Eisenhower, Reagan, or Ford. The creation and expansion of social programs greatly increased transfer payments to the poor, which are included in the estimation of the incomes for comparison with the poverty threshold. Some economists argue that such transfer payments result only in a short-term reduction in poverty, however, and tend to foster long-run dependency on social programs, which may actually result in higher levels of poverty in the future. This theme is common to debates on welfare reform. This thesis may also be supported by the fact that while the Nixon and Ford administrations continued increasing social spending, they did not achieve a commensurate reduction in the percentage of the population below the poverty line, although low poverty levels were maintained.

Q **490. Why has poverty been so stubborn to reduce over the previous 25 years?**

A The standard poverty measure does show even a slight worsening in the percentage of poor compared with 25 years earlier. There have been gradual increases in income inequality and even more pronounced wealth inequality that may have contributed to higher poverty. With outsourcing and increasing globalization, there might also be fewer opportunities for unskilled labor. In addition to these real phenomena, the higher poverty statistic may also have to do with the weaknesses of basing the poverty measurement on cash income than actual poverty. Poverty analysts using consumption data show that the poverty level is actually much lower than commonly reported by the Census Bureau and NIPA (National Income and Product Accounts, under the Department of Commerce). Poverty rates below 9 percent (compared with over 12 percent officially) down to 2.2 percent were estimated using household data surveys based on what people actually consume.

(See 482 Poverty measurement issue no. 3: Which is more important to measuring poverty, how much cash a person receives, or how much he or she consumes? 531 What are the costs of globalization?)

Q **491. Can poverty be eliminated?**

A In principle, the government does eliminate poverty through its assistance programs that help "poor" families meet basic needs. The more precise question is "Can poverty be eliminated without government programs?" During the high levels of social spending in the Nixon and Ford administrations, poverty dropped to historically low levels (11 to 12 percent of the population). In historical terms, it would undoubtedly be a major accomplishment in the future to lower the standard percentage of poverty measure to below 10 percent for a sustained period.

Although prosperous economic times prevailed for all but one or two years since 1983, the poverty level did not return to the historical low of 1973. Many economists fault the poverty line statistic for overstating poverty. A combination of a growing economy, rising levels of education of the poor, and efficiently targeted antipoverty programs should, in principle, always lower the poverty rate, despite what the Census Bureau poverty statistic says. Even if poverty is overestimated, however, antipoverty programs will remain a constant feature of society for the foreseeable future.

Q 492. Is some percentage of poverty acceptable?

A What is an acceptable level of poverty in society is obviously subjective. Poverty has existed historically in all societies, and it would be a first in history for every member of society to have the ability to make freely the decisions necessary to stay out of poverty. In some societies, the poor do not have a choice. They are bound by physical constraints and have no choice but to farm for a living. It is difficult to say how far a society should go to reduce or eliminate poverty. At a minimum, the United States appears committed that every citizen should have adequate food, clothing, shelter, and, for the most part, health care.

INCOME DISTRIBUTION

Q 493. How is income distribution measured?

A An issue closely related to poverty is income distribution, which provides a background against which to view poverty trends and shows how yearly economic production is divided among the population.

The standard measure of income distribution is called the "Gini Index." The Gini Index ranges from 0, when income is perfectly, evenly distributed and every household has the same income, to 1, when one household has all the income. Income distribution by fifths of the population (quintiles) also tells the distribution story.

494. What has been the general trend in income distribution?

A Income inequality decreased somewhat from 1947 to 1968, then increased from 1968 to 1993.

Share of Income Received by Each Fifth and Top 5% of Families

Year	Lowest fifth	Second fifth	Third fifth	Fourth fifth	Highest fifth	Top 5 percent	Gini Index
1947	5.0	11.9	17.0	23.1	43.0	17.5	.376
1957	5.1	12.7	18.1	23.8	40.4	15.6	.351
1967	5.4	12.2	17.5	23.5	41.4	16.4	.358
1977	5.2	11.6	17.5	24.2	41.5	15.7	.363
1987	4.6	10.7	16.8	24.0	43.8	17.2	.393
1992	4.4	10.5	16.5	24.0	44.6	17.6	.403
1997 [a]	4.2	9.9	15.7	23.0	47.2	20.7	.429
1998	4.2	9.9	15.7	23.0	47.3	20.7	.430

[a]A change in methodology increased the inequality estimate by approximately 0.02 to 0.025 index points.
Source: U.S. Census Bureau.

Q **495. What are possible reasons for the increase in income inequality?**

A The following are possible reasons for the increase in family income inequality:

• Transition from industries offering high wages to low-skilled workers to services that employ high-wage college graduates (from automobile assembly to computer jobs).

• Decreased demand for less-skilled, less-educated, high-wage workers within industries (increased mechanization and other efficiency gains).
• Downward wage pressure of intensified global trade and immigration.
• Decline in union membership.
• Decline in real value of minimum wage (although many economists would argue that increasing the minimum wage would decrease employment in low-skilled jobs).
• Change in demographic factors, such as the increase in single parent households.
• Tendency for individuals with higher-than-average earnings to marry other individuals with higher-than-average earnings.

A Relatively, the poor have been getting poorer but not in terms of meeting their basic needs. In a growing economy, as has been largely the case since 1983, distribution has been less equal, but the purchasing power of the lowest fifth of the population has actually increased making most lower-income earners absolutely better off.

Q 497. What is the difference between "mean" and "median" income?

A Mean income is the average income earned: all individuals' incomes are added and divided by the number of individuals. Median income is that income level where half the people are making more and half less than that level. Those concerned about income distribution find median income a better indicator than mean income. Mean income can be distorted by a small percentage of high earners and convey the idea that the average person earns the average income, when, in fact, he or she makes considerably less. For example, if there is one person earning $1 million per year, 10 people earning $50,000 per year, and 11 people earning $45,000 per year, then the mean income would be $90,681, whereas the more representative median income would be $45,000.

WEALTH DISTRIBUTION

Q 498. What is the trend in wealth distribution?

A Wealth distribution is becoming increasingly unequal. The reason behind this trend is that the compounding effect of years of unequal income distribution for the wealthiest percentage of the population has increased their wealth disproportionately faster. One positive development in asset ownership is that an increasing percentage of Americans own stock thanks to a large extent to employer-sponsored retirement plans. As of the end of 1999, nearly 50 percent of all American households owned stock.

Q 499. Why does unequal wealth distribution increase more rapidly than income distribution?

A Unlike income inequality, disparities in wealth distribution accumulate over time. The following example demonstrates the power of the compounding effect. If a rich person makes $100,000 per year and a poor person makes $20,000, then the rich person has 83 percent of the income. If this income disparity continues and the rich person saves 25 percent per year, while the poor person can save only 10 percent, then, assuming a 10 percent return on savings, in 10 years, the rich person has built a stock of wealth of $398,435, while the poor person has only $31,875. The rich person now has 93 percent of the new wealth. With both the stock and real estate booms of the last two decades, the well-off did extremely well. The less well-off, having made few investments, except perhaps in their homes, received only minimal benefits.

Q 500. Is there much difference between mean and median wealth?

A There is a tremendous difference between the two. In 1992 mean wealth was $220,000, while median wealth was only $52,000. This disparity indicates that a small percentage of very rich people push the wealth average up ($220,000), whereas the wealth figure that is more representative of the population is much less ($52,000).

Q 501. How much wealth does the top 1 percent of Americans hold?

A The top 1 percent of the population is estimated to have about 40 percent of total wealth, but only 16 percent of the income. If Social Security and pensions are included as part of wealth, then the share of the top 1 percent declines sharply to 22 percent. This concentration (22 percent) exceeds that of most European countries.

ECONOMIC COSTS OF ILLEGAL DRUGS

The use and trafficking of illegal drugs has plagued America for decades. Drug use rose sharply in the 1960s and 1970s and fluctuated in the 1980s and 1990s. In addition to the high human costs—in terms of the devastation and loss of lives—illegal drugs also hurt the economy. The economic cost of drugs to society include the diminished output of workers and the cost of drug treatment, law enforcement, and assisting victims of crime. Despite the high societal costs for illegal drugs, in terms of economic cost, alcohol abuse may still be the main substance abuse problem in the United States.

Q 502. What is the estimated annual value of the U.S. drug trafficking market?

A On the demand side, Americans spent $49 billion on illegal drugs in 1993. Of the main illegal drugs, $31 billion was spent on cocaine, $9 billion on marijuana, and $7 billion on heroin. Another $2 billion was spent on other illicit drugs and legal drugs used illegally. Estimates of the supply of drugs to the United States show a wider range of $30 to $90 billion.

Q **503. What are the total economic costs associated with illegal drugs?**

A The total loss to the economy related to illegal drugs was $97.7 billion in 1992 (no more recent estimate is available). This cost accounted for about 1.6 percent of GDP in 1992. This estimate includes the related health care costs, production losses, crime, property destruction, and other economic costs.

Economic Costs of Alcohol and Drug Abuse in the United States, 1992 ($ millions)

Health care expenditures	Total costs	Alcohol	Drugs
Alcohol and drug abuse services	$ 9,973	$ 5,573	$ 4,400
Medical consequences	18,778	13,247	5,531
Productivity effects (lost earnings)			
Premature death	45,902	31,327	14,575
Impaired productivity	82,201	67,696	14,205
Institutionalized populations	2,990	1,513	1,477
Incarceration	23,356	5,449	17,907
Crime careers	19,198	—	19,198
Victims of crime	3,071	1,012	2,059
Other effects on society			
Crime	24,282	6,312	17,970
Social welfare administration	1,020	683	337
Motor vehicle crashes	13,619	13,619	—
Fire destruction	1,590	1,590	—
Total	$245,680	$148,021	$97,659

Source: The Lewin Group.

Q **504. Is drug use going up or down?**

A The data available on drug use conflict somewhat, but the trend in drug use probably was down from 1988 to 1993. During this period the amount of spending on cocaine and heroin appeared to decline about 25 percent, but the price of cocaine also fell from $290 per gram in 1988 to $240 per gram in 1993, a 17.2 percent price decline, implying a volume decline of 8 percent. It appeared that much of the decline, according to Drug Use Forecasting data, was due to the increase in incarcerations from 200,000 in 1988 to 400,000 in 1993, with the number of hard-core cocaine users dropping from 2.1 to 1.9 million over the same period.

Q 505. What economic component of illegal drug use costs society the most?

A The major cost of illegal drug use is the loss of production, valued at $69.4 billion in 1992, mainly relating to the early deaths of users, imprisonment, impaired performance, and the choice of a career of crime over that of economic production.

Q 506. Is drug or alcohol abuse more costly to the economy?

A Looking at all related costs, alcohol is about 50 percent more expensive ($148.0 billion for alcohol, $97.7 billion for illegal drugs), when examining the same categories for both. This estimate takes into account productivity losses caused by the legal consumption of alcohol.

COST OF ILLEGALITY OF DRUGS

Q 507. What is the total cost of crime related to drug activities?

A The total cost of crime associated with illegal drugs—including victims' costs, paying for the criminal justice system, and crime-related productivity losses—was estimated at $58.7 billion. This amount is 60 percent of the total economic loss due to illegal drugs. Although the total economic costs of alcohol are 50 percent higher than for illegal drugs, the costs associated with the illegality of drugs are three times higher than for alcohol ($58.7 billion for drugs and $19.8 billion for alcohol).

Q 508. How much does it cost to control illicit drugs?

A The cost of controlling drugs, or the law enforcement side of crimes related to illegal drugs, was $18.1 billion (0.3 percent of GDP) in 1992.

Total Costs of Alcohol and Drug Abuse in Criminal Activity, 1992 ($ millions)

	Total	Alcohol	Drugs
Economic costs to victims			
Medical expenses for victims of violent crimes	$505	$400	$105
Property damage	221	28	193

Total Costs of Alcohol and Drug Abuse in Criminal Activity, 1992 ($ millions)

	Total	Alcohol	Drugs
Criminal justice system			
Police protection	$ 6,191	$ 1,547	$ 4,644
Legal and adjudication	1,701	491	1,210
State and federal correction	8,483	1,790	6,693
Local correction	3,517	2,326	1,191
Federal drug traffic control	3,753	62	3,691
Private legal defense	416	68	348
Crime-related productivity losses			
Homicide victims (premature death)	8,016	6,589	1,427
Other crime victims	3,071	1,012	2,059
Incarcerated offenders	23,356	5,449	17,907
Crime careers	19,198	—	19,198
Total	$78,428	$19,762	$58,666

Source: The Lewin Group.

Q 509. What is the cost of corrections/imprisonment for drug crimes?

A The total cost of federal, state, and local corrections and imprisonment for drug offenses was $7.9 billion in 1992.

Q 510. What is the economic cost of adjudicating drug offenses?

A The cost of adjudicating drug offenses, including private legal defense, was $1.5 billion in 1992.

Q 511. How much does the federal government spend to fight drugs?

A In 1999 the National Drug Control Budget totaled $17.9 billion, with 50 percent being allocated to domestic law enforcement, 33 percent to demand reduction programs, 13 percent for interdiction, and 4 percent for international law enforcement. The following table breaks down the drug control budget by agency:

Department of Justice	$7,708,000
Department of Health and Human Services	2,859,000

Department of Treasury	$ 1,659,000
Veterans' Affairs	1,126,000
Other	4,534,000
Total	$17,886,000

[Q] 512. What are the economic implications of legalizing drugs?

[A] Simplistically, legalizing drugs would save virtually all crime-related costs, or nearly $59 billion (about 1 percent of GDP) in 1992. On the human side, much of the loss of life and property of victims of crime would be averted. Drug offenders would be treated like abusers of any other legal substance (such as alcohol). Of course, the behavior alteration of drugs would continue, and there would be victims related to violent behavior of drug users.

These savings would have to be weighed against a possible increase in drug use due to legalization. Policymakers considering the legalization of drugs would have to consider whether drug use would rise to the level of alcohol use. If so, then legalization of drugs would be a potential catastrophe in productivity losses and have negative social and health consequences.

NATURAL RESOURCES

Land, or more broadly, natural resources, is one of the three factors of production. The other factors of production are labor and capital. Life cannot exist without natural resources, such as fresh water, fertile land, and breathable air. These and other natural resources—such as minerals, fuel, and other raw materials—have economic value. Natural resources can be further processed into useful products and energy. One important application of economics is natural resource management, which combines the disciplines of science and economics. The challenge of natural resource management is to ensure that these resources are used in a sustainable way that provides the public both economic and noneconomic benefits.

[Q] 513. What are natural resources?

[A] Natural resources include minerals, metals, coal, petroleum, timber, fisheries, fodder from grasslands, and miscellaneous goods like natural medicines. Some resources, such as timber, are considered renewable while others, such as coal and petroleum, are not. Some resources fall into both categories depending on the location. Water is a renewable resource in most places but nonrenewable "water mining" occurs in some areas when groundwater from nonrecharging aquifers is used. Natural resources also play a role in many recreational activities, such as beach-going, hiking, fishing, and hunting.

However, some economists broaden the view of natural resources to include services provided by the environment. These services include purification of air and water, detoxification and decomposition of wastes, climate regulation, regeneration of soil fertility, and production and maintenance of biodiversity, from which derive key inputs of agricultural, pharmaceutical, and industrial enterprises. For example, forests help regulate the water cycle by lessening the chance of floods, droughts, erosion, and silting of streams and lakes. This broad view of natural resources may be increasingly used as the importance of these services are realized.

Q 514. What is the value of natural resource production in the United States?

A The total value of mineral production in the United States was nearly $150 billion in 1997, of which more than $100 billion was mineral fuels, crude petroleum ($41 billion), natural gas ($46 billion), and coal ($20 billion). Total nonfuel mineral production included mining and production of metals such as copper, gold, lead, magnesium, silver and zinc, and industrial minerals like asbestos, cement, clay, feldspar, lime, perlite, pumice, sand and gravel, stone, vermiculite, and zeolites.

In 1995, 402 billion gallons per day (Bgal/day) of fresh and saline water were used for public supply, domestic, commercial, irrigation, livestock, industrial, mining, and thermoelectric power. Surface water constituted 324 Bgal/day and groundwater was 78 Bgal/day.

Q 515. What is the value of all natural resources in the world?

A One attempt to calculate the value of earth's ecosystems placed the value of all natural goods and services between $16 to $54 trillion every year. This estimate included everything from fishing, to pollination, to recreation, to the regulation of carbon dioxide. This range of values is roughly equivalent to half to double the entire world GDP of $30 trillion.

Q 516. What is economic damage to natural resources?

A Economic damages include the injury, destruction, or loss of natural resources. Under some laws, whoever is responsible for the damage can be sued. Economic losses can include the reduction of benefits caused by pollution, such as fewer fish or wildlife; and impaired beauty that keeps tourists away, such as the loss of timber. Damage can also include "non-use" or "intrinsic" values, which is the loss of the natural beauty or value of a natural resource, such as damage to Prince William Sound by the *Exxon Valdez* oil spill in 1989 or the loss of visibility at the Grand Canyon from power plant emissions. Assigning a dollar value to this type of economic damage is difficult and the method of quantifying the damage is called contingent valuation.

(See 464 How much pollution is acceptable? 477 Are there other damaging environmental practices that are subsidized?)

Q 517. Is the United States using up its natural resources?

A Eventually all nonrenewable natural resources on the earth that can be economically extracted will by definition be used up. (The energy of the sun will also eventually be used up but this is not expected to happen for another 4.5 billion years.) The real question is, will Americans run out of any critical natural resources before technological advances solve the shortage? Perhaps the most important are fuels such as oil, gas, and coal.

It is tricky to estimate the exact amount of oil and gas in the country. The U.S. Geological Service in a 1995 assessment found that there were approximately 110 billion barrels of recoverable oil on U.S. land and off-shore. Natural gas reserves were measured at about 715 trillion cubic feet. The assessment also concluded that oil production in the United States has been declining since the early 1970s, while natural gas production has not peaked and this resource is more plentiful. The agency also concluded that "even to maintain delivery at present levels, industry will need to increase drilling and the Nation will have to address a variety of technological and land-use considerations." The American Petroleum Institute estimated that proved oil reserves were enough to sustain 1996 levels for 44 more years, or growing production levels for 20 years, assuming no additional discoveries were made.

Coal production and use in the United States is at an all-time high (coal production in 1994 was the highest level ever with a consumption of 930 million short tons). But even with this high usage, the Energy Information Administration in 1995 estimated U.S. coal resources to last at least another 250 years.

Q 518. Is biodiversity an economically valuable natural resource?

A Yes, the natural diverse range of species—being composed of different genetic material—is a very valuable resource. Economically, it is impossible to predict when different genetic material will be needed. Much of the "green revolution" of the 1970s— the boom in Third World agricultural yields credited with alleviating much of the world's hunger—was the result of the introduction of new genes from relatives of familiar food crops that increased yield. But to improve or even maintain the yield, new genes will be needed to combat pests, make crops more marketable, and even improve nutrition. New drugs, such as the cancer-fighting drug taxol that comes from the Pacific yew tree, come from nature. Many people also place high value on the diversity of species, such that society has incurred high economic costs to protect animals and plants that are endangered.

(See 472 What other costs are associated with protecting the environment?)

Q 519. Who owns these natural resources?

A Natural resources in the United States are owned by both the public (through governmental bodies) and private individuals and business. There are 2.3 billion acres of land in the United States. The federal government owns about 660 million acres or 29 percent of the total area. Public lands include national parks, national forests, wildlife refuges, and wilderness areas; other federal land is under the jurisdiction of the Department of Defense. There are 395 million acres of nonfederal forest land.

Q 520. What are the federal lands?

A The government owns a significant amount of land which is considered "public" and includes national parks, national forests, wildlife refuges, wilderness areas, and national monuments and historic areas. Public lands are used for recreation (fishing, hiking, off-road vehicles, and camping), commercial enterprises (mining, grazing, forestry, power transmission rights-of-way, and motion picture filming), and to protect plant and animal species, and archaeological and historic sites.

Q 521. What agencies are involved in managing the federal lands?

A The primary federal agencies managing public lands are the Bureau of Land Management, U.S. Forest Service, U.S. Fish and Wildlife Service, and the National Park Service. In addition, the Department of Defense controls 25 million acres of land.

• **Bureau of Land Management:** manages about 40 percent (264 million acres) of federal land (11 percent of total U.S. acreage)—the most land of any federal agency with jurisdiction. The agency also administers an onshore surface and mineral estate of 264 million acres of public land and 300 million acres of mineral estate under other lands.

- **Forest Service:** manages 191.8 million acres. (Compared with 395 million acres of nonfederal forest land.)
- **Fish and Wildlife Service:** manages 92 million acres in 500 national wildlife refuges.
- **National Park Service:** manages 80.7 million acres of national parks, monuments, preserves, historic sites, memorials, battlefields, cemeteries, seashores, lakeshores, rivers, parkways, and trails.

(See 463 What are the major government agencies concerned with the environment?)

Q 522. What are the economic uses of federal lands?

A Federal lands are used for a variety of purposes including recreation (fishing, hiking, off-road vehicles, and camping), commercial enterprises (mining, grazing, forestry, power transmission rights-of-way, and motion picture filming), and protection of plant and animal species, and archaeological and historic sites. The economic and commercial uses of federal lands have generated considerable controversy, especially in the areas of grazing rights, timber, and minerals. The primary issues are the sustainability of land practices and management, and the prices charged. For example, in 1992 the World Resources Institute estimated that charging market prices for commodities from public lands (such as water, minerals, and timber) would bring in an additional $1.5 billion per year.

Q 523. Is the exploitation of federal lands priced at fair market value?

A Not really. In fact, those who use federal lands tend to get an exceptionally good deal. The Bureau of Land Management (BLM) estimated that in fiscal year 1998 the market value of production on BLM public lands was $11.8 billion, while revenue that year was only $1.3 billion. Ninety-nine percent of revenue came from the sale of energy and minerals. Some critics blame artificially cheap land use prices for the overuse of that land. For example, current grazing fees and management have been alleged to cause overgrazing and, therefore, degradation of public land. Fees charged on federal land by the Forest Service (95 million acres) and BLM (167 million acres) are consistently half or more below the amount charged by private landowners.

However, livestock producers point out that federal fees are lower than those from private business because the federal land is not as productive and is more costly to use. In addition, fee increases may cause smaller ranchers to go out of business. Critics counter that the low fees cost taxpayers between $50 and $500 million per year, contribute to overgrazing, and subsidize a small percentage of livestock operators. This issue has been debated since grazing fees were first introduced in 1906.

524. Why is forest management on public lands controversial?

There is perhaps no area of public land management that is more controversial than forest management. As in the controversy over grazing rights, part of the issue is the cost to taxpayers and the charge of subsidizing private companies. The other major issues concern the purpose of forests and sustainable management. Both the Forest Service and BLM manage forest lands, but it is the Forest Service that seems to be the bigger target of criticism. Part of the Forest Service's problem may stem from the agency's dual mission to protect forests and to produce goods and services. By law the Forest Service is to "manage its lands for environmental protection and for recreational opportunities, as well as to provide continuous levels of certain goods, including timber, oil and gas, minerals, and forage for grazing livestock. No one use of the national forests is given priority in any of these laws."(GAO)

The Forest Service is also accused of mismanagement. According to the Center for Public Integrity, the Forest Service is one of the "most mismanaged, poorly led, politically manipulated, and corrupt agencies in the federal government." There is no doubt that the Forest Service timber program is expensive and that the cost of offering timber for sale often exceeds the revenues brought in, not including the expense of building roads to make the timber accessible. In addition to the money lost, there is an environmental cost to not correctly pricing a natural resource, because underpriced resources are often wasted.

According to a 1999 GAO report, the Forest Service is increasingly emphasizing resource protection and ecological sustainability over production. This has had the effect of dramatically increasing the cost of harvesting timber (less clear cutting, fewer sales, more restrictions on size and location of timber, etc.). However, over time this refocusing may help reduce the controversy over Forest Service management.

INTERNATIONAL ISSUES

GLOBALIZATION

For hundreds of years, expanded trade has been bringing nations together and "shrinking" the world. Recently, the liberalization of trade, the decontrol of major industries, advances in communications and technology, and the emergence of capitalism as the lone-standing economic system have spurred globalization. Is this increasing globalization a good thing? Are there ways to manage the negative aspects of it? Will globalization eventually do away with individual cultures, making the world homogeneous?

Q **525. What is globalization?**

A Globalization is the rapid interconnection of the economies of nations through trade and technology. Globalization is driven by the benefits from free trade and capital flows. Free trade is based on one of the great principles of economics, "comparative advantage."

Q **526. What is comparative advantage?**

A The whole basis for free trade and even specialization rests on comparative advantage, a concept developed by David Ricardo in the early nineteenth century. Comparative advantage states that even if one country can produce all products more cheaply than another, it can still benefit from trading with that country, by trading what it can produce *comparatively* cheaply for what the other country can produce *comparatively* cheaply. The example of the trade of food and clothing between the United States and Europe illustrates:

Labor Input (days per unit produced)

	United States	Europe
Food	1	3
Clothing	2	4

The United States produces both goods more cheaply than does Europe. How then would it benefit the United States to trade with Europe? By virtue of the fact that

Figure 31   Benefits of Comparative Advantage

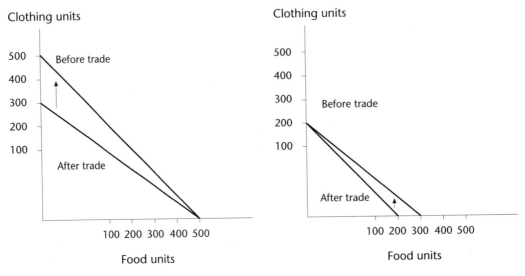

A. U.S. Consumption

B. European Consumption

within the United States, food is produced *relatively,* or *comparatively,* more cheaply than clothing. That is, food is cheaper to produce than clothing in the United States (by a ratio of one to two). Food is also cheaper than clothing in Europe, but only by a ratio of three to four. By the United States specializing in food and trading it to Europe, and by Europe specializing in clothing and trading it to the United States, *both countries can have more of both products.* Figure 31 illustrates how both the United States and Europe achieve higher levels of consumption by specializing in production and then trading.

Specialization by comparative advantage produces enormous economic benefits at the national level and is a necessity for individuals. It would be prohibitively expensive, even impossible, for each individual to produce everything he or she consumes. Comparative advantage shows how to reach a maximum plane of consumption by having each producer specialize in what it does best.

Q **527. Why use a nineteenth-century economics concept to explain the twenty-first century international economy?**

A Comparative advantage is helpful for a couple of reasons. First, comparative advantage truly is the economic basis for globalization. Second, although comparative advantage is not a difficult concept, it is a subtle one. Anything that is subtle must be learned over and over again. Even policymakers forget the principle of comparative advantage. A (hopefully untrue) quote attributed to Abraham Lincoln illustrates this point. "I don't know much about the tariff, but I know this much. When we buy manufactured goods abroad, we get the goods and the foreigner gets the money. When we buy the manufactured goods at home, we get both the goods and the money." This sentiment ignores the fact that the United States does not get the foreigner's market or imports either.

Q 528. How fast is the world "globalizing"?

A It depends on how one measures "globalization." In terms of instantaneous communications and volume of information traveling across borders electronically, globalization is occurring very fast. In terms of capital flows, which is the value of financial resources moving to and from countries, international transactions increased from $15 billion per day in 1973 to $1.2 trillion per day in 1995. Capital flows now exceed trade flows by a 60 to 1 margin. Globalization measured by trade as a percentage of GDP, is happening at a much slower rate. In fact, trade percentages are about where they were in 1914. The year 1914 did mark the end of a golden age of trade after which trade declined. There are several factors that slow down globalization. One is called "home bias," in which governments and national institutions demonstrate greater comfort, and therefore preference for having their needs met domestically.

Share of Imported to Total Intermediate Inputs in Manufacturing (percent)

Country	1974	1984	1993
Canada	15.9%	14.4%	20.2%
Japan	8.2	7.3	4.1
Great Britain	13.4	19.0	21.6
United States	4.1	6.2	8.2

Note: U.S. estimates are for 1975, 1985, and 1995.

Source: "Integration of Trade and Disintegration of Production in the Global Economy," *Journal of Economic Perspective,* Fall 1998, 40.

Q 529. What are some of the more notable examples of globalization?

A Some of the more recent examples of globalization are
 • **The European Economic (and Monetary) Union:** a unified economic market created by eliminating traditional barriers between European countries.

- **The Euro:** a single currency for 11 European countries.
- **The World Trade Organization:** a world trade body that became effective on January 1, 1995, to reduce barriers to international commerce and resolve trade disputes.
  - **NAFTA:** a free trade agreement between the United States, Canada, and Mexico.
  - **Asian financial crisis:** an economic collapse facilitated by rapid expansion of short-term lending and loose capital controls, which would not have occurred in the less globalized, tightly controlled financial markets of the 1950s and 1960s.
  - **Stock Exchange cross-effects:** the phenomenon that what happens overnight in Japan on the NIKKEI often has strong effects on the New York Stock Exchange.
  - **Immigration:** the increased mobility of labor.
  - **Removal of the Bretton Woods System:** paved the way for freer capital movements by eliminating the system of fixed exchange rates.

(See 158 What was the Bretton Woods Agreement?)

530. What are the benefits of globalization?

In general, the main benefit of globalization is higher consumption for less effort, which is achieved through higher efficiency and productivity. Globalization allows international returns to scale, not just domestic returns to scale. This means that workers, investors, and consumers gain more by operating in the larger international market. Although these benefits have been enjoyed for centuries through trade, modern globalization has intensified and accelerated the practice of free trade. The benefits of globalization can be divided into three categories: goods, capital, and labor.

Benefits in Terms of Goods

The decades leading up to 1913 were the golden age of trade. U.S. trade as a percentage of GDP was 6.1 percent in 1913. With the outbreak of World War I, U.S. trade began to decline. The Great Depression depressed trade further. It was a long time before trade recovered its share of the GDP.

U.S. trade as a percentage of GDP has more than doubled during the last few decades, from 9.1 percent in 1960 to 24.2 percent in 1999. Most European countries have trade levels approaching a quarter of GDP. The ratio of merchandise trade to merchandise value added has risen sharply, suggesting a far greater degree of integration, because it shows that the United States is trading a higher percentage of what it produces and consumes. The manufacturing process has been chopped up consid-

BARBIE DOLL: EXAMPLE OF OUTSOURCING

The main raw materials for a Barbie doll (plastic and hair) are obtained from Taiwan and Japan. The assembly of the doll used to be done in those countries, as well as the Philippines, but it has now migrated to lower-cost locations in China, Indonesia, and Malaysia. China also supplies the cotton cloth used for dresses. The molds themselves come from the United States, as do additional paints used in decorating the dolls. Of the $2 export value for the dolls when they leave Hong Kong for the United States, about 35 cents covers Chinese labor, 65 cents covers the cost of materials, and the remainder covers transportation and overhead, including profits earned in Hong Kong. The dolls sell for about $10 in the United States, of which Mattel earns at least $1, and the rest covers transportation, marketing, wholesaling, and retailing in the United States. The majority of the value-added cost is therefore from the U.S. activity. The dolls sell worldwide at the rate of two dolls every second, and this product alone accounted for $1.4 billion in sales for Mattel in 1995.

erably as part of globalization with the surge in outsourcing (farming out tasks to workers outside the company) occurring internationally as well as domestically. The trade in intermediate inputs is also increasing as the vertical structure of production is broken down. Fewer companies are producing products from start to finish under the same roof. This "chopping up" lowers cost and increases efficiency. Trade in intermediate inputs, also equalizes factor prices (the cost of land, labor, and capital) more rapidly. The box above illustrates how what was once a vertical process, the manufacture of a Barbie doll, has now been spread over a number of countries.

Benefits to Capital

The theoretical advantages to a global capital market are accepted by the vast majority of economists. Just as a broader domestic market allows for the greater pooling of risk and the gains from tapping savings surplus areas by savings deficit areas, the international market offers an even broader diversification. For example, if a country has a savings deficit, it has no place to go for an infusion of financial resources unless there is a global capital market. Countries that have surplus savings can invest in or lend to the country in recession in order to boost investment and lessen the recession. An international market also imposes a greater discipline on a country contemplating overspending or weak bank regulation, because the domestic capital has another place to go—that is, outside the country. Floating exchange rates, exchange rates that are determined by the supply and demand of two currencies, are also a key factor in the growth of international capital markets.

Benefits to Labor

With increasing globalization, some parts of the labor force will do better and some worse. Paradoxically, the type of workers that are in greater abundance domestically will be in greater demand under increasing globalization. The reason is that countries will naturally specialize in activities that they can do comparatively more cheaply, that is, where the labor resources are in greater abundance. In industrialized countries, abundance is more apt to be in high-tech, highly skilled services, financial and economic expertise, engineering, medical services, and graduate education. These are high-priced services, but they are in abundance in the United States relative to other countries. Lower-skilled occupations, such as assembly and other factory work, are fairly high priced in the United States. Lower-skilled workers are in relatively greater abundance in less-developed countries.

Q **531. What are the costs of globalization?**

A One "cost" of globalization is a loss of national economic autonomy. For instance, when the European nations joined the European Monetary Union, they lost their power to conduct independent fiscal and monetary policy. This is one reason why Great Britain elected not to join the Union.

In terms of capital, the explosion in short-term liquidity has increased the risk of runs on national currencies as seen in East Asia during the financial crises in the late 1990s. In addition, in a world of mobile capital, independent national monetary policy is affected. It can be very difficult for countries that want to keep the value of their currencies fairly stable with respect to other currencies (fixed-exchange rates).

In terms of labor, globalization makes it easier for countries, through trade, investment, and outsourcing, to substitute foreign lower-skilled workers for domestic lower-skilled workers. Thus, a major "cost" of globalization is that domestic lower-skilled workers might lose jobs, or at the very least, suffer lower wages as their economic bargaining power falls.

(See 589 How does this unified currency (the Euro) affect monetary policy?)

Q **532. Should unskilled workers be compensated when their livelihoods are affected by globalization?**

A One could argue that if unskilled workers are hurt by tight monetary policy, they would not get compensation beyond the usual unemployment compensation. However, the political feasibility of future trade agreements may depend on incorporating policies that compensate lower-skilled workers (as was the case for NAFTA), whether through training, education, income supplements, or combinations thereof.

Q **533. What are the major challenges for the United States and globalization?**

A With the benefits of globalization are many challenges. These major challenges include:

• **Financial volatility in emerging market countries:** The goal will be to manage the mushrooming capital inflows, not to prevent outflows, which would scare away investors who are always concerned about the ease of cashing in an investment.

• **Marginalization of low-income countries:** The poorest countries in the world are at risk of falling farther behind as technology accelerates. Effective poverty alleviation will need to be devised.

• **Labor insecurity in industrialized countries:** Lower-skilled workers will shoulder much of the burden of further globalization. Ways to compensate them will need to be devised.

• **Increasing difficulty for government policy:** Trade, competition, industrial, and R&D policies will become harder to implement as it becomes more difficult to distinguish between foreign and domestic firms. Intra-firm transactions will make tax policy more complicated. There will be greater pressure on government revenue as the international mobility of corporations allows them to minimize tax liability. Trade liberalization also will generate new trade disputes over policies (such as labor and environmental standards) that were once considered purely domestic and in the domain of the individual in national cultures.

Q **534. How can the United States meet the major challenges of globalization?**

A How the United States meets these major challenges will determine whether globalization can maximize the benefits while minimizing the costs. The following are ways of addressing the major challenges of globalization:

• **Financial volatility in emerging market countries:** Financial crisis prevention will be most effective if surveillance of countries' accounts and transparency of their public and private finances can be substantially improved. Only then can trouble be addressed long before the crisis stage. When crises do arise, some of the moral hazard (engaging in risky activities when the cost of failure to the decision-maker is low) could be eliminated by requiring that creditors (often from the United States) who took the risks in the first place, take a mandatory loss, probably in the form of rescheduling the debt of the country in crisis. Capital controls on speculative *inflows* would be another safeguard against currency runs that precipitate crises.

• **Marginalization of low-income countries:** Low-income countries need help, especially in the form of debt relief. Countries that are poor but are committed to economic integration could also be helped with the kind of infrastructural investments that would attract sufficient private capital to keep them on pace with global technological changes. Further trade liberalization by the industrialized countries, such as eliminating tariffs on the 50 poorest countries' exports, would help nurture their development at a small cost to importing countries. Broader participation in international trade and investment agreements would also help keep the poorer countries from being marginalized.

• **Labor insecurity in industrialized countries:** The World Trade Organization (WTO) can resolve trade disputes resulting from traditional trade barriers, but disputes arising from labor and environmental standards probably need to be worked out through other institutions. The WTO will likely need additional resources to fulfill its unexpectedly active role as a dispute-settlement body.

• **Increasing difficulty for government policy:** Additional negotiations are needed to establish rules/guidelines for international competition for investment. Broad participation of countries, not just the Organization for Economic Cooperation and Development (OECD), or industrialized, countries, would help the effectiveness of these negotiations. The OECD convention on outlawing bribery, a very common business practice throughout the world, could be important for better allocation of investment between and within countries.

Q **535. Can the world be fully integrated/globalized?**

A It is probably impossible for the world to become completely integrated. There will always be transportation and transactions costs that will prevent complete equalization of prices, wages, and goods availability, even if all nations decide to reduce their economic autonomy to a minimum. Also, there are some things that simply cannot be transported physically or electronically, such as land. Only indirectly through trade can the production attained from land, such as minerals and agriculture, be used by someone far away. That is not to say that many cultural distinctions will not disappear. For example, globalization may have something to say about whether the stone-age tribes of the Amazon, or the Pygmies in central Africa, will be left to their own devices or whether they will be gradually assimilated into the vast world economy.

NAFTA AND ITS RECORD ON TRADE AND JOBS

When the North American Free Trade Agreement (NAFTA) was being debated in 1993, a number of critics contended that a large number of American jobs would be lost to Mexico if the free trade agreement was implemented. NAFTA became effective in 1994, but whether it has brought about the loss of U.S. jobs is not clear. The available data on trade and jobs show what has happened *since* NAFTA began, but not necessarily entirely *because* of NAFTA.

NAFTA consists mainly of tariff reduction and investment rules between the three nations, but there are many other non-NAFTA factors that affect trade volume and jobs, such as currency fluctuations. The long-term technological transition in the United States from low to high-tech industries and to the service sector was also long under way before NAFTA. Generally, economists believe that net job gain or loss from NAFTA will not be large in the long term, but that labor will be allocated more efficiently, and, therefore, will be more productive in all participating countries.

Q 536. What is NAFTA?

A NAFTA is an agreement between the United States, Canada, and Mexico to eliminate all tariffs and reduce other trade barriers gradually over 15 years (beginning in 1994) between the three countries. The bill made numerous changes in U.S. law to conform to the trade pact signed two years earlier by President George Bush. In addition to trade barrier reduction, NAFTA has provisions governing investments in other NAFTA countries, environmental and safety regulations, and opening up the services market.

(See 539 What does NAFTA do?)

Q 537. When and how did NAFTA pass?

A NAFTA was passed by the House on November 17, 1993, by a vote of 234–200 and three days later by the Senate by a vote of 61–38. It was signed by President Bill Clinton on December 8, 1993. It went into effect on January 1, 1994. Congress processed

NAFTA under "fast-track" procedures that did not allow amendments and required an up-or-down vote within 90 days of the bill's introduction.

Q 538. Why is NAFTA a priority economic issue?

A First, in terms of the size of the market it covers, NAFTA claims a combined GDP of more than $10 trillion and a total of 390 million consumers. Thus, the NAFTA region is comparable in size to the European Union, although economic relationships are not as well developed nor as comprehensive under NAFTA. Second, NAFTA demonstrates the U.S. commitment to the already well-established trend toward globalization where countries increasingly specialize in what they do best and relinquish industries to other countries that do those activities best. By doing so, the United States has ensured this trend in specialization will continue into the twenty-first century. Third, NAFTA is controversial because of its potential effect on U.S. jobs, expanding trade deficits, and environmental degradation.

(See 525 What is globalization? 528 How fast is the world "globalizing"?)

Q 539. What does NAFTA do?

A The following are the major provisions of NAFTA:
  • **Tariffs:** Some tariffs were eliminated immediately; others were to be eliminated between five and 15 years. Tariffs on certain sensitive U.S. products, such as glassware, ceramic tile, and footwear would be phased out over a 15-year period.
  • **Investments:** Each country agrees to place no special requirements on foreign investors, treating them as they do domestic investors. Any expropriation would be compensated at fair market value through binding international arbitration rather than the host country's court system.
  • **Rules of Origin:** NAFTA countries are prohibited from operating merely as an export platform to reach other NAFTA countries' markets.
  • **Health and Environmental Standards:** NAFTA countries pledged to work toward common, but nonbinding, standards to protect the food supply and the environment. There was agreement that such standards would not be reduced to attract investment and that they had to be as stringent as those provided in to the General Agreement on Tariffs and Trade (GATT).
  • **Safeguards:** Antidumping proviso allows NAFTA countries to reinstate tariffs if one member were to flood another member's market with a product.
  • **Services:** NAFTA countries are to allow greater openness particularly in banking, telecommunications, and trucking areas (directed mainly at Mexico).

- **Intellectual Property:** NAFTA countries are required to protect copyrights for 50 years, patents for 20 years, and trademarks for 10 years (directed mainly at Mexico).

- **Side Agreements:** Established Commissions for Environmental and for Labor Cooperation responsible for monitoring compliance, investigating complaints, and imposing fines and sanctions against governments rather than businesses (directed mainly at shoring up weak labor and environmental protections).

Q **540. What trade benefits has the United States reaped since NAFTA went into effect?**

A The main benefit for the United States has been increased U.S. exports to both Mexico and Canada. During the first five years of the agreement (1994–1998), exports increased by 50 percent. Exports to Mexico have grown by 11.9 percent on average per year, and exports to Canada have grown by 6.4 percent annually. The growth in U.S. exports to Mexico is particularly impressive because Mexico suffered a severe financial crisis during 1994–1995. In addition, the United States was able to compensate for a shortfall in imports of light manufactures from Thailand and Malaysia by buying the goods from Mexico. The shortfall was related to the Asian financial crisis.

(See 576 Has the Asian crisis hurt the United States?)

Q **541. What have been the trade costs of NAFTA?**

A The main "cost" of NAFTA has been the rising trade deficit as imports have risen even faster than exports. In the case of Mexico, small trade surpluses in 1993 and 1994 developed into a trade deficit of more than $17.6 billion in 1998. With Canada, the U.S. trade balance went from a $13.4 billion deficit in 1993 to a $36.9 billion deficit by 1998. However, the trade deficit increase was not confined to NAFTA countries. The trade deficit as a whole increased sharply for the United States with most of its world trading partners, owing to the strong dollar and purchasing power of American consumers. In addition, a U.S. trade deficit is not necessarily bad, as U.S. consumers benefit from cheaper, more plentiful imports.

U.S. Trade with Canada and Mexico, 1993–1999 ($ billions)

Trading partner	1993	1994	1995	1996	1997	1998	1999	Average growth
Mexico								
U.S. exports to	$41.64	$50.84	$46.31	$56.76	$71.38	$75.37	$81.38	11.8%
U.S. imports from	40.75	50.36	62.76	74.11	87.17	93.02	109.02	17.8
Trade balance	0.89	0.48	-16.45	-17.35	-15.79	-17.65	-27.64	
Canada								
U.S. exports to	100.19	114.26	126.02	132.58	150.12	137.77	145.73	6.4
U.S. imports from	113.62	131.96	148.30	159.75	171.44	174.69	198.24	9.7
Trade balance	-13.43	-17.70	-22.28	-27.16	-21.35.	-36.92	-52.51	

Source: U.S. International Trade Commission.

542. Is the United States losing jobs because of NAFTA?

Yes, the United States is losing jobs in some areas. Between 38,000 and 420,000 jobs have been lost according to some estimates. During the first five years of the agreement, the Bureau of Labor Statistics (BLS) certified 191,000 jobs in 1,638 plants as threatened by imports from, or plant relocations to, Canada or Mexico (not necessarily because of NAFTA, but rather all imports from Canada and Mexico). Apparel and electronics accounted for 40 percent of the threatened jobs, which, ironically, were two industries where export increases from the United States were the largest. The BLS estimated that about 20 to 30 percent of those threatened employees actually collected unemployment. The rest either did not lose their jobs, or found new jobs before collecting benefits. Thus, the certifiable job loss estimated by the BLS has been about 60,000. This number omits those who lost jobs who did not apply, or were ineligible for certification. The number of these additional job losses is believed to be about 40,000. So, about 100,000 lost jobs because of NAFTA would seem a realistic figure.

543. Is the United States gaining jobs because of NAFTA?

Although there has been no definitive study, the United States probably is gaining considerably more jobs than it has lost. From 1993 to 1998, an estimated 680,000 jobs were gained by increased exports to Mexico and Canada, representing 6 percent of the total 12 million jobs created in the total U.S. economy during that period. At the same time, the manufacturing sector recorded an increase of 582,000 jobs. The

BLS does not estimate job gain by specific industry, but the industries where U.S. exports to Canada and Mexico increased the most probably indicate where the jobs were gained.

Increases in U.S. Exports to Mexico and Canada by Major Industry, 1993–1997

Industry	$ billions	% change	% of NAFTA export gain
Transport equipment	$16	54%	20%
Electronics	15	72	18
Nonelectrical machinery	15	69	18
Apparel	2	102	2

Source: Department of Commerce, Office of Trade and Economic Analysis.

Q 544. If imports are increasing faster than exports, why has there been a gain in U.S. jobs?

A If GDP and employment are rising, as they were during the 1993–1998 period, then the new imports are just added to domestic production, not substituted for domestic production. In addition, as the United States approached full employment in the 1990s, it became increasingly difficult to find workers who could have produced goods to substitute for the increased imports from Canada and Mexico, and it is not clear that the wages would be sufficiently attractive to cause workers to shift toward import substitutes. That is why even though imports have increased much faster than exports, there is a substantial net gain in jobs.

It is interesting to note that the job loss estimates are based on the number of workers in the NAFTA certification program, while job gain estimates are based on the number of jobs required to support the export gains. The reason for the different estimation method is that the increased imports do not necessarily come at the expense of jobs.

Q 545. Is there a cushion for U.S. workers who lose their jobs?

A Yes, the NAFTA Transitional Adjustment Assistance Program (TAA) identifies workers who are eligible for training and income replacement when imports are expected to "contribute importantly to the potential for job loss."

Q 546. Are American workers forced to compete with people, including children, working in sweatshops?

A It is rare that American workers produce goods that compete with goods produced in sweatshops overseas, including those that operate with child labor. In the mid 1990s, the news media exposed the practice of low-wage workers producing $150 designer (Nike) athletic shoes in a factory outside Jakarta, Indonesia, which dramatized income inequality between producers and consumers. What the reporters failed to point out were the alternatives available to the adult factory workers. In most cases these workers' second-best alternative was working for a lower income in the rice fields. It is difficult, if not impossible, for companies in labor-intensive industries that are paying $100 a day for labor in the United States to compete with companies paying $1 a day, or even much more in developing countries. This is why very labor-intensive industries shift overseas.

Q 547. Does NAFTA cause or accommodate trade and job shifts between countries?

A By reducing tariffs and investment restrictions, NAFTA accommodates the trade and labor flows dictated by the international free market price and wage framework. For example, if a U.S. worker earns $12 an hour ($1,920 per month) to produce brooms, there naturally will be a strong incentive to relocate to Mexico where a worker makes $80 a month to make brooms. This is a natural occurrence of a low-tech industry finding it hard to survive in a high-wage economy. The tariff reductions under NAFTA would not be chiefly responsible for the loss of that type of job.

Q 548. What are the main environmental concerns about NAFTA?

A From the beginning, NAFTA critics raised environmental concerns about Mexico's willingness to enforce environmental safeguards, especially in the areas of ozone depletion, industrial emissions, deforestation, and food contamination. The NAFTA side agreements on environmental safeguards were criticized for being weak in dealing with noncompliance. Fines for failure to enforce environmental safeguards could be assessed only after a lengthy process of dispute consultation, and even then, fines could not be enforced. In addition, the side agreements specified that no fines could be imposed if a government failed to enforce its environmental (or labor) laws because it had expended resources on other priorities.

From a purely competitive point of view, different levels of environmental protection could make a difference in the cost of production, which could lead to unfair trade advantages under NAFTA. However, if a country was found to have failed to enforce environmental safeguards, the NAFTA side agreements authorize the other two countries to raise tariffs on that country's goods. In summary, Mexico's association with NAFTA should improve the country's environmental protection, but the weak sanctions might also encourage some relocation of polluting industries from the United States to Mexico in order to circumvent costly environmental compliance.

(See 478 Is there really a trade-off between jobs and the environment?)

Q 549. What are the expected future benefits from NAFTA?

A Analysts believe that trade-related output increases for the United States, Canada, and Mexico will continue at a moderate pace overall, as will the supply of goods and services from Canada and Mexico. Net employment increases for the United States are not expected to be appreciable.

Q 550. What is "fast-track"?

A Fast-track authority allows the president to submit a negotiated trade treaty to Congress for an up-or-down vote within 90 days, and without amendment. NAFTA, itself, was passed by Congress under fast-track authority. Fast-track authority was first passed by Congress in 1974 and was renewed periodically. Proponents of fast-track maintain that trade negotiators have a much easier time drafting a treaty with foreign governments, knowing that the provisions will not be changed by Congress. Thus, foreign governments would find it easier to deal with the United States. The most recent effort to renew presidential fast-track authority was defeated in the House on September 25, 1998. Fast-track renewal lost the support of free trade, labor, and environmental groups over questions of the president's power to deal with issues in these areas. The future of fast-track was uncertain at the beginning of 2000.

Q 551. What are the major future issues for NAFTA?

A The major future issue for NAFTA is whether the trade agreement should be expanded to include other Latin American countries. The debate over whether to renew fast-track in 1998, for example, also included whether to add Chile to NAFTA, which was regarded as the best next candidate to join. Other future issues for NAFTA include the continued compliance with the tariff reductions and improvements in investment code and environmental standards as provided for in NAFTA. There has been no serious attempt to nullify NAFTA by the U.S. Congress.

IMMIGRATION: COSTS AND BENEFITS FOR THE UNITED STATES

Less than 2 percent of Americans claim ancestry to the indigenous peoples of America. America was originally settled and developed by Europeans, who made the United States a nation of immigrants. Beginning in the second half of the twentieth century, a new wave of immigrants began arriving, many from non-European parts of the world. Does the twenty-first century call for a new approach to immigration? Does the inscription on the Statue of Liberty have the same force as when it was erected in the late nineteenth century?

While the cultural and political aspects of immigration are weighty, economists are concerned mainly with the effect of immigration on the U.S. economy. Do the economic benefits of immigration outweigh its costs for the United States? Economists assess the economic contribution of immigrants on one side, and the wage depression and displacement of workers who are already citizens of the United States on the other. At the federal and state level, the impact of immigration on public assistance is also calculated. Do immigrants provide badly needed labor in activities for which there may not be enough U.S. citizens—such as construction, road crews, seasonal agriculture, and computer technology and other higher-skilled occupations—or are immigrants simply driving down the standard of living for many of the U.S. lower-skilled laborers?

DIMENSIONS OF IMMIGRATION

Q 552. What is the difference between an alien and an immigrant?

A An alien is *any person not a citizen or national of the United States* (Immigration and Nationality Act of 1952). Immigrants are *permanent residents of the United States, but are not citizens.* Nonimmigrants are *people admitted temporarily as visitors for a specific purpose*, such as tourists, foreign students, diplomats, temporary agricultural workers, intracompany business personnel, and exchange visitors. Aliens include both immigrants and nonimmigrants. Illegal aliens are those who are not documented as immigrants or nonimmigrants.

Q 553. What is a green card?

A A green card is a permit enabling a foreign national to live and work permanently in the United States.

Q **554. How many immigrants live in the United States?**

A Between 1970 and 1998, the number of immigrants living in the United States almost tripled, increasing from 9.6 million to 26.3 million, or 9.8 percent of the total U.S. population, according to the Center for Immigration Studies.

Q **555. How many people officially immigrate to the United States each year?**

A Legal immigration ranged between 720,461 in 1995 up to 915,900 in 1996 (Department of Justice). About half of these immigrants were new arrivals. The other half were already in the United States but had their status adjusted to immigrant.

Q **556. How does today's immigration rate compare with the all-time peak year of 1913?**

A About 1.3 million people immigrated in 1913, which came to 13 immigrants per 1,000 resident population. Today's immigration rate is about 3 per 1,000 residents.

Q **557. Which countries are the largest source of legal immigrants?**

A Mexico is the number one source of immigrants to the United States and accounts for 27 percent of all immigrants living in the United States. During 1994–1997, Mexico accounted for about 16 percent of legal immigrants (about 130,000 per year). The Philippines follows with 6.5 percent (50,000 annually), then China, Vietnam, and India with about 5 percent (40,000 annually) each.

Q **558. Which states absorb the most legal immigrants?**

A The top states for receiving immigrants are (1994–1997 annual average): California—195,000, New York—137,500, Florida—70,500, Texas—61,750, and New Jersey—47,000.

Q **559. How many illegal immigrants live in the United States?**

A Illegal alien would probably be a more accurate term, because immigrants have permission to reside permanently and work in the United States. There are an estimated 5 million (a range of 4.6 to 5.4 million) undocumented (illegal) aliens in the United States, making up 1.9 percent of the population (or 16 to 19 percent of total immigrants). The population of undocumented immigrants is growing at about 275,000 to 300,000 per year.

Q 560. Which countries are the largest source of illegal immigrants?

A Mexico is the source of more than half the illegal immigrants, an estimated 2.7 million, that currently live in the United States. El Salvador is a distant second at 335,000. Guatemala is third at 165,000, and Canada is fourth with 120,000.

Q 561. Which states have absorbed the most illegal immigrants?

A California is first with about 2 million residing illegally in state. Texas is second at 700,000. New York is third at 540,000, and Florida is fourth at 350,000.

Q 562. What are the fastest growing ethnic groups in the United States that are still immigrating at a high rate?

A Hispanics and Asians are increasing the fastest. Assuming immigration continues at its current pace and with reasonable birthrate and other necessary assumptions, the Asian population will rise from its current three percent, to eight percent of the U.S. population by 2050, and Hispanics from nine to 25 percent.

Q 563. Does the United States limit immigration?

A Yes, there is a complex set of limits based on family relationships, skills needed in the economy, and diversity. The United States limits immigration to 675,000 annually, not including refugees. There is also a ceiling of about 25,000 per country. Immediate relatives of U.S. citizens are not subject to numerical limits and are the main reason that total immigration exceeds the overall 675,000 limit, as well as the per country ceiling. Immediate relatives are spouses, unmarried minor children, and parents of adult U.S. citizens. In 1997, 535,771, or 67 percent, of the 798,378 total immigrants were relatives of U.S. citizens (322,440 were immediate relatives). Refugees and asylum cases accounted for 112,158 immigrants, employment preference (needed skills criterion) accounted for 90,607, and diversity considerations accounted for 49,374.

Q **564. What kinds of federal benefits can immigrants receive?**

A The welfare law (the Personal Responsibility and Work Opportunity Reconciliation Act) passed on August 22, 1996, changed eligibility requirements for immigrants. Most legal immigrants are barred from Supplemental Security Income (SSI) and food stamps until they naturalize or meet the 10-year work requirement. Immigrants who were receiving SSI on or before August 22, 1996, continue to be eligible for SSI. Immigrants receiving food stamps on August 22, 1996, can continue to receive them, but only if they are over 65, or under 18, or become disabled. Immigrants who arrived after August 22, 1996, cannot receive Temporary Assistance for Needy Families (TANF) and Medicaid for five years, after which their state can decide whether to provide these benefits. Refugees remain eligible for SSI, Medicaid, and food stamps for seven years after arrival, and for other programs, five years.

ECONOMIC COSTS AND BENEFITS

Q **565. What are the economic costs of immigration?**

A The commonly cited costs of immigration are the public sector transfer payments to immigrants and the reduction in working conditions, pay level, and job availability for people who are already citizens of the United States.

Economic models demonstrate that an increase in labor supply through immigration lowers the going wage rate and may throw native-born Americans out of work. However, these models have not been proven empirically for an aggregate of all wage categories. With all the variables affecting employment, isolating the effects of immigration is difficult. The positive effects of immigration could also counteract its wage depressing effects. For example by keeping wages low and profits up, investment might be increased in an industry that uses "cheap" immigrant labor. This increase in investment would increase the demand for labor, and, therefore, employment and earnings.

According to the National Academy of Sciences, immigrants do depress the wages of the low-skilled Americans, especially workers with less than a high school degree, by about 5 percent. With the downward pressure on wages in lower-skilled occupations accentuated by increasing globalization (farming out low-wage-intensive manufacturing), and to some extent, deregulation of certain major industries, a continuing inflow of immigrants can be very discouraging to low-skilled, citizen laborers with stagnating earnings.

Most studies of the impact of immigrants on the federal budget have found them not to be a fiscal burden. However, at the state and local level, immigration is costly to taxpayers in the states that absorb the bulk of immigrants, such as California, Florida, and Texas. The taxes that immigrants pay are less than the government services they use, primarily in health care and public schools. The National Academy of Sciences study found that the average household in California pays an extra $1,178 in taxes because of immigrants. People that immigrate in families tend to be costly because of the educational needs for their children. People that immigrate singly tend not to be a fiscal burden even at the state and local levels. The 1996 welfare bill's curtailment of benefits to immigrants should result in a more favorable budget balance with respect to immigrants.

(See 402 What has been the effect of deregulation on labor? 531 What are the costs of globalization?)

Q 566. What are some of the intangible benefits of immigration?

A Immigrants increase competition for jobs with native-born Americans. For most immigrants, when they first arrive, they tend to compete at lower levels such as in manual labor or retail services. Ambitious immigrants work to see their children educated and later compete on more professional levels. This tends to disrupt the human tendency to become complacent, maintaining a continuous injection of drive and competition into the U.S. workforce.

Q 567. How does the current immigration policy increase the potential for economic benefits?

A Whether by design or accident, the system of preferences (immigrant selection system) can be seen as a way to select immigrants that are likely to be more economically productive. The family preference, for example, means that these immigrants are more likely to have the support and guidance of family members who are established in the United States and are familiar with its culture and institutions, which are important for success in the workforce.

The selection criterion of economic skills needs is explicitly designed for maximum economic benefit. For example, immigration helps meet the shortfall in computer workers. Immigrants include some of the most highly skilled people from other countries such as doctors, engineers, entertainers, and star athletes. The home countries cannot compete with the lavish incentives in the United States, and they are forced to mourn the loss of their skill base. But their "brain drain" is America's gain.

Q 568. How do costs and benefits balance out?

A Some studies compare the taxes that immigrants pay with the federal benefits they receive. Of course, for immigrants, or for anyone to be paying their way, it is not enough just to pay taxes equal to or greater than the cost of direct services and welfare payments they receive. There is much more to the cost of government than mere welfare payments and social services. Taxes must also cover defense, foreign policy, and all the other services that government provides (about another 75 percent of the government budget). Yet, paying only for direct services is the threshold for many studies.

There is no clear consensus on whether costs or benefits are higher. Most reports are anecdotal and there is no recent comprehensive analytical study on the costs and benefits of immigration, but the evidence leans toward the view that immigrants create more economic benefits than costs. That is not to say that immigrant productivity is on a par with that of persons who were born in the United States, are assimilated, and understand the institutions. One study by the National Academy of Sciences looked at the "bottom line" of immigration and found a total positive overall economic impact, but a net drain on state versus federal treasuries.

Lifetime Impact of the Average Immigrant on Government Budgets

Impact on state and local treasuries	-$25,000
Impact on federal Treasury	+105,000
Total impact	+$80,000
Total impact by education level	
Less than high school	-$13,000
High school graduate	+51,000
More than high school	+198,000
Overall average impact	+$80,000

Source: National Academy of Sciences/National Research Council.

THE ASIAN FINANCIAL CRISIS: IMPACT ON THE UNITED STATES

The Asian financial crisis greatly surprised the international financial community. There was plenty of front-page news coverage of the crisis. Countries that had been the "miracle Asian tigers" were suddenly viewed as corruptly and ineptly run. Yet it was hard to find a clear systematic explanation of how it happened and what it cost. The phrase "bailout" was thrown around without clear explanation. The central question about the crisis was whether it signaled new vulnerabilities caused by increasing globalization, or whether it was merely a localized crisis that could be quickly contained using conventional financial interventions. Are there protective measures the United States could take to avoid being adversely affected by future foreign crises?

Q 569. What was the Asian financial crisis?

A During mid- to late 1997, a severe financial crisis drove the economies of five Asian nations—Thailand, Malaysia, Philippines, Indonesia, and South Korea—to the brink of collapse. Except for the Philippines, these countries had seen their economic growth soar over the previous three decades, averaging 6 percent or more in real terms. But in 1997, stock markets and currencies plummeted and several of the countries were on the precipice of default on their international loans. In 1998, all five of the countries fell into deep recession. Indonesia, for example, lost twenty years of gains in poverty reduction as close to half the population of 200 million fell below the official poverty line. The Indonesian GDP declined 12 percent in fiscal year 1998 after more than 25 years of rapid growth. In all five countries, businesses collapsed and wages fell, while prices for basic commodities increased. The stock markets in Korea, Thailand, and Malaysia dropped more than half their value. Indonesia's currency lost 80 percent of its value, while the currencies in the other four countries dropped 40 percent or more in value.

Q 570. Why did the Asian financial crisis happen?

A The long-term causes of the Asian financial crisis were a punishing combination of poor financial management, crony capitalism, and adverse regional economic trends. The immediate cause was that Asian companies borrowed too much from foreign lenders and did not protect themselves in the event of an economic decline.

Specifically, companies in these Asian nations borrowed foreign hard currency without taking prudent financial measures to protect themselves in case their currency fell. That is, they did not hedge their liabilities. Hedging can be done by purchasing a financial contract (for delivery of dollars at a given rate in their national currencies) that counteracts the risk of their currencies' devaluation. The majority of corporations in these Asian nations found the much lower (than domestic) international interest rates very attractive and were convinced that the exchange rate would remain predictable and they did not need to hedge (which, like buying insurance, is a costly thing to do). The main external factor in the simultaneous meltdown of the Asian tigers was the drag of Japan's prolonged recession. Japan is a major economic partner of East Asian countries, and its recession translated into less Japanese investment in and less Japanese trade with the crisis countries.

The impressive performance of the East Asian economies, which had recorded sustained growth of around 6 percent over the 20 years prior to the crisis, may have led their governments and international analysts to underestimate the potential for a crisis, even though there were clear signs of growing economic vulnerability. The problems of rising external debt, slowing export growth, and declining international competitiveness seemed outweighed by robust GDP growth, a budget surplus, a healthy trade balance, ample foreign exchange reserves, and moderate inflation.

(See 533 What are the major challenges for the United States and globalization?)

Q 571. Did anybody anticipate the Asian financial crisis?

A Not really, and this failure raised serious questions about the performance of international financial institutions, especially the International Monetary Fund (IMF) and the World Bank, of which the United States is by far the largest shareholder. These two institutions are responsible for conducting up-to-date analyses of countries that borrow from them. While the IMF and the World Bank were dubbing Asia's economic success as the "Asian miracle," the forces of crony capitalism and poor financial management were laying the groundwork for the deep recessions to come. Even President Clinton, as late as November 1997 (as the crisis neared full swing), at the Asia Pacific Economic Cooperation (APEC) Summit, characterized the Asian crisis as "a few small glitches in the road." In the course of a few months, these countries went from being the "Asian tigers" to the "sick kittens" that, according to the World Bank and IMF, urgently needed fundamental restructuring of their economies.

Although they did not predict the crisis, some economists did doubt the sustainability of rapid Asian growth. These economists provided evidence that showed that the East Asian growth was simply a result of resource mobilization; East Asian countries continued to save and invest more and more, including investing more in education. This investment is what fueled growth, not technological progress, or some new innovative economic paradigm. There was no unusually high growth in efficiency of these economies. Mobilizing saving and investment has limits. When the saving and investment rates "maxed out," combined with the excessive financial risk

ANATOMY OF A CRISIS: CASE OF INDONESIA

Indonesia's financial crisis began when neighboring Thailand and the Philippines decided to "float" their currencies. As international mutual fund managers withdrew further investment from much of East Asia, Indonesia's currency, the rupiah (Rp), devalued by 7 percent. Indonesia then decided to float the rupiah and tighten monetary policy, resulting in overnight interest rates as high as 81 percent.

In spite of these actions, the rupiah devaluation accelerated. The reason is that Indonesian corporations had financed their short-term external debt without hedging the exchange rate. Therefore, when the rupiah started its freefall, Indonesian corporations' losses began to skyrocket. Several corporations sought to hedge by buying foreign currencies, but it was too late and it further weakened the rupiah. When the rupiah was floated, corporations' purchases of foreign currencies soared, further accelerating the devaluation and making creditors more reluctant to lend to Indonesian corporations.

In October 1997, an IMF rescue program closed six troubled Indonesian banks. Instead of raising confidence in the banking system, depositors began to withdraw their money in large amounts. This run on banks prompted the central bank to issue increasing amounts of emergency credits to prop up the banks. Foreign banks cut their credit lines to Indonesian banks in response and the rupiah fell to Rp4,000/US$. Investors saw the inflationary implications and started dumping the rupiah, pushing it still downward.

Political uncertainties about President Suharto, who intended to stand for a seventh five-year term, and an unrealistic budget presented in January, added capital flight to Indonesia's economic problems. In the first three weeks of January alone, the rupiah fell from Rp4,850/US$ to Rp13,600/US$, even as President Suharto agreed to carry out a second-round of IMF reforms.

On January 27, 1998, the Indonesian government announced a plan to restructure banks and to resolve private corporate debt. Debate over establishing a currency board and the announcement of a third IMF package on April 8 also bolstered foreign exchange markets. The foreign exchange rate continued to fluctuate sharply, but at the much lower range of 7,500/US$ to 8,500/US$.

Rapid decline was reignited as the political situation deteriorated. Student protests, mass demonstrations, and violent rioting erupted, in which an estimated 1,200 people died. The rupiah lost 50 percent of its value from Rp8,000/US$ in early May to Rp16,000/US$ by mid-June. Fortunately, the peaceful transition of power and restraint of the army staved off further decline.

taking and other economic defects of Asian corporations, the collapse of the Asian economies was bound to happen.

Q 572. What is a "bailout"?

A Financial bailouts are money transfers to governments of countries in economic crisis to help stave off creditors and avoid default. Bailouts are designed to win back the confidence in international financial markets so that the crisis does not get worse. Bailouts are not the same as handouts, but are funding packages that come with heavy strings attached. In order to get the bailout money, governments have to agree to correct the economic practices that caused the economic crisis in the first place.

Q 573. Who takes the lead in organizing the bailouts?

A Usually, the International Monetary Fund advances the most money and takes the lead in figuring out the changes that have to be made to the sick economy. Bailouts often include funding from the World Bank and other multilateral organizations as well. The way it works is that a country gets an installment of the bailout money after it carries out an agreed set of economic reforms. Sometimes, as in the case of the Mexican bailout in 1994–1995, the United States takes the lead. As the major shareholder of both the IMF and the World Bank, the United States can also intervene indirectly, using the resources of these two institutions to conduct bailouts.

Q 574. How much were the Asian bailouts?

A Of the countries that received bailouts the amounts were

Korea	$57 billion
Indonesia	$43 billion
Thailand	$17 billion

Q 575. Who pays for the bailouts?

A For the Asian financial crisis, most of the money was paid out by the multilateral institutions, mainly by the IMF, but also by the World Bank and the Asian Development Bank. Not all of the amounts of the bailouts were disbursed. In the case of Korea, less than $40 billion was actually disbursed. Most of the remainder was pledged by the G-7 (the top industrial countries, including the United States). However, these funds would only be tapped in the Korean case should there be a second wave of crisis. Although the G-7 money was not tapped, the pledge of it apparently had a reassuring effect on international creditors.

Q 576. Has the Asian crisis hurt the United States?

A The Asian crisis hurt the United States in terms of net exports to East Asia. With their income falling and the prices for U.S. products increasing, the United States exported $15 billion less to the East Asian countries in crisis in 1998 compared with 1997, a drop of 28 percent. The trade deficit between the United States and the five countries doubled to $38.6 billion. On the flip side, U.S. consumers gained by being able to buy cheaper East Asian imports.

Still, the overall impact on the United States was minor mainly because of the economic size of the five countries. Although the area is populous, with more than 400 million people combined, the total GDP of the five countries amounts to $1,064 billion, or only 13.8 percent of the U.S. GDP, and 3.5 percent of world GDP.

Trade Balance with East Asian Partners ($ billions)

Country	1996	1997	1998	1999
Korea				
Imports	$22.5	$22.9	$23.7	$31.1
Exports	25.4	24.3	16.0	22.0
Trade balance	2.9	1.3	-7.7	-9.1
Thailand				
Imports	11.3	12.5	13.4	14.3
Exports	6.9	7.2	5.0	4.7
Trade balance	-4.4	-3.3	-8.3	-9.6
Indonesia				
Imports	8.1	9.1	9.3	9.4
Exports	3.9	4.4	2.2	1.9
Trade balance	-4.2	-4.6	-7.0	-9.6
Malaysia				
Imports	17.8	17.9	18.8	21.4
Exports	7.9	10.3	8.5	8.6
Trade balance	-9.8	-7.6	-10.3	-12.8

Trade Balance with East Asian Partners ($ billions)

Country	1996	1997	1998	1999
Philippines				
Imports	$ 8.2	$ 10.4	$11.9	$12.4
Exports	5.8	7.1	6.5	7.0
Trade balance	-2.4	-3.3	-5.3	-5.4
Total				
Imports	67.9	72.8	77.1	88.6
Exports	50.0	53.3	38.3	44.2
Trade balance	-17.8	-19.5	-38.6	-44.4

Source: U.S. International Trade Commission.

Q 577. Is the Asian crisis over?

A By the end of 1999, the crisis of imminent default by any of the countries was over, and much fundamental reform had been achieved. However, some of the underlying causes were still evident, such as crony capitalism, where corporations depend on favors from the government in the form of guaranteed markets and other protections from competition, and cheap loans for risky, highly leveraged ventures. It seems that once the scare of collapse subsided, special interests dug in to slow down economic reform. Still, all five countries that were in recession in 1998 achieved positive, albeit low, growth in 1999.

Q 578. What circumstances could cause another regional/global financial crisis?

A If a noncompetitive environment is allowed to continue in potential crisis countries, and international creditors fail again in their risk measurement, then it certainly could and probably will happen again. With the heavy outstanding debt burden of some countries' corporate sectors, a downswing in the global business cycle would make bailouts less affordable for the rich countries providing the money, and the lack of support could precipitate actual default in a number of countries.

Q 579. What steps have been taken to avert another crisis?

A International financial institutions, such as the IMF and World Bank, support long-term economic reform measures backed with technical assistance and bailout money.

Although a bit late, the reforms should reduce the chance for future crises. In addition, governments can more closely monitor capital movements and regulate financial practices including:

• Improving the surveillance of the flow of capital in and out of developing countries. In standard international economics, developing countries should always receive more capital than they pay out, because capital is scarce in developing countries and abundant in rich countries such as the United States. When developing countries start to pay out more capital (as occurred in the Asian financial crisis), alarms should go off.

• Collecting more timely, accurate, and comprehensive data to evaluate public and private finances that would provide the early warning signs. This is what international analysts call "transparency."

• Supervising and regulating the finances of private businesses to be consistent with the best international practices.

• Focusing capital controls on short-term capital inflows, not long-term inflows. Outflows should not be restricted as restrictions tend to scare away investors.

• Making any capital controls temporary and only in conjunction with "structural reforms" of the financial sector that include eliminating government-directed lending by the banking sector and inadequate capital standards, and improving the above-mentioned surveillance, transparency, and supervision and regulation.

Once financial crises are under way, the negative consequences can be minimized with the following measures:

• Better collaboration between the IMF and the World Bank that takes into account the IMF's short-term perspective and the World Bank's longer-term perspective.

• Minimizing moral hazard by making the creditors who underestimated risk take losses, either through mandatory loan rescheduling or partial cancellations of loans.

(See 534 How can the United States meet the major challenges of globalization?)

THE USE OF ECONOMIC SANCTIONS

When foreign powers commit grave wrongs against the United States or the world community, political pressures on the U.S. government to respond can run high. Short of military action, the U.S. recourse is often in the form of economic sanctions. The effectiveness of economic sanctions as a tool toward attaining political goals, however, needs to be evaluated. Policymakers need to be aware of the record of economic sanctions and under which conditions economic sanctions are likely to succeed or fail.

Q 580. What are the various types of economic sanctions?

A Economic sanctions include increasing tariffs against, or totally banning imports from, the sanctioned country (as in the case of Cuba); prohibiting exports or supplies to the sanctioned country; decreasing U.S. economic aid; freezing assets (as was done against Iran in 1979 after the overthrow of the Shah and the taking of hostages from the U.S. embassy); denying most-favored-nation (MFN) trading status (as is sometimes threatened against China); and prohibiting investment or credit either to or from the country. Noneconomic sanctions include placing travel and visa restrictions on those traveling to and from the country; setting arms embargoes; and withdrawing diplomatic relations.

Q 581. How are economic sanctions applied?

A Economic sanctions can be applied unilaterally, that is, with only one country imposing the sanction, or multilaterally. Sanctions can also be applied secondarily, that is, sanctions imposed on countries that undermine the imposition of the sanctions on another country.

Q 582. Why are sanctions applied?

A The United States has applied sanctions for human rights violations (Serbia, Cuba); aggression (Iraq against Kuwait); noncompliance with an armistice agreement (Iraq); and environmental transgressions (ivory ban, ban on imports of products from any endangered species). Sanctions have also been applied to force compliance with treaty provisions. Trade agreements, such as the North American Free Trade Agreement (NAFTA) and the General Agreement on Tariffs and Trade (GATT), require that sanctions be imposed against countries that break the rules. Sanctions appear to be applied as much to accomplish the goal of behavior modification as they are to express displeasure with these activities. Sanctions often fail when based on an urge to express outrage and when the criteria of a reasonable prospect for success are not paramount.

Q 583. What is the record of sanctions?

A The success of sanctions has been mixed, with some cases of outright failure. Sanctions are often imposed under conditions that undermine their effectiveness. Sanctions have largely failed against the Soviet Union, Cuba, Iran, Vietnam, and China.

Sanctions have had mixed success in South Africa (during Apartheid), Iraq, and Haiti, but there have been no instances of where economic sanctions brought offenders to their knees.

Q **584. When are economic sanctions least effective?**

A Economic sanctions are least effective in the following situations, exemplified by recent history:

- Unilateral sanctions tend to be weak because the sanctioned country can simply take its business elsewhere. For example, France is a major supplier of military hardware to countries that the United States has declared off limits, such as Iran. When other countries fill the gap left by American sanctions, American businesses and workers are hurt.

- Broad sanctions aimed at an offending leader of a country often hurt the innocent populace of a country and strengthen the despot. U.S. sanctions against Iraqi dictator Saddam Hussein after the 1991 Gulf War did not succeed in turning Iraq against its leader.

- Sanctions tend to lose their power over time, but they are difficult to remove if the objective has not been accomplished. U.S. sanctions against the Communist rule in Cuba, which began in the 1960s, have not been successful.

- Sanctions may invite retaliation when two parties have equal power. In 1980, President Carter won imposition of the boycott of the Summer Olympics in Moscow against the Soviet Union (for its invasion of Afghanistan). Some Western powers did not cooperate with the boycott. Four years later, the Soviet Union retaliated by boycotting the 1984 Summer Olympics in Los Angeles.

- When the sanctioned country can adapt to the sanctions, the sanctions may have long-term negative consequences for the sanctioning country. For example, when OPEC imposed its oil embargo against the United States in 1973, the United States was damaged in the short run and even suffered a serious recession (though there were additional causes). Over time, the United States developed greater fuel efficiency, OPEC lost most of its power, and, for the next quarter century, the price per barrel of oil remained far below what it was during the crisis.

- Secondary sanctions against those countries (which might even be allies) that do not support the sanctions are especially problematic and may backfire. The OPEC oil embargo was originally imposed on countries for not boycotting Israel.

Q **585. When are sanctions most effective?**

A The most effective types of sanctions are the following:

• Sanctions that are multilateral. Multilateral, focused sanctions tend to offer the most concentrated force.

• Sanctions following defeat in war. After Iraq's defeat in the 1991 Persian Gulf War, sanctions against the country, backed up by military force, worked to some extent. Weapons inspections took place and Iraqi weapon-making capability was reduced. But the weapons inspections, which were suspended several times, were eventually ended.

• Sanctions against a weak target country. Sanctions in the early 1994 were effective against the government of Haiti, but they had the disastrous consequence of a mass exodus of Haitians by boat to American shores.

• Sanctions against a target country that has a lot to lose, such as an export market, and the costs to the sanctioning country are minor.

• Sanctions with minor goals, such as winning the release of a hostage or political prisoner.

• Sanctions that encourage compliance with trade treaties. The threat of sanctions may be effective because sanctions are seldom triggered.

Q **586. How can economics guide the decision to impose sanctions on a country?**

A The decision whether or not to perform any economic activity adheres to the same principle: the benefits must outweigh the costs. Benefits may be maximized (or costs minimized) when: (1) sanctions have the support of enough other nations such that a true embargo is achieved; (2) when sanctions are focused on the offending party (as opposed to the entire population of a country), such as a particular company or individual; and (3) when sanctions zero in on a key vulnerability. The latter may require improvements in intelligence gathering to uncover what that vulnerability is. Sanctions in place must also be continually evaluated to determine whether benefits still exceed costs. Relying on such a cost-benefit approach may reduce the temptation to impose self-destructive sanctions as a means to express outrage with the conduct of another nation, company, or individual.

THE EURO AND ITS EFFECTS ON THE U.S. ECONOMY

Globalization and economic integration continue to move forward at the dawn of the twenty-first century. Europe leads the way in forming a borderless, regional economic trading bloc. A key element to Europe's economic integration is its use of a single, unified currency, the Euro. The Euro was established under the Maastrich Treaty, signed in 1992.

Q 587. What is the Euro?

A The Euro is the currency of the European Economic and Monetary Union (EMU). The EMU's 11 members adopted the new currency on January 1, 1999. Four members of the European Union (EU) will not be initial members of EMU: Denmark, Greece, Great Britain, and Sweden. The EMU differs from the EU in that the EU is a broader economic and political entity.

Q 588. Has the Euro fully replaced the currencies of these countries?

A Not yet. Although many financial transactions are currently denominated in Euros, the Euro will not be the only currency among the participating countries until July 1, 2002. Until then, the 11 countries' currencies are pegged to the Euro at a fixed rate that does not change over the period. The fixed rates are:

Conversion Rates between the Euro and Currencies of Participating Countries

Country	Currency	Conversion rate for 1 Euro
Austria	Austrian Schilling	13.760
Belgium	Belgian Franc	40.340
Finland	Markkaa	5.946
France	French Franc	6.560
Germany	German Mark	1.956
Ireland	Irish Pound	0.788
Italy	Lire	1936.270
Luxembourg	Lux. Franc	40.340
Netherlands	Guilder	2.204
Portugal	Escudo	200.482
Spain	Peseta	166.386

Q 589. How does this unified currency (the Euro) affect monetary policy?

A The eleven countries in what has become known as "Euroland" now share is a common monetary policy. This unified monetary policy is run by the European System of Central Banks (ESCB), whose members are the 11 heads of each nation's central bank and the European Central Bank located in Frankfurt, Germany. The Central Bank structure in Euroland is similar to that in the United States with the Federal Reserve Board (analogous to the ESCB Governing Council) and the 12 Federal Reserve Banks.

Q 590. How will the Euro behave compared with the dollar?

A As with most major currencies, the Euro is traded freely (or floats) with the dollar. Whether the dollar will increase or decrease in relation to the Euro depends on variables such as the basic short-term interest rate and the balance of payments in the United States compared with Europe. When interest rates are higher in the United States than in Europe (as they were at the end of the 1990s), the dollar usually increases relative to the Euro. The reason is that investors in other countries want to take advantage of the higher U.S. rates and will therefore trade their currencies for dollars needed to buy the U.S. securities. As the demand for U.S. dollars rises, the value of the dollar rises relative to the Euro. However, when the United States records large balance of payments deficits (again as it did at the end of the 1990s), compared with European surpluses, the United States trades back dollars to buy imports from other countries. So the supply of dollars increases and the value of the dollar falls relative to the Euro. The two effects should more or less cancel each other out. Thus, in the near future, there should be little movement between the dollar and the Euro.

Q 591. How will the Euro affect trade?

A The Euro will facilitate trade with Euroland countries because the currency will be the same for the 11 countries. This means that none of the 11 trading countries have to be concerned with uncertainties about future exchange rates and their impact on contract values that have a lag between signing and delivery. In addition, prices of all goods will be in the same currency. Thus, the effect will probably be an increase in intra-Euroland trade, which initially may dampen trade between Euroland and external countries, because more demand will be satisfied within Euroland. The dampening effect will likely dissipate over time because the advantage of convenience of dealing in a single currency is limited.

Q **592. Why should the United States be concerned about the effect of the Euro on the dollar's role as an international reserve currency?**

A The United States should be concerned to some extent, because the dollar's role as a reserve currency carries important advantages. Since the 1950s, the United States has enjoyed the luxury of the dollar being adopted as an international reserve currency with little competition. Other countries did not have such a luxury because if they ran trade or balance of payments deficits, they had to compensate almost immediately, usually by selling off their gold reserves. The United States, on the other hand, could just issue dollars that their creditors were and are willing to hold. The dollar now makes up 57 percent of the world's foreign exchange reserves. The United States gains at least two advantages from the dollar's role as a reserve currency. First, the countries willing to accept dollars as a reserve currency represent an expanded pool of credit for the United States, which keeps U.S. borrowing rates lower than they otherwise would be. Private holdings of dollars alone are about $4 trillion. Second, there is about $250 billion in U.S. paper currency held abroad that bears no interest. At an interest rate of 5 percent, the United States is avoiding $12.5 billion in interest costs annually.

Q **593. How will the Euro affect the U.S. dollar as a reserve currency?**

A Countries that already link their currencies to European currencies are likely to adopt the Euro as their main reserve currency, so that will not affect the dollar's share of reserve currencies. Countries in Asia and Latin America have closer ties to the United States than to Europe and will likely continue to hold a majority of dollars over other reserve currencies. Although these countries may find that diversification with more Euros is desirable, economists do not envision more than a gradual shift. The supply of a reserve currency increases only if the source country of the currency runs a balance-of-payments (BOP) deficit. Because the United States typically runs BOP deficits compared with European surpluses, U.S. dollars are currently rising as a reserve currency.

Q **594. What are the pros for the Euro?**

A The pros of the Euro include:

• **Transaction costs:** Having to deal with only one currency will reduce the cost of converting one currency into another. This will benefit businesses as well as tourists.

- **No exchange rate uncertainty**: Eliminating exchange rates between European countries eliminates the risks of unforeseen exchange rate revaluations or devaluations.
- **Transparency and competition:** The direct comparability of prices and wages will increase competition across Europe, leading to lower prices for consumers and improved investment opportunities for businesses.
- **Strength:** The new Euro will be among the strongest currencies in the world, along with the U.S. dollar and the Japanese yen. It will soon become the second-most important reserve currency after the U.S. dollar.
- **Capital market:** The large Euro zone will integrate the national financial markets, leading to higher efficiency in the allocation of capital in Europe.
- **No competitive devaluations**: One European country can no longer devalue its currency against that of another member country in a bid to increase the competitiveness of its exporters.
- **Fiscal discipline**: With a single currency, other governments have an interest in bringing countries with a lack of fiscal discipline into line.
- **European identity**: A European currency will strengthen European identity.

Q 595. What are the cons for the Euro?

A The cons of the Euro include:

- **Cost of introduction**: Consumers and businesses will have to convert their bills and coins into new ones, and they will have to convert all prices and wages into the new currency. This will involve some costs as banks and businesses need to update computer software and records for accounting purposes.
- **Nonsynchronicity of business cycles**: Europe may not constitute an "optimum currency area" because the business cycles across the various countries do not move in synch.
- **Fiscal policy spillovers**: Since there will only be a Europe-wide interest rate, individual countries that increase their debt will raise interest rates in all other countries. EU countries may have to increase their intra-EU transfer payments to help regions in need.
- **No competitive devaluations**: In a recession, a member country can no longer stimulate its economy by devaluing its currency and increasing exports.
- **Central Bank independence**: Previously, the anchor of the European Monetary System was the independence of the German Bundesbank and its strong focus on price stability. Even though the new European Central Bank (ECB) is supposed to be

independent, it will have to prove its independence. This independence will, at the very least, involve temporary costs as the ECB will have to be extremely tough on inflation.

- **Excessive fiscal discipline**: When other governments exert pressure on a government to reduce borrowing or even pay fines if the budget deficit exceeds a reference value, this may have the perverse effect of increasing an existing economic imbalance or deepening a recession.

V
Evaluating Economic Performance

This chapter looks at how to conduct a reasonable evaluation of economic performance over a given time period—such as during a presidential administration. It is important to establish a critical approach to determining how well the economy is doing or has done. In the political arena, as in spectator sports, people want to know who is winning and who is losing, and who did the best and worst. But if one wants to compare the relative performance of presidents or political parties, then all relevant information should be taken into account in a logical, consistent, and fair way.

SETTING THE STANDARD TO RATE A PRESIDENT'S PERFORMANCE

Q 596. What does the news media report on for economic performance?

A The news media tend to cover three indicators—GDP growth, the unemployment rate, and the inflation rate—as the bottom line of economic performance. Many other indicators—such as the Dow Jones Industrial Average, interest rates, housing starts, and the trade balance—are also reported, but not as widely as the "big three." Economic news reports are also mainly in the form of daily, weekly, monthly, and quarterly updates, leaving the newswatcher without a standard against which to compare the new data. What the economic reports mean—whether they are really good or bad for the economy—is often not easy to determine from news reports.

Q 597. What does the public need to know to evaluate economic performance?

A There are a number of ways to measure performance, but they all should have three elements: (1) a standard by which to measure performance; (2) measures that capture overall performance; and (3) a way to combine all the measures into a single performance measure.

The following example is a three-step method to assess economic performance during presidential administrations:

- **Step 1:** Select a range of economic indicators broad enough (10 to 20) to capture the major aspects of economic performance.
- **Step 2:** Obtain and compare annual indicators for past administrations to provide a standard by which to measure the performance period.
- **Step 3:** Establish the indicators' relative importance in measuring the economy by using weights.

The third step is the most subjective, but it makes it possible to blend the indicators into a single composite ranking.

Q 598. Which indicators should be used in judging presidential performance?

A A good sampling of both private and public sector indicators, such as the indicators used in Chapter 2, can present a readable picture of presidential performance.

Q 599. What is a reasonable time period for a historical context sufficient to evaluate economic performance?

A Probably at least two business cycles. With business cycles becoming longer, that would be about 15 to 20 years. If that period also needs to be placed in context, 30 years would be needed. Additional time periods up to the full postwar era would be relevant and beneficial.

Q 600. Can all the indicators be combined into one score?

A The task of describing economic performance in one "score" is a subjective exercise. Each indicator has to be assessed for how important it is to overall performance. Is inflation more or less important than unemployment? How important are deficits compared to improvements in productivity? These decisions must be made in order to combine all the indicators, through weights, into a single score. Then overall performance of presidents, political parties, and Congresses can be compared. Because of the subjectivity of this exercise, such a ranking is not included here.

Q **601. How does one measure the effects of a president's policies that persist after the president leaves office?**

A It is difficult to account for the effects of a president's policies accurately over time. Different policies have different lag effects on different indicators. The way to account for delayed effects is to look at how indicators behave in response to the policy, not just in the year in which the policy was introduced, but also in the following year and continuing into the future. For this reason, in the case of the economic records of presidents, it is probably better to examine indicators beginning in the year following that in which the president took office. For example, the economic record of President George Bush would carry through 1993 as the effects of policies from his administration dissipate, and the policies of his successor are formulated. Thus, President Bill Clinton's record would begin in 1994 and conclude at the end of 2001.

Q **602. Why does it not make sense to compare presidents before President Truman with those after?**

A The Great Depression and World War II constitute a "break-point" in economic comparisons. After these two enormous events, the U.S. position in the world changed. America entered the modern economy with an unrivaled economic position in the international economy, captained by mature monetary and fiscal policies that benefited from the lessons of the depression. The administration of Franklin Roosevelt was dominated by such extraordinary events as to make his administration incomparable to others. Prior to Franklin Roosevelt, the economic world was very different. All the basic tools of monetary and fiscal policy had been in place for 20 years (since 1913, with the Federal Reserve and the Federal income tax), but their usefulness in smoothing swings in the business cycle was not sufficiently understood. In addition, from a practical point of view, for many indicators, data either were not collected, or are not comparable, prior to World War II.

Q **603. How does one assign responsibility for economic results?**

A Measuring indicators during an administration shows what happened on a president's watch, but not necessarily whether the president was actually responsible. Responsibility can be determined only by analyzing what were the economic impacts of a specific policy that the president's administration, itself, devised and implemented.

Q 604. What does a president's economic record mean to the daily lives of Americans?

A Some of the main economic questions on people's minds are these: Can I earn enough money for the things I need and want? Am I building financial security? Am I saving enough for my children's education, my retirement, or my some-day elderly parents? To many Americans, a good economic performance by a president means an affirmative answer to these questions. In the aggregate, a good economic record means greater security and a higher living standard. For example, with strong growth and low unemployment, people have more economic options, and, with greater purchasing power, greater potential for both consumption and savings. In a low inflation economy, consumption and savings decisions are easier to make. Low interest rates facilitate home purchases and borrowing for education. That is why a good economic performance is considered the best political asset for any political leader. At the same time, there are many Americans, who while employed, may not be getting ahead or increasing their financial security. A good economic record may still mean that many are left out. Poverty and income and wealth distribution statistics must also be examined.

Q 605. What is the ultimate question of presidential economic performance?

A The ultimate question is also the most difficult to answer. To know whether a president really turned in a good performance is to know *what was possible to achieve under the circumstances in which the president governed.* If a president were in office during a worldwide recession, it would be unreasonable to expect that the average economic performance would compare favorably to that of presidents who did not face a recession. If a president inherited high inflation and wanted to eliminate it, the required contractionary policies would slow GDP growth. A president might also have had good success with policies to stimulate savings and investment, but for some reason, the benefits were not realized until after he left office. A true measure of economic performance must take these factors into account. Examining what happened on the president's watch is only the first step.

TRACKING THE ECONOMY: TRUMAN TO CLINTON

The rankings of presidents in this section show how each president performed with respect to each major indicator (factoring in a one-year time lag from when they took office). For each indicator, there are two rankings: (1) the average value achieved during the administration (Rate); and (2) the degree (percentage) of improvement or decline in the indicator from the previous administration (Trend). Growth rates are adjusted for inflation. All rankings are from best to worst.

Q **606. How did the ten most recent presidents rank on GDP growth?**

A The rate here is the average annual GDP growth, adjusted for inflation. The average growth from 1946 to 1999 was 3.4 percent.

Rate		*Trend*	
1. Kennedy	5.2%	Truman	5.8%
2. Ford	4.8	Ford	4.8
3. Johnson	4.6	Kennedy	3.5
4. Clinton	3.8	Clinton	1.7
5. Truman	3.7	Reagan	1.0
6. Reagan	3.4	Bush	-1.1
7. Carter	2.9	Carter	-2.0
8. Eisenhower	2.6	Eisenhower	-2.3
9. Nixon	2.2	Johnson	-2.7
10. Bush	1.8	Nixon	-3.4

Q **607. How did the ten most recent presidents rank on employment growth?**

A The rate here is the average annual employment growth. The average from 1946 to 1999 was 1.8 percent.

Rate		*Trend*	
1. Ford	3.5%	Ford	4.8%
2. Johnson	2.3	Kennedy	2.3
3. Carter	2.2	Reagan	1.0
4. Reagan	1.9	Johnson	0.3
5. Clinton	1.9	Clinton	0.1
6. Kennedy	1.8	Bush	-0.6
7. Truman	1.6	Eisenhower	-1.6
8. Nixon	1.6	Carter	-2.6
9. Eisenhower	0.9	Truman	-3.1
10. Bush	0.4	Nixon	-3.7

Q 608. How did the ten most recent presidents rank on unemployment?

A The rate here is the average annual unemployment rate. The average from 1946 to 1999 was 5.7 percent.

Rate		Trend	
1. Johnson	3.8%	Clinton	-2.6%
2. Truman	4.0	Reagan	-2.3
3. Clinton	5.1	Johnson	-1.7
4. Eisenhower	5.4	Kennedy	-1.5
5. Kennedy	5.5	Ford	-1.4
6. Nixon	5.9	Truman	-1.0
7. Bush	6.6	Carter	0.6
8. Carter	6.7	Bush	1.6
9. Reagan	7.2	Eisenhower	3.8
10. Ford	7.4	Nixon	4.9

Q 609. How did the ten most recent presidents rank on inflation?

A The rate here is the average annual inflation rate. The average from 1946 to 1999 was 4.2 percent.

Rate		Trend	
1. Kennedy	1.2%	Truman	-7.5%
2. Eisenhower	1.4	Reagan	-5.5
3. Clinton	2.4	Ford	-2.6
4. Johnson	3.4	Bush	-1.8
5. Bush	3.8	Clinton	-0.8
6. Reagan	3.9	Eisenhower	0.2
7. Truman	4.5	Kennedy	0.3
8. Ford	6.0	Nixon	3.6
9. Nixon	6.4	Carter	3.8
10. Carter	10.1	Johnson	4.2

Q 610. How did the ten most recent presidents rank on the real prime interest rate?

A The rate here is the average annual real prime interest rate. The average from 1946 to 1999 was 2.6 percent.

	Rate			*Trend*	
1. Truman	-2.6%		Nixon		-3.5%
2. Ford	0.6		Bush		-2.9
3. Nixon	1.0		Reagan		-2.0
4. Johnson	2.5		Johnson		-0.8
5. Eisenhower	2.5		Kennedy		-0.3
6. Carter	3.0		Eisenhower		1.1
7. Kennedy	3.3		Ford		1.4
8. Bush	3.6		Clinton		2.8
9. Clinton	5.6		Carter		7.5
10. Reagan	6.3		Truman		8.6

Q 611. How did the ten most recent presidents rank on savings?

A The rate here is the annual personal savings rate as a percentage of disposable income. The average from 1946 to 1999 was 8.1 percent.

	Rate			*Trend*	
1. Nixon	10.0%		Nixon		2.8%
2. Carter	9.8		Carter		2.1
3. Ford	9.1		Kennedy		0.5
4. Reagan	8.8		Eisenhower		-0.1
5. Johnson	8.5		Bush		-0.4
6. Kennedy	8.3		Johnson		-1.0
7. Eisenhower	8.0		Truman		-1.4
8. Bush	8.0		Ford		-1.9
9. Truman	7.4		Reagan		-3.3
10. Clinton	4.5		Clinton		-4.7

Q 612. How did the ten most recent presidents rank on investment?

A The rate here is the annual gross domestic private investment rate as a percentage of GDP. The average from 1946 to 1999 was 15.8 percent.

	Rate			Trend	
1. Carter	18.4%		Ford	3.7%	
2. Ford	16.9		Clinton	3.2	
3. Reagan	16.7		Kennedy	1.0	
4. Clinton	16.4		Truman	0.7	
5. Johnson	16.0		Johnson	0.5	
6. Nixon	15.9		Carter	0.4	
7. Truman	15.3		Eisenhower	0.1	
8. Kennedy	15.2		Bush	-1.5	
9. Eisenhower	14.8		Nixon	-1.8	
10. Bush	14.1		Reagan	-2.3	

Q 613. How did the ten most recent presidents rank on productivity growth?

A The rate here is the average annual productivity growth rate, adjusted for inflation. The average growth from 1947 to 1999 was 2.5 percent.

	Rate			Trend	
1. Kennedy	4.3%		Clinton	3.2%	
2. Truman	4.1		Nixon	3.1	
3. Eisenhower	2.7		Kennedy	0.9	
4. Johnson	2.7		Carter	0.5	
5. Ford	2.4		Eisenhower	-0.1	
6. Nixon	2.4		Truman	-0.6	
7. Clinton	2.2		Bush	-1.0	
8. Bush	1.9		Reagan	-1.0	
9. Reagan	1.7		Ford	-2.0	
10. Carter	0.9		Johnson	-4.2	

Q 614. How did the ten most recent presidents rank on compensation growth?

A The rate here is the average annual compensation growth rate, adjusted for inflation. The average growth from 1947 to 1999 was 1.9 percent.

	Rate			Trend	
1. Truman	3.4%		Truman	5.2%
2. Kennedy	3.1		Clinton	3.2
3. Eisenhower	3.0		Kennedy	0.8
4. Johnson	2.7		Bush	0.5
5. Ford	2.1		Ford	0.3
6. Nixon	1.4		Nixon	-0.5
7. Clinton	1.4		Carter	-1.2
8. Bush	1.2		Reagan	-1.7
9. Reagan	0.8		Johnson	-2.4
10. Carter	0.5		Eisenhower	-2.6

Q 615. How did the ten most recent presidents rank on poverty?

A The rate here is the percentage of population below the poverty line. The average from 1959 to 1998 was 14.5 percent. (Truman is not included, and only the last three years of the Eisenhower administration are included.)

	Rate			Trend	
1. Ford	11.7%		Johnson	-6.9%
2. Nixon	11.9		Kennedy	-2.9
3. Carter	12.5		Clinton	-2.4
4. Clinton	13.6		Reagan	-1.2
5. Reagan	13.9		Ford	-0.7
6. Johnson	14.2		Eisenhower	-0.5
7. Bush	14.4		Nixon	0.2
8. Kennedy	19.8		Bush	2.3
9. Eisenhower	22.1		Carter	2.5

616. How did the ten most recent presidents rank on stock market growth?

A The rate here is the annual growth in the Dow Jones Industrial Average, adjusted for inflation. The average growth from 1946 to 1999 was 3.5 percent.

Rate		Trend	
1. Clinton	16.3%	Nixon	46.4%
2. Eisenhower	10.6	Reagan	38.9
3. Reagan	10.4	Eisenhower	22.1
4. Kennedy	4.8	Clinton	12.1
5. Bush	3.9	Truman	10.7
6. Truman	2.1	Carter	4.6
7. Johnson	-5.2	Kennedy	-5.1
8. Nixon	-5.3	Bush	-10.7
9. Ford	-7.2	Johnson	-32.1
10. Carter	-8.8	Ford	-49.1

Q **617. How did the ten most recent presidents rank on the trade balance?**

A The rate here is the average annual trade balance as a percentage of GDP. The average from 1946 to 1999 was -0.3 percent, that is, a modest deficit was the average performance.

Rate		Trend	
1. Truman	1.5%	Nixon	1.0%
2. Kennedy	0.6	Eisenhower	0.8
3. Eisenhower	0.3	Carter	0.7
4. Johnson	0.1	Bush	0.4
5. Nixon	0.0	Kennedy	0.2
6. Ford	-0.6	Johnson	-0.9
7. Bush	-0.7	Reagan	-1.0
8. Carter	-0.8	Clinton	-1.9
9. Clinton	-1.5	Ford	-2.0
10. Reagan	-2.1	Truman	-3.3

Q 618. How did the ten most recent presidents rank on exports?

A The rate here is the average annual exports volume as a percentage of GDP. The average from 1946 to 1999 was 7.0 percent.

Rate		Trend	
1. Clinton	11.0%	Nixon	3.3%
2. Bush	9.9	Carter	1.9
3. Carter	9.2	Eisenhower	0.9
4. Reagan	8.0	Clinton	0.8
5. Ford	8.0	Bush	0.6
6. Nixon	6.6	Kennedy	0.3
7. Truman	5.1	Johnson	-0.1
8. Johnson	5.0	Reagan	-0.4
9. Kennedy	4.8	Ford	-0.5
10. Eisenhower	4.4	Truman	-2.2

Q 619. How did the ten most recent presidents rank on size of the federal budget?

A The rate here is the average annual federal budget as a percentage of GDP. The average from 1946 to 1999 was 19.6 percent.

Rate		Trend	
1. Truman	16.9%	Truman	-4.4%
2. Eisenhower	17.8	Clinton	-2.8
3. Kennedy	18.6	Eisenhower	-2.0
4. Johnson	18.8	Reagan	-1.0
5. Nixon	19.5	Ford	-0.6
6. Clinton	19.9	Kennedy	0.1
7. Ford	21.1	Bush	0.3
8. Carter	21.2	Johnson	0.8
9. Bush	22.0	Carter	1.5
10. Reagan	22.3	Nixon	2.0

Q 620. How did the ten most recent presidents rank on federal budget growth?

A The rate here is the average annual growth in the federal budget. The average growth from 1947 to 1999, adjusted for inflation, was 2.2 percent. (The year 1946 is omitted because the budget fell precipitously because of the drop in military spending after World War II, a phenomenon that distorts average annual budget growth.)

Rate		*Trend*	
1. Truman	0.0%	Ford	-10.7%
2. Eisenhower	0.0	Johnson	-7.2
3. Clinton	1.3	Bush	-4.1
4. Bush	1.9	Eisenhower	-4.0
5. Reagan	2.6	Reagan	-0.4
6. Ford	2.8	Kennedy	1.5
7. Nixon	3.0	Clinton	2.0
8. Kennedy	4.1	Carter	2.4
9. Carter	4.2	Nixon	14.5
10. Johnson	5.2	Truman	44.6

Q 621. How did the ten most recent presidents rank on the federal budget deficit?

A The rate here is the average annual federal budget deficit as a percentage of the total budget. The average from 1946 to 1999 was -7.6 percent.

Rate		*Trend*	
1. Truman	2.4%	Clinton	25.4%
2. Eisenhower	-2.0	Truman	20.3
3. Clinton	-3.6	Johnson	6.8
4. Johnson	-4.4	Eisenhower	5.1
5. Kennedy	-5.3	Ford	2.9
6. Nixon	-7.8	Carter	1.5
7. Carter	-11.3	Kennedy	-1.6
8. Ford	-16.5	Reagan	-1.7
9. Reagan	-19.0	Bush	-4.8
10. Bush	-19.3	Nixon	-17.8

Q **622. How did the ten most recent presidents rank on the national debt?**

A The rate here is the average annual gross federal debt as a percentage of GDP. The average from 1946 to 1999 was 56.4 percent.

Rate		Trend	
1. Carter	33.5%	Truman	-50.3%
2. Ford	36.0	Eisenhower	-16.2
3. Nixon	36.0	Johnson	-10.7
4. Johnson	42.6	Kennedy	-5.9
5. Reagan	45.4	Clinton	-4.8
6. Kennedy	51.4	Nixon	-3.7
7. Bush	61.8	Carter	-3.3
8. Eisenhower	61.9	Ford	1.0
9. Clinton	65.3	Bush	13.3
10. Truman	92.7	Reagan	20.5

Q **623. How did the ten most recent presidents rank on taxes?**

A The rate here is the annual average federal tax receipts as a percentage of GDP. The average from 1946 to 1999 was 17.8 percent.

Rate		Trend	
1. Truman	16.6%	Nixon	-1.8%
2. Eisenhower	17.4	Reagan	-1.3
3. Ford	17.6	Eisenhower	-0.9
4. Kennedy	17.6	Bush	-0.7
5. Bush	17.7	Kennedy	-0.3
6. Johnson	18.0	Ford	0.1
7. Nixon	18.0	Truman	1.1
8. Reagan	18.0	Carter	1.6
9. Carter	18.8	Johnson	2.2
10. Clinton	19.1	Clinton	2.4

Q **624. How did the ten most recent presidents rank on Social Security?**

A The rate here is the average annual growth in the Social Security trust fund, adjusted for inflation. The average growth from 1946 to 1999 was 4.8 percent.

Rate		*Trend*	
1. Reagan	19.8%	Reagan	57.6%
2. Bush	17.2	Johnson	11.9
3. Clinton	11.7	Kennedy	3.9
4. Truman	7.4	Carter	2.2
5. Johnson	6.2	Clinton	2.1
6. Eisenhower	0.7	Truman	0.7
7. Nixon	-2.0	Ford	-6.7
8. Kennedy	-2.7	Eisenhower	-9.4
9. Ford	-16.6	Nixon	-24.2
10. Carter	-19.6	Bush	-30.9

POLITICAL PARTIES AND THE ECONOMY

Q **625. Which party had the most recessions during its tenure in the White House?**

A Under Republican presidents there were seven recessions from 1946 to 1999. During the same period there were only two recessions under Democratic presidents.

Q **626. Which party had the most recessions during its majority control of Congress?**

A Eight of the nine recessions from 1946–1999 occurred under a Democratic House, and only one occurred under a Republican House. Seven of the nine recessions took place under a Democratic Senate, and only two under a Republican Senate.

Q 627. What was the economic record of various political combinations of governmental control with respect to economic growth, inflation, and unemployment?

A The following lists every possible combination of party control of the House, Senate, and the presidency from 1946 to 1999 (note that three combinations did not occur during this period):

Presidency	Senate	House	Years of party combination	GDP growth	Inflation	Unemployment
Rep.	Rep.	Rep.	2	3.2%	0.2%	5.0%
Rep.	Rep.	Dem.	6	3.4	3.8	7.9
Rep.	Dem.	Rep.	0	NA	NA	NA
Rep.	Dem.	Dem.	20	2.7	4.4	6.0
Dem.	Dem.	Dem.	20	3.5	5.2	4.8
Dem.	Dem.	Rep.	0	NA	NA	NA
Dem.	Rep.	Dem.	0	NA	NA	NA
Dem.	Rep.	Rep.	7	3.2	2.8	4.9
Average for period				3.3	4.3	5.7

Q 628. Which has more influence on the economy, Congress or the President?

A Congress generally has more influence because it makes a greater number of economic legislative and spending decisions and has final approval of the way bills and budgets are written. Presidents can veto bills, but Congress can override their vetoes with a two-thirds majority. And, despite the more concentrated power of the presidency (located in a single person versus power spread out between 525 members of Congress), Congress tends to initiate more economic proposals.

However, strong presidents can periodically exert greater influence over the economy than Congress, as in the cases of President Ronald Reagan's tax cut and tax reform and Lyndon Johnson's Great Society programs. Even in those instances, the presidents relied heavily on Congress. President Reagan's tax cut was similar to one that had been proposed by Representative Jack Kemp and Senator William Roth (the Kemp-Roth tax cut), several years earlier. Successful passage of President Johnson's Great Society programs depended on a very supportive Congress with a large Democratic majority. Another advantage of the president is the power of appointment to key economic posts, including the Fed chairman, governors of the Fed, and senior management of other economic agencies. Still, the Senate may approve, or reject, these appointments.

(See 22 Do the president's and Congress's policies affect the business cycle?)

TODAY'S ECONOMY AND PRIORITIES FOR TOMORROW

Q 629. Was the economy of the 1990s truly "great" compared to that of other periods?

A The U.S. economy in the 1990s exhibited elements of a "great" performance, with the lowest unemployment and inflation in decades, and an unprecedented boom in the stock market. However, the economy also displayed weak points, with low savings rates, high debt, and high real interest rates. A number of indicators also pointed to mediocre performance, such as the level of investment and the rate of poverty reduction. In comparison to the 1946–1999 period, growth in the 1990s was slightly below average (3.0 percent versus the average of 3.4 percent). "Satisfying" would probably be a better adjective to describe the economy of the 1990s.

In addition, there appear to be few new developments in the 1990s that would pave the way for growth in the medium and long term. The 1990s seem to be more a beneficiary than a source of such developments. Four developments in particular that began in the late 1970s and early to mid-1980s paid long-term dividends on which much of the prosperity of the 1990s was based: the end of, or victory in, the cold war resulting in huge defense budget savings ($100–$200 billion annual "peace dividend"); reduction in energy prices from the breakup of the oil cartel (the Organization of Petroleum Exporting Countries—OPEC); deregulation of major industries (airlines, financial institutions, telecommunications, etc.); and widespread corporate restructuring. The one long-term economic development of the 1990s was the meteoric rise of the Internet and the efficiencies gained with the faster and greater flow of information. Globalization—whose source belongs as much to the 1980s as the 1990s—is another factor in economic prosperity.

(See 529. What are some of the more notable examples of globalization?)

Q 630. What was President Clinton's greatest economic initiative?

A President Clinton's 1993 budget deal—the Omnibus Budget Reconciliation Act of 1993—which set the stage for deficit reduction, was probably his greatest economic initiative. NAFTA and the welfare reform bill were also significant, but the former was initiated in a prior administration and the latter passed with the help of a Republican majority in Congress. Certainly, President Clinton also deserves the credit for their passage.

The underlying premise of Clinton's 1993 budget plan was that the economy could not grow its way out of the deficit problem—something had to be done to rein in the deficits. The Clinton economic team devised a plan that was a combination of tax increases and spending cuts and freezes. Despite dire predictions of some opponents of the plan, the tax increases and tight budget did not undermine the economic expansion, and deficits were erased far ahead of schedule. At the outset of the plan, it was expected that by fiscal 1998, the fifth year of the program, the spending adjustments were to account for $87 billion and tax increases, $59 billion, for a total of $146 billion, annually.

(See 212 What was welfare reform and what did it do? 536 What is NAFTA?)

Q 631. What spending adjustments did Clinton make to help eliminate federal budget deficits?

A Effectively, there was a five-year freeze on discretionary spending such that real FY 98 spending was to be $2.5 billion below that of FY 93. This change was expected to lower inflation-adjusted spending by 13 percent. Major budget cuts occurred in defense spending, programs for the federal workforce, and the delay of COLAs for federal workers. These discretionary changes were to be worth about $36 billion in budget savings annually. On the mandatory spending side, Medicare was cut the most, $18 billion (also by FY 98), along with cuts in agricultural and veterans' programs, and student loans, with a total savings of $25.6 billion by FY 98. When the $25 billion of expected reduction in debt service was added in, the annual spending side savings added up to $87 billion by FY 98.

Q 632. Which taxes did President Clinton raise and by how much?

A The various taxes levied under the 1993 budget bill with projected revenue gains projected by fiscal 1998 were as follows:

• Marginal tax rates were increased for the top income brackets. Revenue = $27.2 billion:

Marginal Tax Rate

Taxable income	Before tax increase	After tax increase
$0–$36,900	15.0%	15.0%
$36,900–$89,150	28.0	28.0
$89,150–$140,000	31.0	31.0
$140,000–$250,000	31.0	36.0
More than $250,000	31.0	39.6

• The corporate tax rate was raised by 1 percent, some loopholes were closed, and some tax incentives were given. (Revenue = $8 billion.)

• The Medicare tax rate (2.9 percent) was applied to all earnings, not just the first $135,000. (Revenue = $7.2 billion.)

• The gasoline tax was increased by 4.3 cents per gallon. (Revenue = $5 billion.)

• The taxable portion of Social Security benefits was raised for the top 13 percent of recipients. (Revenue = $4.5 billion.)

Q 633. Was Clinton's 1993 tax increase the largest in history?

A In terms of absolute nominal dollars, the value of Clinton's 1993 tax increase was the largest in history. A more meaningful measure of the burden imposed by the tax increase is the percent of GDP taken in tax revenues before and after the Clinton tax increase. This increase can then be compared against earlier tax increases. In fact, the bracket creep of the mid- to late 1970s saw higher tax increases on individuals as a percentage of GDP, but bracket creep was a passive increase that did not take place by act of Congress, but rather by the lack of indexing the tax brackets to inflation.

Looking at the average tax share of GDP for all years under Clinton compared with that of the preceding Bush administration, Clinton did raise taxes substantially, 1.5 percentage points of GDP higher than the average during the Bush term. Comparing tax year 1993 with tax year 1999, tax receipts as a percentage of GDP moved up 2.4 percentage points, a hefty increase by historical standards. Part of the reason for this increase was the result of a positive trend, the steady growth in the economy that pushed taxpayers into higher brackets. This adjustment should be taken into account in citing Clinton's tax increase as "the largest in history."

U.S. Congress. There are also congressional committees, with separate staffs, that deal directly or indirectly with economic matters: Committee on Agriculture, Committee on Appropriations, Committee on Banking and Financial Services, Committee on the Budget, Committee on Commerce, Committee on Education and the Workforce, Committee on Resources, Committee on Small Business, Committee on Transportation and Infrastructure, Committee on Ways and Means, Joint Committee on Taxation, and the Joint Economic Committee. *(www.house. gov* and *www.senate.gov)*

INDEPENDENT FEDERAL AGENCIES

Environmental Protection Agency (EPA): protects human health and safeguards the natural environment. The EPA was created in 1970 to consolidate the environmental activities carried out by six different agencies. Environmental protection contributes to making communities and ecosystems diverse, sustainable, and economically productive. The United States plays a leadership role in working with other nations to protect the global environment. *(www.epa.gov)*

Export-Import Bank of the United States (Ex-Im Bank): helps finance the overseas sales of U.S. goods and services, provides guarantees of working capital loans for U.S. exporters, guarantees the repayment of loans, and makes loans to foreign purchasers of U.S. goods and services. Ex-Im Bank also provides credit insurance that protects U.S. exporters against the risks of nonpayment by foreign buyers for political or commercial reasons. Ex-Im Bank does not compete with commercial lenders, but assumes the risks they cannot accept. *(www.exim.gov)*

Federal Communications Commission (FCC): regulates interstate and international communications by radio, television, wire, satellite, and cable. The FCC's jurisdiction covers the 50 states, the District of Columbia, and U.S. possessions. The FCC was established by the Communications Act of 1934. *(www.fcc.gov)*

Federal Deposit Insurance Corporation (FDIC): maintains the stability of and depositors' confidence in the nation's banking system. To achieve this goal, the FDIC has insured deposits and promoted safe and sound banking practices since 1933. *(www.fdic.gov)*

Federal Reserve (The Fed): as the nation's central bank, provides the United States with a safer, more flexible, and more stable monetary and financial system. The Fed conducts monetary policy; supervises and regulates banking institutions and protects the credit rights of consumers; maintains the stability of the financial system; and provides certain financial services to the U.S. government, the public, financial institutions, and foreign official institutions. The Fed also produces monetary aggregate and interest rate statistics including the prime rate. The Fed was established by Congress in 1913. *(www.bog.frb.fed.us)*

Federal Trade Commission (FTC): enforces a variety of federal antitrust and consumer protection laws. The FTC seeks to ensure that markets function competitively, and are vigorous, efficient, and free of undue restrictions. The FTC also works to enhance the smooth operation of the marketplace by eliminating acts or practices that are unfair or deceptive. *(www.ftc.gov)*

Securities and Exchange Commission (SEC): administers the federal securities laws as an independent, nonpartisan, quasijudicial regulatory agency. These securities laws protect investors in securities markets that operate fairly and ensure that investors have access to disclosure of all material information concerning publicly traded securities. The SEC also regulates firms engaged in the purchase or sale of securities, people who provide investment advice, and investment companies. *(www.sec.gov)*

Social Security Administration (SSA): administers the $400 billion Social Security (OASDI) program and the $20 billion Supplemental Security Income program. Created by the Social Security Act of 1935, the SSA became an independent federal agency in 1995. *(www.ssa.gov)*

U.S. International Trade Commission (USITC): as an independent, quasijudicial federal agency, provides trade expertise to both the legislative and executive branches of government, determines the impact of imports on U.S. industries, and directs actions against certain unfair trade practices, such as patent, trademark, and copyright infringement. USITC analysts and economists investigate and publish reports on U.S. industries and the global trends that affect them. The agency also updates and publishes the Harmonized Tariff Schedule of the United States. *(www.usitc.gov)*

MAJOR INTERNATIONAL INSTITUTIONS

Organization for Economic Cooperation and Development (OECD): seeks to promote the highest sustainable economic growth and employment and a rising standard of living in member countries, while maintaining financial stability; contributes to sound economic expansion in member as well as nonmember countries in the process of economic development; contributes to the expansion of world trade on a multilateral, nondiscriminatory basis in accordance with international obligations; researches and monitors the world economy; and provides a forum for economic discussion that may lead to international economic agreements. The OECD, established in 1961 as an organization of 29 industrialized countries, is headquartered in Paris. *(www.oecd.org)*

World Trade Organization (WTO): monitors the rules of international trade and compliance with trade agreements. Created in 1995 as a result of the Uruguay Round of the General Agreement on Tariffs and Trade (GATT), WTO marked one of the biggest reforms of international trade since GATT was created in 1948. GATT deals only with trade in goods. The WTO Agreements now cover services and intellectual property as well. The main principles which WTO follows are nondiscrimination ("most-favored-nation" treatment and "national" treatment), freer trade, predictable policies, competition, and extra provisions for less-developed countries. *(www.wto.org)*

REGIONAL DEVELOPMENT BANKS

African Development Bank (AFDB): a multinational development bank supported by 77 nations (member countries) from Africa, North and South America, Europe, and Asia. The AFDB was established in 1964 and headquartered in Abidjan, Cote d'Ivoire; its mission is to promote economic and social development through loans, equity investments, and technical assistance. *(www.afdb.org)*

Asian Development Bank (ADB): a multilateral development finance institution, located in Manila, Philippines. ADB was founded in 1966 by 31 member governments to promote the social and economic progress of the Asian and Pacific region. The Bank's membership has grown to 57, of which 41 are from within the region and 16 from outside the region. The United States is tied with Japan as the largest shareholder with 16 percent of total shares. *(www.adb.org)*

Inter-American Development Bank (IADB): the oldest and largest regional development institution established in December 1959 to help accelerate economic and social development in Latin America and the Caribbean. *(www.iadb.org)*

United Nations (UN) Organizations

The UN system, which is composed of the UN, specialized agencies (such as the World Bank and the IMF), and the UN programs and funds, works in a variety of ways to promote economic and social goals. The mandates of the specialized agencies cover virtually all areas of economic and social endeavor. The agencies provide financial and technical assistance and other forms of practical help to countries around the world. Working in cooperation with the UN, these agencies help formulate policies, set standards and guidelines, foster support and mobilize funds. The United States, as a member of the UN, often uses UN agencies to carry out economic development activities. *(www.un.org)*

Food and Agriculture Organization (FAO): works to improve agricultural productivity and food security, and to better the living standards of rural populations. FAO is based in Rome, Italy. *(www.fao.org)*

International Monetary Fund (IMF): promotes international monetary cooperation, exchange stability, and orderly exchange arrangements; fosters economic growth and high levels of employment; and provides temporary financial assistance to countries under adequate safeguards to help ease balance of payments adjustments. The IMF is a specialized agency that is technically a part of, but mostly independent of, the UN system. Established in 1946, the IMF has 182 member countries with the United States as the largest shareholder. *(www.imf.org)*

U.N. Development Program (UNDP): administers and coordinates UN technical assistance programs. Founded in 1965, UNDP is the UN's largest program with a staff of 5,300 in its New York headquarters and its 132 offices throughout the world. It serves 170 countries and provides $6.5 billion in development assistance. *(www.undp.org)*

U.N. Industrial Development Organization (UNIDO): helps improve living conditions and promote global prosperity by offering tailor-made solutions for the sustainable industrial development of developing countries and countries with economies in transition. UNIDO helps formulate policies and programs to improve working conditions and employment opportunities, and set labor standards used by countries around the world. *(www.unido.org)*

World Bank: commits more than $20 billion in development assistance loans each year to help developing countries strengthen their economies and expand their markets. Although World Bank loans are available only to governments, the World Bank also works with local communities, NGOs and, through the International Finance Corporation, private enterprise to encourage sustained growth. The United States is the largest shareholder of the World Bank, which is considered a sister organization of the IMF. *(www.worldbank.org)*

MAJOR ECONOMIC THINK TANKS (RESEARCH ORGANIZATIONS)

The following is a partial list of some of the more prominent think tanks in economic policy. Think tanks are especially useful sources in covering current economic issues because they provide greater depth of coverage than the mass media does. It is important to note, however, that many or most think tanks and their publications have some ideological slant, despite their nonpartisan claims.

American Economics Association (AEA): organized in 1885 at Saratoga, N.Y., and incorporated in 1923 in Washington, D.C., the AEA now has 22,000 economists as members and 5,500 institute subscribers. More than 50 percent of the membership is associated with academic institutions, 35 percent with business and industry, and the remainder largely with federal, state, and local government agencies. The AEA publishes the *American Economic Review, Journal of Economic Perspectives,* and the *Journal of Economic Literature.(http://rfe.wustl.edu)*

American Enterprise Institute (AEI) for Public Policy Research: founded in 1943 in Washington, D.C., AEI is one of America's largest and most respected think tanks. It is dedicated to preserving and strengthening the foundations of freedom through scholarly research and open debate. AEI research covers economics and trade; social welfare; government tax, spending, regulatory, and legal policies; U.S. politics; international affairs; and U.S. defense and foreign policies. The institute's 50 resident scholars and fellows include some of America's foremost economists, legal scholars, political scientists, and foreign policy experts. *(www.aei.org)*

Brookings Institution: founded in 1916 as the Institute for Government Research (taking the name of Brookings in 1927), Brookings is committed to publishing independent and analytical findings for the information of the public. In its conferences and activities, Brookings serves as a bridge between scholarship and public policy, bringing new knowledge to the attention of decisionmakers and affording scholars a better insight into public policy issues. *(www.brookings.org)*

Cato Institute: founded in 1977 as a nonpartisan public policy research foundation headquartered in Washington, D.C., the institute is named for *Cato's Letters,* which are libertarian pamphlets that helped lay the philosophical foundation for the American Revolution. The institute has grown to be an internationally recognized institution of research and policy analysis with 55 adjunct scholars and 14 fellows. *(www.cato.org)*

Conference Board (CB): founded in 1916, CB is a business membership and research network headquartered in New York. Membership includes 3,000 businesses in 67 countries. Its mission is to improve the business enterprise system and to enhance the contribution of business to society. CB produces an index of leading indicators and a consumer confidence index that the media quotes widely. *(www.conference-board.org)*

Heritage Foundation: founded in 1973, the Heritage Foundation is a nonpartisan, tax-exempt institution and one of the nation's largest public policy research organizations. Its mission is to formulate and promote conservative public policies based on the principles of free enterprise, limited government, individual freedom, traditional American values, and a strong national defense. *(www.heritage.org)*

Hoover Institution on War, Revolution and Peace: founded in 1919 at Stanford University by Herbert Hoover, who later became the thirty-first president of the United States, the institution contains a library, archives, and center of scholarship and public policy research committed to generating ideas that define a free society. The Hoover Institution has 60 resident scholars-specialists in economics, political science, history, international relations, law, and other disciplines who study, analyze, write, and publish on current public policy issues as well as historical topics. *(www.hoover.org)*

Institute for International Economics (IIE): founded in 1981, IIE is a private, nonprofit, nonpartisan research institution devoted to the study of international economic policy. The institute's total staff of about 50 includes more than two dozen researchers. Its agenda emphasizes macro-

sidered in the index's value. Stock splits do not affect the DJIA. Although only 30 stocks are included, the companies represented are so large as to account for more than 20 percent of total market value.

Economies of scale. The principle that the bigger a company is, the lower are its production costs. Put more technically, the average unit cost of production decreases as the amount, or scale, of production increases. The sources of economies of scale may be either internal or external. Internal economies of scale occur when a company's cost of producing one unit of output falls until all of the company's machine and plant capacity are fully utilized. External economies of scale occur when an industry becomes large enough so that services and capacities develop that support the industry's productivity. This support might include a better-trained labor pool, a side industry that produces needed components, or a trade association that circulates important industry information.

Efficient market hypothesis. The theory that holds that prices prevailing in the market reflect all available information. The implication is that the market cannot be beaten, or that speculators cannot make excess profits, because whatever information one player has, all have.

Euro. The transnational currency of the European Monetary Union. The Euro will be put into physical use, replacing national currencies in January 2002. During the transition period, the Euro will hold a fixed value vis-à-vis the currencies of the 11 countries where the Euro is effective. One Euro equals 13.7 Austrian Schillings, 40.3 Belgian Francs, 5.9 Finnish Markkaa, 6.6 French Francs, 1.9 German Marks, 0.78 Irish Pounds, 1,936 Italian Lire, 40.3 Luxembourgian Francs, 2.2 Dutch Guilders, 200.5 Portuguese Escudos, and 166.4 Spanish Pesetas. In 1999 the Euro fluctuated vis-à-vis the U.S. dollar at around 1 Euro per dollar.

Eurodollars. Bank deposit liabilities denominated in U.S. dollars but not subject to U.S. banking regulations. For the most part, banks offering Eurodollar deposits are outside the United States, but since 1981, non-U.S. residents can conduct business with international banking facilities in the United States. Eurodollar deposits are owned by individuals, corporations, and governments. The Eurodollar market grew rapidly in the 1960s and 1970s when U.S. financial regulations were very tight. The estimated size of the Eurodollar market is $2 trillion, which is about one-third of the M3 money supply.

Federal Reserve. The U.S. central bank founded in 1913 to provide a flexible and stable monetary and financial system. Its main functions are to (1) conduct monetary policy; (2) supervise and regulate banking institutions and protect the credit rights of consumers; (3) maintain the stability of the financial system; and (4) provide certain financial services to the U.S. government.

Fee-for-service. The traditional health care relationship where patients choose their doctors and pay for their services, either directly, or through a third party, usually an insurance company.

Flexible spending account (FSA). An account offered by employers to set aside, out of the employee's paycheck, pretax dollars to pay for insurance premiums and other expenses including child care. It is a way for employees to avoid taxes on medical coverage. FSAs have a use it or lose it provision, such that whatever money the employee does not use is returned to the employer.

Flow variable. A variable that has a time dimension; it is measured as so much per unit of time. For example, deficits are measured during the course of a year. GDP is measured by quarter or year. In other words, a flow variable has to have a time dimension to give it meaning. (See Stock variable.)

Game theory. A branch of economics where one person's, or group's, actions materially affect another's. For example, if a village depends on a pond for fish, the villagers must be careful not to overfish or they will wipe out the fish supply. Game theory examines individual behavior faced with such situations. Will individuals, fearing that others will do the same, act greedily and take as many fish as possible? These individuals know that the fish stock may be wiped out, but at least they will get fish for themselves. Game theory looks into strategies that help to obtain optimal results in these situations. Game theory is often applicable to environmental protection issues and wage bargaining between employers and unions.

Gross domestic product (GDP). The total monetary value of all goods and services produced in a nation during a single year.

Health maintenance organization (HMO). An organization that is both a health care provider and an insurer. Doctors receive a fixed fee per beneficiary rather than fees for services. The incentive to provide unnecessary medical care is eliminated, but an incentive to underprovide services is introduced.

Hedge. A hedge is the purchase or sale of a derivative security (such as options or futures) in order to reduce or neutralize all or some portion of the risk of holding another security. A hedge fund is a fund holding derivative securities. (See Call option; Put option.)

Inflation. A rise in the general price level of goods and services. The government's main measure of inflation is the Consumer Price Index (CPI). (See Consumer Price Index.)

International Monetary Fund (IMF). An institution set up under the Bretton Woods system for the purpose of creating a favorable environment for trade by helping countries maintain stable exchange rates. Countries experiencing balance of payments difficulties may receive medium-term (often for five years) financing from the IMF until the difficulties could be solved, such as through improved monetary policy.

Keynesian. A branch of economics based on the work of John Maynard Keynes (1883–1946), an English economist who held that demand, rather than supply, drove the economy. Keynes believed that it was up to government to supply the necessary additional demand for goods and services to eliminate unemployment.

Lag effect of economic policies. Economic variables usually do not respond immediately to economic policies. There is almost always some time lag. A tax cut, for instance, may take six months or a year to have a significant impact on the growth of GDP, and the effects may last for years. An increase in investment expenditure during one year does increase GDP in the same year, but that increase in investment also contributes to higher growth in future years. Thus, both tax cuts and investment have lag effects, as do most economic policies.

Lagging indicator. A process that reaches a peak or a trough *after* the general economy does. *The Survey of Current Business* publishes a lagging indicators index which, on average, follows peaks by six months and troughs by about 10 months. The lagging indicators index includes the prime interest rate, the change in the consumer price index for services, the average duration of unemployment, and the ratio of consumer installment credit outstanding to personal income. Lagging indicators serve as a confirmation of the cyclical fluctuations in the economy. (See Leading indicator.)

Leading indicator. A process that reaches a peak or a trough *before* the general economy does. *The Survey of Current Business* publishes a leading indicators index which, on average, leads peaks and troughs by about 11 months. Leading indicators are useful predictors of the future direction of the economy. Examples of leading indicators are: the number of permits for building new houses, the Standard & Poor's 500 stock average, plant and equipment orders, average weekly claims for unemployment insurance, consumer expectations index, and growth in the money supply (M2). A change in the direction of the indicator should be sustained for at least three months before the indicator becomes predictive. (See Lagging indicator.)

Macroeconomics. The study of an entire national economy rather than the individuals and firms that make it up. Macroeconomics is especially concerned with the factors influencing economic (GDP) growth, including fiscal and monetary policy. Macroeconomics deals also with the determination of economy-wide inflation, employment, and the balance of payments. (See Microeconomics.)

Managed competition. A feature of President Clinton's 1994 health care proposal whereby individuals choose among competing health plans that are required to charge the same premium to every applicant regardless of medical history. Because of this strict requirement, many analysts feared that health plan providers would find ways to screen out people with high-cost conditions.

Marginal tax rate. The rate at which the last dollar of income is taxed. For example, under a system with two tax brackets (25 percent tax on the first $40,000 of income and 40 percent above that amount), a person who earns $100,000 per year is, therefore, in the 40 percent tax bracket. The last dollar earned was taxed at 40 percent, hence a 40 percent marginal tax rate. (See Average tax rate.)

Market value. The last reported price at which an asset was sold. In stocks and bonds, market value is the current quote. The market value is normally based on the market's expectation of what the return on the company or asset will be. (See Book value.)

Means-tested programs. Programs that provide cash or services to people who meet a test of need based on income and assets. Most means-tested programs are entitlements, such as Medicaid, the food stamp program, Supplemental Security Income, family support, and veterans' pensions. A few means-tested programs, such as subsidized housing and various social services, are funded through discretionary appropriations.

Medical savings accounts (MSAs). Accounts from which people pay medical bills. Annual deposits are usually made by employers in lieu of more generous insurance coverage. Employees get to keep whatever money they do not spend from their account (unlike flexible spending accounts). Under some proposals, these deposits would be tax free and unspent funds would grow over a person's lifetime and be available for postretirement health care, incorporated into a pension fund or into the account holder's estate.

Microeconomics. The study of economics on a disaggregated level. In other words, microeconomics focuses on single economic agents such as individual firms, households, and individuals. In particular, microeconomics examines optimizing behavior of these agents, that is, utility maximization of individuals and profit maximization of firms, which in turn, determines prices. Microeconomics deals mainly with demand theory; theory of the firm and factors of production, land, labor, and capital; and how they can be efficiently combined in the production process.

Misery index. A measure of economic performance that adds the inflation rate to the unemployment rate. Devised during Jimmy Carter's 1976 presidential campaign, the index had reached 14 percent. Four years later, when Carter ran for reelection, the misery index stood at more than 20 percent.

Monetarist. An economist who stresses monetary causes of cyclical fluctuations and inflations, believes that stabilization policy is not needed, and believes that monetary policy is superior to fiscal policy in achieving policy goals. (See Chicago School of Economics.)

Nominal. The actual value of an indicator, that is, one from which inflation has not been removed.

North American Free Trade Agreement (NAFTA). An agreement to reduce obstacles and promote trade between the United States, Canada, and Mexico. NAFTA negotiations began with Canada during the Reagan administration in the 1980s. Mexico saw advantages of participating and was able to join in the agreement. The final agreement was reached during the Bush administration in 1992, and the treaty was ratified in late 1993 under President Clinton.

Off-budget. Government spending or revenues excluded from the budget totals by law. The revenues and outlays of the two Social Security trust funds and the transactions of the U.S. Postal Service are off-budget.

Payroll tax. A tax levied on the wage bill, or payroll. Payroll taxes include Social Security and Medicare and unemployment insurance, and are separate from the income tax.

Poverty line. The income level below which a person or a family cannot meet its basic needs and is, therefore, poor. Poverty lines, or thresholds, are based on family size. If a family is below the threshold income for that family size, then each person in the family is counted as poor.

Producer surplus. The revenue that the producer receives from a producing a good or service that is above the minimum amount the producer is willing to accept to supply the same amount of that good. It can be measured by estimating the theoretical, lowest price at which the producer is willing to produce the good or service. This price is subtracted from the actual price charged. For example, if a producer charges $70 for a radio that could have been sold for $50 in order to attain the minimum profit, the producer surplus is therefore $20 ($70 - $50) per radio. (See Consumer surplus.)

Production possibility frontier. Also called the transformation curve, it represents the possible combinations of products the economy can produce when operating at maximum efficiency.

Progressive tax. A tax whose rate increases with income level. The federal income tax is a progressive tax because it has several tax brackets with higher rates at higher income levels. Progressive taxes reduce differences in after-tax income across the population.

Purchasing power. Usually applied to the strength of a currency or to consumers' ability to buy things. The currency of a country with low inflation gains purchasing power compared with the currencies of countries with high inflation. Consumers' purchasing power is enhanced by savings, low inflation, and productivity growth. When consumers have an increase in purchasing power, the economy can expect a surge in growth.

Put option. An option to sell an asset at a specified exercise price on or before a specified exercise date. (See Call option.)

Random walk. The characteristic of an indicator that shows no pattern over time. Stock prices are said to follow a random walk. The only thing that can affect a stock's price is news about the firm that cannot be anticipated and, thus, is random.

Rational expectations. A theory in economics that holds that individuals will form expectations that will be correct on average. A consequence of rational expectations is that government policy seeking to stimulate demand will fail. For example, if the government expands the money supply by 5 percent, the public will recognize it and conclude that prices will rise. They will demand higher wages and/or prices for their goods. With the resulting 5 percent inflation, there would be no positive impact on employment of increasing the money supply.

Real. A descriptive term usually applied to an economic indicator in which the effects of inflation have been taken out. For example, if the noninflation adjusted GDP growth rate is 10 percent, but the inflation rate is 5 percent, then the *real* GDP growth rate is about 5 percent.

Year	Real growth in compensation per hour	Number below poverty line (thousands)	% of population below poverty line	Dow Jones Industrial Average (end of year)	Dow Jones Industrial Average (inflation adjusted)	Balance on goods & services ($ millions)	Real balance on goods & services ($ millions)
1945				192.91	1502.41	-800	-6,230
1946				177.20	1274.29	7,100	51,058
1947				181.16	1138.78	10,800	67,889
1948	0.5%			177.30	1031.01	5,400	31,401
1949	2.8%			200.13	1177.90	5,200	30,605
1950	5.9%			235.41	1367.76	700	4,067
1951	1.5%			269.23	1449.73	2,400	12,923
1952	4.4%			291.90	1542.50	1,000	5,284
1953	5.6%			280.90	1472.59	-800	-4,194
1954	2.7%			404.39	2105.23	300	1,562
1955	3.0%			488.40	2552.80	400	2,091
1956	5.1%			499.47	2572.08	2,300	11,844
1957	3.1%			435.69	2171.96	4,000	19,940
1958	1.7%			583.65	2830.31	400	1,940
1959	3.5%	39,490	22.4%	679.36	3271.54	-1,680	-8,090
1960	2.4%	39,851	22.2%	615.89	2916.31	2,418	11,450
1961	3.0%	39,628	21.9%	731.14	3427.76	3,355	15,729
1962	3.6%	38,625	21.0%	609.18	2827.70	2,448	11,363
1963	2.2%	36,436	19.5%	767.21	3515.55	3,300	15,121
1964	3.8%	36,055	19.0%	874.13	3954.08	5,484	24,807
1965	2.2%	33,185	17.3%	969.26	4315.35	3,863	17,199
1966	3.6%	28,510	14.7%	785.69	3399.47	1,872	8,100
1967	2.6%	27,769	14.2%	905.11	3798.42	1,441	6,047
1968	3.8%	25,389	12.8%	943.75	3800.94	-1,265	-5,095
1969	1.4%	24,147	12.1%	800.36	3055.39	-1,218	-4,650
1970	1.8%	25,420	12.6%	838.92	3029.89	1,218	4,399
1971	1.9%	25,559	12.5%	890.20	3079.59	-3,014	-10,427
1972	3.0%	24,460	11.9%	1020.02	3419.28	-7,992	-26,791
1973	2.2%	22,973	11.1%	850.86	2685.71	609	1,922
1974	-1.2%	23,370	11.2%	616.24	1752.38	-3,149	-8,955
1975	1.0%	25,877	12.3%	852.41	2221.79	13,551	35,320
1976	3.0%	24,975	11.8%	1004.65	2475.04	-2,281	-5,619
1977	1.3%	24,720	11.6%	831.17	1922.69	-23,670	-54,754
1978	1.8%	24,497	11.4%	805.01	1730.64	-26,119	-56,152
1979	0.3%	26,072	11.7%	838.74	1620.09	-23,974	-46,308
1980	-0.3%	29,272	13.0%	963.99	1640.54	-14,893	-25,345
1981	0.1%	31,822	14.0%	875.00	1,350.04	-14,978	-23,110
1982	1.4%	34,398	15.0%	1,046.54	1,520.45	-20,542	-29,844
1983	0.1%	35,303	15.2%	1,258.64	1,771.89	-51,653	-72,716
1984	0.3%	33,700	14.4%	1,211.57	1,635.31	-102,015	-137,694
1985	1.4%	33,064	14.0%	1,546.67	2,015.07	-114,211	-148,799
1986	3.3%	32,370	13.6%	1,895.95	2,424.06	-131,882	-168,618
1987	0.4%	32,221	13.4%	1,938.83	2,392.75	-142,260	-175,566
1988	1.0%	31,745	13.0%	2,168.57	2,570.87	-106,285	-126,002
1989	-1.5%	31,528	12.8%	2,753.20	3,114.46	-80,723	-91,315
1990	0.6%	33,585	13.5%	2,633.66	2,826.60	-71,422	-76,654
1991	1.0%	35,708	14.2%	3,168.80	3,263.86	-20,697	-21,318
1992	2.7%	38,014	14.8%	3,301.11	3,301.11	-27,857	-27,857
1993	-0.1%	39,265	15.1%	3,754.09	3,644.75	-60,489	-58,727
1994	-0.2%	38,059	14.5%	3,834.44	3,628.42	-87,096	-82,416
1995	-0.6%	36,425	13.8%	5,117.12	4,710.29	-84,255	-77,556
1996	0.5%	36,529	13.7%	6,448.27	5,762.73	-88,965	-79,507
1997	1.5%	35,574	13.3%	7,908.25	6,908.60	-88,308	-77,145
1998	4.0%	34,476	12.7%	9,181.43	7,897.82	-149,566	-128,656
1999	3.1%	NA	NA	11,497.10	9,677.69	-256,800	-216,162
Growth/average	1.9%		14.5%				

Year	Trade volume as % of GDP	U.S. exports as % of GDP	Federal budget outlays ($ millions)	Federal outlays as % of GDP	Federal budget deficit ($ millions)	Federal deficit as % of budget
1945	6.1%	2.9%	92,712	41.9%	(47553)	-51.3%
1946	9.1%	6.1%	55,232	24.8%	(15,936)	-28.9%
1947	10.4%	7.3%	34,496	14.7%	4,018	11.6%
1948	9.1%	5.5%	29,764	11.6%	11,796	39.6%
1949	8.5%	5.2%	38,835	14.3%	580	1.5%
1950	7.8%	4.0%	42,562	15.6%	(3,119)	-7.3%
1951	8.9%	4.8%	45,514	14.2%	6,102	13.4%
1952	8.5%	4.4%	67,686	19.4%	(1,519)	-2.2%
1953	7.9%	3.8%	76,101	20.4%	(6,493)	-8.5%
1954	7.8%	4.0%	70,855	18.7%	(1,154)	-1.6%
1955	8.0%	4.1%	68,444	17.3%	(2,993)	-4.4%
1956	8.8%	4.6%	70,640	16.5%	3,947	5.6%
1957	9.1%	5.0%	76,578	17.0%	3,412	4.5%
1958	8.3%	4.2%	82,405	17.9%	(2,769)	-3.4%
1959	8.5%	4.1%	92,098	18.7%	(12,849)	-14.0%
1960	9.1%	4.8%	92,191	17.7%	301	0.3%
1961	8.9%	4.8%	97,723	18.4%	(3,335)	-3.4%
1962	8.9%	4.7%	106,821	18.8%	(7,145)	-6.7%
1963	9.0%	4.8%	111,316	18.5%	(4,756)	-4.3%
1964	9.3%	5.1%	118,528	18.5%	(5,915)	-5.0%
1965	9.3%	4.9%	118,228	17.2%	(1,411)	-1.2%
1966	9.6%	4.9%	134,532	17.8%	(3,697)	-2.7%
1967	9.7%	5.0%	157,464	19.4%	(8,642)	-5.5%
1968	10.1%	5.0%	178,134	20.5%	(25,161)	-14.1%
1969	10.1%	5.0%	183,640	19.3%	3,242	1.8%
1970	10.8%	5.5%	195,649	19.3%	(2,842)	-1.5%
1971	10.8%	5.3%	210,172	19.4%	(23,033)	-11.0%
1972	11.3%	5.3%	230,681	19.6%	(23,372)	-10.1%
1973	13.2%	6.6%	245,707	18.7%	(14,908)	-6.1%
1974	16.8%	8.3%	269,359	18.7%	(6,135)	-2.3%
1975	15.8%	8.3%	332,332	21.3%	(53,242)	-16.0%
1976	16.4%	8.2%	371,792	21.4%	(73,732)	-19.8%
1977	16.8%	7.8%	409,218	20.7%	(53,659)	-13.1%
1978	17.4%	8.1%	458,746	20.7%	(59,185)	-12.9%
1979	18.8%	8.9%	504,032	20.1%	(40,730)	-8.1%
1980	20.5%	10.0%	590,947	21.7%	(73,835)	-12.5%
1981	19.8%	9.7%	678,249	22.2%	(78,977)	-11.6%
1982	18.0%	8.7%	745,755	23.1%	(127,989)	-17.2%
1983	17.1%	7.8%	808,380	23.5%	(207,818)	-25.7%
1984	18.0%	7.7%	851,874	22.1%	(185,388)	-21.8%
1985	17.1%	7.2%	946,423	22.9%	(212,335)	-22.4%
1986	17.3%	7.2%	990,460	22.5%	(221,245)	-22.3%
1987	18.4%	7.7%	1,004,122	21.6%	(149,769)	-14.9%
1988	19.6%	8.7%	1,064,489	21.2%	(155,186)	-14.6%
1989	20.0%	9.3%	1,143,671	21.2%	(152,481)	-13.3%
1990	20.4%	9.6%	1,253,198	21.8%	(221.229)	-17.7%
1991	20.4%	10.0%	1,324,403	22.3%	(269,362)	-20.3%
1992	20.6%	10.1%	1.381,684	22.2%	(290,402)	-21.0%
1993	20.7%	9.9%	1,409.512	21.5%	(255,111)	-18.1%
1994	21.8%	10.3%	1,461,902	21.0%	(203,275)	-13.9%
1995	23.3%	11.1%	1,515,837	20.7%	(164,007)	-10.8%
1996	23.5%	11.2%	1,560,572	20.3%	(107,510)	-6.9%
1997	24.4%	11.7%	1,601,282	19.6%	(21,990)	-1.4%
1998	23.8%	11.0%	1,652,611	19.1%	69,187	4.2%
1999	24.2%	10.7%	1,703,040	18.7%	124,414	7.3%
Growth/average	14.3%	7.0%		19.6%		-7.6%

Office of Management and Budget. *Report to Congress on the Costs and Benefits of Federal Regulations.* Washington, D.C.: Government Printing Office, 1997.

Peoples, James. "Deregulation and the Labor Market." *Journal of Economic Perspectives,* Summer 1998, 111–130.

Taylor, Jeremy. *The Banking System in Troubled Times.* Westport, Conn.: Quorum, 1989.

White, Lawrence J. *The S&L Debacle: Public Policy Lessons for Bank and Thrift Regulation.* New York: Oxford University Press, 1991.

Winston, Clifford. "U.S. Industry Adjustment to Economic Deregulation." *Journal of Economic Perspectives* 12, no. 3 (1998), 89–110.

CIVIL LITIGATION

"In Defense of Punitive Damages in Products Liability: Testing Tort Anecdotes with Empirical Data." *Iowa Law Review* 78, 1.

Eaton, Thomas A., and Susette M. Talarico, *A Profile of Tort Litigation in Georgia and Reflection on Tort Reform.* Georgia Law Review Association. Athens: University of Georgia, 1996.

CORPORATE WELFARE

Stansel, Dean, and Stephen Moore. "Federal Aid to Dependent Corporations." Fact sheet. Washington, D.C.: Cato Institute, 1997.

U.S. Congress. House. Committee on the Budget. *Corporate Welfare.* 104th Cong., 2nd Sess., March 7, 1996.

HEALTH CARE

Fallows, James. "A Triumph of Misinformation." *Atlantic Monthly,* January 1995.

"Highlights of the National Health Expenditures Projections, 1997–2007." *www.hcfa.gov.*

Kaitz, David. *Social Security: Brief Facts and Statistics.* CRS Report for Congress. Washington, D.C.: Government Printing Office, 1998.

Portability: Is Kassebaum/Kennedy the Answer? Brief Analysis No. 196. Washington, D.C.: National Center for Policy Analysis, 1996.

Ruhm, Christopher J. "Policy Watch, The Family and Medical Leave Act." *Journal of Economic Perspectives* (1998).

Twight, Charlotte. "Medicaid's Progeny: The 1996 Health Care Legislation." *Independent Review* II, no. 3 (1998).

ENVIRONMENTAL PROTECTION

Arnold, Frank. "Does Environmental Protection Cause Unemployment, Plant Closures, and Reduce International Competitiveness?" in *Environmental Protection: Is It Bad for the Economy?* Online report. Washington, D.C.: U.S. Environmental Protection Agency, July 9, 1999.

Dallas, Burtraw, and Michael Toman. *Benefits from Reduced Air Pollutants in the U.S. from Greenhouse Gas Mitigation Policies.* Resources for the Future Climate Issue Brief #7. Washington, D.C.: Resources for the Future, 1998.

Davies, J. Clarence, and Jan Mazurek. *Pollution Control in the United States: Evaluating the System.* Washington, D.C.: Resources for the Future, 1998.

Fodor, Eben. "The Three Myths of Growth." *Planning Commissioners Journal* 21 (1996), 18.

Hertzman, Clyde. *Environment and Health in Central and Eastern Europe.* Washington, D.C.: World Bank, 1995.

McMahon, Edward T. "Stopping Sprawl by Growing Smarter." *Planning Commissioners Journal* 26 (1997), 4.

Morgenstern, Richard D., et al. *Are We Overstating the Economic Costs of Environmental Protection?* Resources for the Future Discussion Paper 97-36. Washington, D.C.: Resources for the Future, 1997.

———. *Jobs versus the Environment: Is There a Trade-off?* Resources for the Future Discussion Paper 99-01. Washington, D.C.: Resources for the Future, 1998.

Oates, Wallace E., ed. *The RFF Reader in Environmental and Resource Management.* Washington, D.C.: Resources for the Future, 1999.

Office of Management and Budget. *Report to Congress on the Costs and Benefits of Federal Regulations.* Washington, D.C.: Government Printing Office, 1997.

Repetto, Robert, and Duncan Austin. *The Costs of Climate Protection: A Guide for the Perplexed.* Washington, D.C.: World Resources Institute, 1997.

Vogan, Christine R. "Pollution Abatement and Control Expenditures, 1972–94." *Survey of Current Business,* September 1996, 48.

U.S. Department of Commerce. Bureau of the Census. *Measuring the Productivity Impact of Pollution Abatement.* Statistical brief. Washington, D.C.: Government Printing Office, 1993.

U.S. Environmental Protection Agency. *Clean Water Needs Survey Report to Congress.* Washington, D.C.: Government Printing Office, 1996.

U.S. Environmental Protection Agency. *Economic Benefits of Runoff Controls.* Washington, D.C.: Government Printing Office, 1995.

U.S. Environmental Protection Agency. *Environmental Investments: The Cost of a Clean Environment.* Washington, D.C.: Government Printing Office, 1990.

U.S. Environmental Protection Agency. *Global Warming Fact Sheet: The Kyoto Protocol on Climate Change.* Washington, D.C.: Government Printing Office, 1999.

POVERTY AND INCOME

Burton, C. Emory. *The Poverty Debate—Politics and the Poor in America.* Westport, Conn.: Greenwood Press, 1992.

Dalaker, Joseph, and Mary Naifeh. *Poverty in the United States.* Washington, D.C.: Bureau of the Census, 1997.

Jorgenson, Dale W. "Did We Lose the War on Poverty?" *Journal of Economic Perspectives* 12, no. 1 (1998), 79–96.

Triest, Robert K. "Has Poverty Gotten Worse?" *Journal of Economic Perspectives* 12, no. 1 (1998), 97–114.

U.S. Department of Commerce. Bureau of the Census. *Poverty in the United States: 1992.* Current Population Reports, Consumer Income, Series P-60, No. 185. Washington, D.C.: Government Printing Office, 1993.

Weinberg, Daniel. *A Brief Look at Post-War U.S. Income Inequality.* Census Bureau Series P60-191, Household Economic Studies. Washington, D.C.: Government Printing Office, 1996.

Wolff, Edward N. "How the Pie Is Sliced: America's Growing Concentration of Wealth." *www.epn.org/prospect.*

ILLEGAL DRUGS

Harwood, Henrick, Douglas Fountain, and Gina Livermore. *The Economic Costs of Alcohol and Drug Abuse in the United States 1992.* Rockville, Md.: Lewin Group, 1994.

Office of National Drug Control Policy. *National Drug Control Strategy Budget Summary.* Washington, D.C.: Government Printing Office, 1999.

Rhodes, William, et al. *What America's Users Spend on Illegal Drugs, 1988–93.* Bethesda, Md.: Abt Associates, 1995.

Individual Retirement Account (IRA), 268, 312
Indonesian financial crisis, 571
Indoor air quality, 475
Industrial countries, 32
Industrial innovations, 350
Industry sector, 8
Inflation
  acceptable rate, 33
  average rate per decade, 32
  bracket creep, 188
  CPI, 250, 325, 326, 327
  defined, 29
  economic performance indicator, 596
  Federal Reserve role, 99, 293, 294, 298
  interest rates and, 294
  Korean War, 163, 165
  market trader fear of, 99
  measurement, 30
  1946 to 1999, 31
  post–World War II, 155
  rates, by president, 608
  real costs, 292
  related to unemployment, 296
  unemployment and, 294, 296
  Vietnam War, 177, 178
Information technology, 349. *See also* Innovations
Initial public offering (IPO), 92
Innovations
  agricultural, 351
  benefits versus damages, 345
  business contributions, 358
  business hindrances, 357
  commercial versus military, 362
  defense industry, 360, 361, 362
  development strategies, 366, 367, 368
  economic policies, 343
  economic value, 342, 364
  entertainment, 352
  financial justification, 344
  future possibilities, 369, 636
  government role, 365
  household, 352
  industrial, 350
  institutional sources, 359
  medical, 348
  office and information technology, 349
  product development, 346, 353

science and economic strategy interface, 354
  types, 347
  U.S. dominance, 363
  unpredictability, 353
  unsuccessful, 370
Intellectual property, 539
Interest ceilings, 50, 162
Interest payments, 122
Interest rates
  determinants, 39
  economic performance measure, 49
  effect on growth, 48
  effect on investment, 48
  effect on saving, 48
  1946 to 1999, 50
  related to money supply, 42
  related to saving and investment, 301, 306
Interest-bearing public debt securities, 316, 318
Intergovernmental Panel on Climate Change (IPCC), 461
Interior, Department of the, 463
Internal Revenue Service (IRS), 190, 265
International Bank for Reconstruction and Development, 158
International Development and Humanitarian Assistance, 125
International Monetary Fund (IMF)
  Asian financial crisis, 571
  bailouts, 573, 575, 579
  establishment of, 158, 181
International trade. *See* Trade
Internet, 361, 364, 629
Interstate Commerce Commission, 147
Interstate Highway Act, 166
Investment
  average rates by decade, 65
  as economic indicator, 8
  exclusions, 56
  as GDP component, 7, 342
  importance, 300
  influences, 302, 307, 311
  interest rate effects, 48, 301, 306
  lag effect, 67
  lagging indicator, 59
  measures, 53, 58
  NAFTA, 539, 547
  1946 to 1999, 64
  optimal rate, 301

private sector, 367
  rates, by decade, 308
  rates, by president, 612
  saving versus, 57
  target rate, 66
  tax incentives, 312
Investment tax credit, 179, 199

Jacob, Mary Phelps, 352
Jenkins, C. F., 352
Job Corps, 174
Johnson, Lyndon
  Great Society, 174, 178, 489, 628
  Medicare, 451
  1968 tax surcharge, 31, 178
  Vietnam War, 175, 176, 177, 178
Jones, Paula, 213
Junk bonds, 39, 347
Justice Department, 511

Kapany, Narinder S., 350
Keating, Charles, 196
Kemp, Jack, 628
Kemp-Roth tax cut, 190, 628
Kennedy, John F.
  New Frontier, 174
  1964 tax cut, 20, 153, 172, 173, 294
  social programs, 489
  space race, 171
  Vietnam War, 175
Keynes, John Maynard, 152, 305
Keynesianism, 148, 152, 156, 173, 294, 296
Korean War
  economic impact, 70, 165
  history, 163, 168
  inflation controls, 163
Kyoto Protocol, 461

Labor Department, 208, 209, 478
Labor force
  deregulation effects, 402
  downsized, 372, 377
  globalization effects, 531, 532
  immigrant issues, 565, 566, 567
  participation rate, 23, 295
  restructuring effects, 371
  unionization, 402
  unskilled workers, 530, 532
Laffer, Arthur, 195
Laffer Curve, 195
Lag effect, 67
Lagging indicator, 59
Land use, 476

NOTE: Locator references point to question numbers in the text.

Lasers, 353
Lawyers, 416, 417, 418, 419
Leading indicators, 59
Leisure measures, 333
Lewinsky, Monica, 213
Liability law, 467
Lincoln, Abraham, 527
Litigation
  cost of legal services, 412, 413
  direct and indirect costs, 414
  product liability cases, 411, 420
  tort case length, 415
Local taxation, 143
London Stock Exchange, 92
Low-density development, 476

Maastrich Treaty, 586
MacArthur, Douglas, 164
Manufacturing sector, 68, 376
Marconi, Guglielmo, 353
Marginal tax rates, 632
Marine Animal Protection Act, 462
Marketable debt, 316
Marshall Plan, 157, 160, 161
Maturity, interest rate, 39
McDonald's, 409, 410, 411
McDonald's effect, 381
Mean income, 497
Mean wealth, 500
Means-testing, 251, 481
Median income, 497
Median wealth, 500
Medicaid
  beneficiaries, 452
  creation of, 451
  expenditures, 44
  immigrant eligibility, 564
  outlays, 227, 483
Medical equipment costs, 430, 437
Medical innovations, 348
Medical malpractice insurance, 414
Medical savings accounts, 443, 444
Medicare
  beneficiaries, 452
  creation of, 174, 451
  described, 450
  funding, 454, 631
  outlays, 227
  payroll tax for, 234
  reform proposals, 254
  as social insurance tax, 141
  tax rate, 632
  trust fund, 453, 455, 456
Mercury program, 171

Microsoft, 404
Mihaly, D., 352
Military-industrial complex, 170
Mineral production, 514
Mobile source, 458
Modigliani, Franco, 38
Money supply
  business cycle and, 45
  defined, 36
  measures, 37, 43, 145
  1948 to 1999, 44
  regulation by the Fed, 38, 46
Monsanto/Johns-Manville, 411
Morgan, Thomas, 348
Mortgage rates, 40
Most-favored-nation (MFN) trading
  status, 159, 580

NAFTA Transitional Adjustment
  Assistance Program (TAA), 545
NAIRU, 297
National Academy of Sciences, 565,
  568
National Aeronautics and Space
  Administration (NASA), 169, 356,
  463
National Association of Home
  Builders, 473
National Association of Security
  Dealers (Nasdaq), 89
National Bureau of Economic
  Research (NBER), 367
National debt. See Debt
National deficit. See Deficit
National Drug Control Budget, 511
National Environmental Policy Act
  (NEPA), 462
National Historic Preservation Act
  (NHPA), 462
National Income and Product
  Accounts (NIPA)
  controversy, 324
  investment measures, 53, 57
  poverty level estimates, 490
  savings measures, 55, 57, 335, 336,
    337
National Labor Relations Board, 147
National Park Service, 521
National retail sales tax (NRST)
  arguments against, 281
  arguments for, 280
  compliance costs, 274
  defined, 279
  overview, 272, 275

National Science Foundation, 356
National Teachers Corps, 174
Natural gas production, 517
Natural gas rate deregulation, 399,
  400, 401
Natural monopoly, 403, 404
Natural resources
  biodiversity, 518
  defined, 513
  economic damages, 516
  economic value measures, 342, 343
  global value, 515
  ownership, 519
  public lands, 520, 521, 522, 523, 526
  renewable, 513
  U.S. production value, 514
  U.S. shortages, 517
Natural Resources Defense Council,
  475
Naturalization, 564
Net exports, 7, 8
Net interest payments, 118, 119
Net investment, 54
Net saving, 54, 55
New Deal programs, 147, 153
New York Stock Exchange (NYSE), 89
Newman, M., 349
NIKKEI, 92, 529
Nixon, Richard
  social programs, 489, 491
  Social Security, 220
  Vietnam War, 176, 177
  wage and price controls, 31, 179,
    180
  Watergate scandal, 183
Nonaccelerating inflation rate of
  unemployment (NAIRU), 297
Noncash benefits, 480
Nondiscretionary spending, 124
Nonnative species, 472
Non-point source, 458
Nonwage benefits, 382
North American Free Trade
  Agreement (NAFTA)
  certification program, 544
  costs, 541
  defined, 207, 529, 536
  economic sanctions, 582
  environmental concerns, 539, 548
  fast-track, 537, 550
  future benefits, 549
  future issues, 551
  history, 537
  intellectual property, 539

NOTE: Locator references point to question numbers in the text.

investments, 539
partners, 207, 536, 541
as priority economic issue, 538
provisions, 539
rules of origin, 539
safeguards, 539
services, 539
side agreements, 539
sweatshops, 546
tariffs, 112, 539
trade and labor flows, 547
U.S. jobs gained, 543, 544
U.S. jobs lost, 542, 545
U.S. trade benefits, 540
North American Treaty Organization (NATO), 168
Northern Spotted Owl, 472
Nursing home care, 430, 436

O'Neill, Tip, 198
Ocean Dumping Act, 462
Ocean transport, 407
Off-budget item, 123, 239, 244
Office innovations, 349
Office of Management and Budget (OMB)
  budget projections, 243
  environmental programs, 463
  EPA compliance costs, 459
  national debt tracking, 319
  regulation cost-benefit estimates, 394
Office of Science and Technology Policy, 463
Office of Thrift Supervision, 401
Oil embargo, 182, 183, 185, 584
Oil lease royalties, 119
Oil Pollution Act (OPA), 462
Oil production, 517
Oil shock, 186
Okun, Arthur, 38
Old-Age and Survivors Insurance (OASI), 219
Old-Age Survivors and Disability Insurance (OASDI), 219
Omnibus Budget Reconciliation Act, 203, 630
On-budget item, 123, 239, 244
Operation Desert Storm, 204
Opportunity cost, 303, 472
Organization for Economic Cooperation and Development (OECD), 320, 534

Organization of Petroleum Exporting Countries (OPEC), 182, 186, 584, 629
Organized labor, 239
Out-of-court settlements, 410, 414, 421
Output per hour worked, 68
Outsourcing, 371, 378, 490, 530, 531
Over-the-counter (OTC) market, 88
Overvaluation, 102, 103

Page, Robert, 350
Patients Bill of Rights, 206
Pay-as-you-earn individual income tax, 153
Pay-as-you-go system, 216, 222, 234
Payroll tax, 136
Peace dividend, 629, 635
Peaks, 18, 19
Pension funds, 236
Permanent income hypothesis, 304
Permit trading, 466
Persian Gulf War, 204, 584
Personal consumption tax (PCT)
  arguments against, 288
  arguments for, 287
  compliance cost, 274
  defined, 286
  overview, 272, 275
Personal Earnings and Benefit Statements (PEBES), 239
Personal income tax, 136, 188
Personal Responsibility and Work Opportunity Reconciliation Act, 212, 564
Personal saving, 55, 61, 62, 63
  decline, 308, 309, 335
  rates of other nations, 310
  rates ranked by president, 611
Physical resources, 118, 119
Physicians' services, 430, 433
Pincus, Gregory, 348
Play-or-pay health plan, 443
Point source, 458
Political parties, 625, 626, 627, 628, 630
Pollution
  abatement costs, 459, 469
  cost trends, 470
  economic damages, 516
  indirect costs, 471
  legally acceptable amount, 464
  opportunity and additional costs, 472
  technology and, 345

types, 458
Pollution Prevention Act (PPA), 462
Population weights, 327
Potomac River, 475
Poverty
  acceptable percentage, 492
  defined by government, 79
  double cost, 485
  gap between rich and poor, 87
  globalization and, 533, 534
  as important issue, 479
  measurement issues, 480, 481, 482
  reasonable range, 84
  reduction or elimination, 490, 491
  related to business cycle, 86
  self-perpetuation, 486
  tax cuts and, 487, 488
Poverty line indicator, 79, 338, 339, 342, 481, 483
Poverty programs, 489
Poverty threshold
  based on pretax income, 481
  calculations, 81
  development, 80
  family of four, 85
  1950 to 1988, 82
  percentage, by president, 615
  population, by decade, 83
Preferences system, 567
Preferential treatment, 477
Preferred stock, 88
Prescription drug costs, 430, 435
Presidents
  budget process, 320
  business cycle policy effects, 20
  environmental programs, 463
  influence on economy, 628
  policy tools, 298
  political party affiliations, 625, 627
Presidential economic ratings
  budget deficit, 621
  budget growth, 620
  budget size, 619
  compensation growth, 614
  context, 605
  employment, 607
  exports, 618
  GDP growth, 606
  impacts versus responsibility, 603
  importance to citizenry, 604
  inflation, 609
  investment, 612
  market growth, 616
  measurement indicators, 598, 600

NOTE: Locator references point to question numbers in the text.

national deficit, 622
personal savings rate, 611
policy effects, 601, 603
post–World War II, 602
poverty, 615
productivity growth, 613
real prime interest rate, 610
single score, 600
Social Security, 624
taxes, 623
time period, 599
trade balance, 617
unemployment, 608
Price-earnings (PE) ratio, 102
Prime interest rate, 51
Prime rate, 40
Private sector investment, 367
Process costs, 394
Procyclical policies, 145, 211
Producer price index (PPI), 30
Product development, 346, 355, 356
Product liability, 411, 420
Productivity
    acceptable levels, 72
    defined, 68
    growth, by decade, 71
    growth, by president, 613
    output per hour worked, 68
    standard of living and, 69
Productivity index, 66
Programmed trading, 201
Progressive taxes, 271
Property values, 473
Public lands. See Federal lands
Publicly held federal debt, 127
Punklett, Roy, 350

Quality improvement, 326
Quotas, 112, 159

Radio, 353
Railroad deregulation, 399, 400, 401,
    402
Rand Corporation, 410
Reagan, Ronald
    balanced budget amendment, 211
    budget deficits, 133, 191, 192
    energy policy, 186
    inflation, 33, 188
    military buildup, 122, 190, 192
    social programs, 489
    Social Security trust fund, 235
    tax cut, 20, 190, 192, 194, 195, 628
    tax reform, 199, 628

"trickle down" theory, 487, 488
Real interest rate, 41, 52, 132
Real prime interest rate, 50, 610
Republican Party, 626, 627, 630
Recession
    deficits, 135, 635
    defined, 10
    Japan, 570
    labor productivity, 70
    1946 to 1999, 11
    1974 to 1975, 183
    1981 to 1982, 150, 191, 488
    political parties and, 625
Recourse Conservation and Recovery
    Act (RCRA), 462
Reengineering, 385
Refugees, 563, 564
Regulation
    cost and benefit measures, 393
    costs and benefits, 394
    government entities, 392
    importance, 391
    tax code compliance cost, 395
Report on Monetary Aggregates, 38
Research and development (R&D)
    categories, 355
    defense industry, 360, 361, 362
    government expenditures, 356, 359
    government incentives, 367
    industrial sector, 359
Resolution Trust Corporation (RTC),
    401
Resource mobilization, 571
Resources for the Future, 461, 464,
    467
Restructuring. See Corporate
    restructuring
Retained earnings, 55
Revenue neutrality, 260
Ricardo, David, 526
Risk, 39
Risk assessment, 217
Rivers and Harbors Act, 462
Rock, John, 348
Roosevelt, Franklin D., 145, 146, 217
Roth, William, 628
Russian financial crisis, 299

Sabin, Albert, 348
Safe Drinking Water Act (SDWA),
    462
Safety regulations, 391, 420
Salary. See Compensation
Salk, Jonas, 348

Salmon conservation, 472
Sarnoff, David, 353
Saving
    acceptable rates, 63
    exclusions, 56
    gross private savings, 55, 61, 62, 308
    importance, 300, 334
    influences, 302, 311
    interest rates, 48, 301, 306
    investment versus, 57
    measures, 55, 58, 334
    1946 to 1999, 61
    optimal rate, 301
    personal, 55, 61, 62, 611
    rates by decade, 62, 308
    role in tax system, 267
Saving rate measure, 309, 335, 335,
    336, 337
Savings and loan crisis, 196, 197, 401
Schawlow, Arthur L., 350
Securities, 316
Securities and Exchange Commission
    (SEC), 147, 374
Serviceman's Readjustment Act, 155
Services sector, 8
Shah of Iran, 186, 580
Share, 88
Shelby, Richard, 276
Shockley, William, 350
Single-payer health plan, 443
Sixteenth Amendment, 261
Small business deductions, 268
Smith, Adam, 4
Smoot-Hawley Tariff, 145
Social insurance taxes, 141
Social Security
    administrative costs, 232
    advisory council, 246, 247
    annual growth by decade, 223
    Clinton proposals, 252, 253
    COLA, 250
    creation of, 147, 217
    debate, 239, 240, 241, 242
    defined, 216
    The Economist's view of, 225
    growth of outlays, 220, 221
    importance, 225
    independence, 231
    means-testing, 251
    1980s funding changes, 198
    payback periods, 228
    privatization proposals, 239, 245,
        247, 248, 249

NOTE: Locator references point to question numbers in the text.

reform proposals, 245, 247, 248, 249, 254
revenue sources, 226, 234
size of program, 227, 240
surpluses, 234, 244
Social Security Act, 217, 246, 451
Social Security Administration, 219, 239, 242
Social Security taxes, 141, 256, 632
Social Security Trust Fund
  budget project effects, 243
  as contingency fund, 216
  defined, 219
  effect on economy, 255
  fluctuations, 222
  future, 636
  growth, by president, 624
  key dates, 233
  national debt component, 127
  1999 balance, 224
  origins, 234
  relation to national debt, 244
  surpluses, 219, 234, 235, 240, 242, 255
  tax allocation issues, 256
  tax increases, 237
Solid waste disposal, 469
Soviet Union
  cold war, 168, 170
  Czech rebellion, 168
  dissolution, 168
  Olympics boycott, 584
  space race, 169, 171, 360
Space race, 169, 171, 360
Specialization, 536, 538
Species diversity, 518
Spin-off, 372
Spironolactone, 353
Split-off, 372
Split-up, 372
Sprawl, 476
Sputnik, 169, 360
Stagflation, 184
Standard and Poor's 500 (S&P 500), 91, 101, 102
Standard of living, 2, 69
State taxation
  federal, local and, 143
  sales tax, 279
  system, 273
Steptoe, Patrick, 348
Stock, 88
Stock exchange cross-effects, 529
Stock index, 90, 91

Stock market
  acceptable rate, 96
  appreciation, 335
  Asian financial crisis, 569
  corporate restructuring, 98
  defined, 89
  growth patterns, 94, 95
  growth, by president, 616
  major indexes, 9
  1929 collapse, 144
  1987 crash, 200, 201
  1990s boom, 97, 100, 101
  overvaluation, 102
  reported by news media, 93
  risks, 337
  trader reactions, 102
Stock prices, 379, 383
Stranded assets, 406
Structural deficit, 193
Subsidies
  farm, 425
  federal land, 522
  sugar import control, 477
Sugar import control program, 477
Suharto, President, 571
Superfund, 462, 467
Supplemental Security Income (SSI), 227, 230, 246, 483, 564
Supplementary Medical Fund (SMF), 453
Supplementary Medical Insurance (SMI-Part B), 450
Supply, 6
Supply-side economics, 190, 195
Surface Mining Control and Reclamation Act (SMCRA), 462
Sustainable management, 522, 524

Tariffs
  as economic sanction, 580
  and GATT, 159
  Great Depression, 145
  and NAFTA, 539, 547
  as trade control, 112
Tax breaks, 426, 443
Tax code
  assessment, 636
  change process, 291
  complexity, 264, 266, 271
  compliance costs, 265, 266, 271, 395
  criticisms, 263, 267
  milestones, 262
  proponent arguments, 268, 269

  proposed alternatives, 312
  tax bracket reduction, 262
Tax cuts
  Kemp-Roth, 190, 628
  Kennedy, 20, 153, 172, 173, 294
  Reagan, 20, 190, 192, 194, 195, 628
Tax Foundation, 265, 266
Tax policy, 20
Tax reform
  avoiding double taxation, 289
  broadening the tax base, 289
  counterarguments, 268, 269
  defined, 257
  economic incentives, 270
  estimated compliance costs, 274
  importance, 258
  major proposals, 259, 260, 272, 273, 274, 275, 289
  Reagan, 199
  recent or pending legislation, 290
  value considerations, 271
Tax Reform Act of 1986, 199
Tax shelters, 199
Taxation. *See* Federal taxation; Local taxation; State taxation
Technology. *See* Innovations
Telecommunications, 353, 402, 403
Telephone, 353
Temporary Assistance to Needy Families (TANF), 227, 564
Term structure, 317
Thrift industry, 196
Thrifts, 196, 197, 401
Tort, 408
Tort reform, 409, 410
Townes, Charles A., 350
Toxic Substances Control Act (TSCA), 462
Toyota, 165
Tradable emissions, 466
Tradable permits, 466
Trade. *See also* Globalization
  comparative advantage, 525
  competitiveness, 111
  components, 104
  defined, 104
  gold standard, 47
  "good," 110
  importance, 105
  intra-Euroland, 591
  NAFTA, 207
  percentage of GDP, 528, 530
  volume, 108, 110

NOTE: Locator references point to question numbers in the text.

Trade balance, 106, 107, 109, 576, 617

Trade controls, 112

Trade deficits, 106, 541, 576

Trade policy, 145, 157

Transfer costs, 394

Transfer payments, 114, 121, 423, 479, 489

Transistor, 353, 354

Transparency, 579

Treasury bills, 313

Treasury Department
  drug control, 511
  financial instruments, 316
  responsibility for national debt, 319
  Special Issues, 219, 235, 237, 244, 255, 256, 316
  World War II interest rates, 162

"Trickle down" theory, 487, 488

Troughs, 18, 19

Trucking industry, 399, 400, 401, 402

Truman, Harry, 133, 163, 164, 165

Tupper, Earl W., 352

Turing, A., 349

Undistributed offsetting receipts, 118, 119

Unemployment
  causes, 22
  defined, 21
  economic performance indicator, 596
  Great Depression, 144, 146, 148, 149, 150
  inflation and, 294, 296
  measurement, 21
  1974 to 1975 recession, 183
  participation rate, 295
  post–World War II, 154, 155

Unemployment insurance, 141, 483

Unemployment rate
  acceptable, 28
  averages by decade, 27
  averages by president, 608
  1946 to 1999, 24
  versus participation rate, 23

Unified budget, 239

Unionization, 402

United Nations (UN), 164

United Nations Monetary and Financial Conference, 158

Universal health care, 205, 206

Universal service, 406

Unlimited saving account (USA), 272, 274, 312

Urban transport, 407, 420

Value-added tax (VAT)
  applications, 283
  arguments against, 285
  arguments for, 285
  compliance costs, 274
  defined, 281
  invoice method, 283
  overview, 272, 275

Velocity of money, 43, 46

Vertical equity, 170

Vietnam War
  cost, 176, 177
  duration, 168
  inflation, 178
  progression, 176
  U.S. involvement, 175

Vietnamization, 176

Vista Volunteers, 174

Volcker, Paul, 33, 298

Voodoo economics, 194

Voting Rights Act, 174

Wage and price controls
  Nixon, 31, 179, 180

Truman, 163, 165

Wage stagnation, 382

Wages. *See* Compensation

Wales, Nathaniel, 352

War bonds, 148

Warsaw Pact, 168

Wastewater treatment, 469

Watergate scandal, 183

Watson, James, 348

Wealth distribution
  compounding effect, 499
  mean and median wealth, 500
  by percent of population, 501
  poverty level and, 479
  trend to inequality, 498

Wealth inequality, 490

Welfare, 423, 427

Welfare reform, 212, 489

Wholesale price index (WPI), 30

Wilmut, Ian, 348

Wilshire 5000, 91

Withholding tax, 153

World Bank
  Asian financial crisis, 571, 575, 579
  development institution, 160
  establishment of, 158, 181

World Resources Institute, 461, 522

World Trade Organization (WTO), 529, 534

World War II
  economic changes, 153, 156, 157
  interest rates, 162
  pollution and health study, 474
  taxation, 148

Y2K computer problem, 214, 215, 411

NOTE: Locator references point to question numbers in the text.